STEVE MUDWAY

BEHOLD, I HAVE FORETOLD YOU ALL THINGS

A STUDY OF ISRAEL AND THE MILLENNIUM

STEVE MUDWAY

BEHOLD, I HAVE FORETOLD YOU ALL THINGS

A STUDY OF ISRAEL AND THE MILLENNIUM

MEREO
Cirencester

Mereo Books

1A The Wool Market Dyer Street Cirencester Gloucestershire GL7 2PR
An imprint of Memoirs Publishing www.mereobooks.com

"Behold, I have foretold you all things": 978-1-86151-753-1

First published in Great Britain in 2017
by Mereo Books, an imprint of Memoirs Publishing

Copyright ©2017

Steve Mudway has asserted his right under the Copyright Designs and Patents Act 1988 to be identified as the author of this work.

A CIP catalogue record for this book is available from the British Library.

This book is sold subject to the condition that it shall not by way of trade or otherwise be lent, resold, hired out or otherwise circulated without the publisher's prior consent in any form of binding or cover, other than that in which it is published and without a similar condition, including this condition being imposed on the subsequent purchaser.

The address for Memoirs Publishing Group Limited can be found at
www.memoirspublishing.com

The Memoirs Publishing Group Ltd Reg. No. 7834348

The Memoirs Publishing Group supports both The Forest Stewardship Council® (FSC®) and the PEFC® leading international forest-certification organisations. Our books carrying both the FSC label and the PEFC® and are printed on FSC®-certified paper. FSC® is the only forest-certification scheme supported by the leading environmental organisations including Greenpeace. Our paper procurement policy can be found at www.memoirspublishing.com/environment

Typeset in 11/15pt Bembo
by Wiltshire Associates Publisher Services Ltd. Printed and bound in Great Britain by Printondemand-Worldwide, Peterborough PE2 6XD

INTRODUCTION

It has never been a secret in the scriptures that the Jewish nation will one day be blessed above all nations on the earth. They are after all God's chosen people, so it is reasonable to expect that eventually they will be recognised as such. This truth may seem to have been somewhat tarnished by the extraordinary series of events that are interwoven with the history of the nation Israel, which consists of a catalogue of disasters and misfortune which may lead the casual observer to conclude that their hour has come and gone, or that their very survival as a nation is in doubt. However their resilience, resourcefulness and continued presence will one day stand as a testimony to God's faithfulness toward them. Even a brief study of what He has pronounced against them in their own scriptures should they desert Him ought to be enough to convince the earnest inquirer that as He has remained true to His Word regarding His stated judgements of them, so He can also be relied upon to refine and purge them according to His promises, so that eventually they will reflect His glory on earth, as was intended for them from their beginning.

The Bible, with the possible exception of the writings of Paul the apostle, concerns itself almost exclusively with either the history or the future of the Jewish people, and their relationship with God. Much as some might prefer to think otherwise, it tells us that all other nations are destined to come under its own umbrella of blessing, and eventually become subject to the Lord's overall rule, so that the peace on earth we presently seek by other means will then become a reality.

Of course national pride and modern economic reality stand against this idea, which, when weighed against present circumstance, seems ridiculous. How likely does it seem that nations with such vast resources such as Russia, China or America will ever be subject to a country as tiny as Israel? Or how likely does it seem that the Jewish people, whom even their own scriptures describe as being 'stiff-necked', will become the international role model for the future? Standing where we are now, with Israel being considered for investigation for war crimes by an international court and is despised for its perceived arrogance towards the Palestinian people, it appears most unlikely that there will ever be a time where Israel's pre-eminence can be possible, in any sense.

Clearly something will have to change for Israel to take its rightful place as God's nation on this earth.

Steve Mudway, Gloucester, 25th October 2016
alphaandomega70@hotmail.com

CONTENTS

INTRODUCTION

Chapter 1	John the Baptist: The voice in the wilderness	1
Chapter 2	The Sermon on the Mount: Teaching on the Kingdom of Heaven	12
Chapter 3	The Parables: Mysteries of the Kingdom of Heaven	48
Chapter 4	The Mount of Olives: When shall these things be?	69
Chapter 5	Isaiah: Israel in God's blessing	89
Chapter 6	Ezekiel: Four visions, Gog and Magog	144
Chapter 7	Ezekiel: Fifth vision, the Third Temple and its ordinances	177
Chapter 8	Zechariah: And many nations shall be joined unto the Lord in that day	207
Chapter 9	Malachi: Behold, I will send my messenger	232
	Endnotes	242

CHAPTER ONE

John the Baptist: The voice in the wilderness

The first and most obvious place to start to look for the future of the Jewish nation must be in the four Gospels, which contain the Lord's words concerning His people. We can take comfort from what He said in regard to end of days prophecy: [1]*But take ye heed, Behold I have foretold you all things*, so that everything we discover as we seek to develop our knowledge of prophecy can be measured against His words, which we will take as a benchmark for our further study.

Although He began to talk about the Kingdom of God from the very start of His ministry and His parables are full of references to the end days, it is not until Peter and the others understood that He was who He claimed to be: *Thou art the Christ, the son of the living God*, that He began to talk about His death, resurrection and the coming events of the kingdom in any detail:

Matthew 16:13-28 *When Jesus came into the coasts of Caesarea Philippi, he asked his disciples, saying, Whom do men say that I the Son of man am? And they said, some say that thou art John the Baptist: some, Elias; and others, Jeremias, or one of the prophets. He saith unto them, But whom say ye that I am? And Simon Peter answered and said, Thou art the Christ, the Son of the living God. And Jesus answered and said unto him, Blessed art thou, Simon Bar-jona: for flesh and blood hath not revealed it unto thee, but my Father which is in heaven. And I say also unto thee, That thou art Peter, and upon this rock I will build my church; and the gates of hell shall not prevail against it. And I will give unto thee the keys of the Kingdom of Heaven: and whatsoever thou shalt bind on earth shall be bound in heaven: and whatsoever thou shalt loose on earth shall be loosed in heaven. Then charged he his disciples that they should tell no man that he was Jesus the Christ. From that time forth began Jesus to shew unto his disciples, how that he must go unto Jerusalem, and suffer many things of the elders and chief priests and scribes, and be killed, and be raised again the third day. Then Peter took him, and began to rebuke him, saying, Be it far from thee, Lord: this shall not be unto thee. But he turned, and said unto Peter, Get thee behind me, Satan: thou art an offence unto me: for thou savourest not the things that be of God, but those that be of men. Then said Jesus unto his disciples, If any man will come after me, let him deny himself, and take up his cross, and follow me. For whosoever will save his life shall lose it: and whosoever will lose his life for my sake shall find it. For what is a man profited, if he shall gain the whole world, and lose his own soul? or what shall a man give in exchange for his soul? For the Son of man shall come in the glory of his Father with his angels; and then he shall reward every man according to his works. Verily I say unto you, There be some standing here, which shall not taste of death, till they see the Son of man coming in his kingdom.*

Of course it is easy to get into difficulties in interpreting the significance of what was said to Peter, but it should be clear to most that the 'rock' that the church was going to be built upon was not Peter himself, but his testimony *Thou art the Christ, the son of the living God*. Peter and the others were far from being 'rocks' at this time despite their best efforts, and it would be hard to argue, in the light of forthcoming events, that Peter was responsible for building any church, whether it consisted of Jew or Gentile, for he manifestly [2]fell short of the commission that he was given, and the mantle was taken up by Paul. His testimony to the Lord however has withstood the test of time, and is that very rock of which the Lord spoke. We must be clear that what the Lord was talking about in these verses is confined to the church or assembly of Israel, although the scope of His words leaves room for the fact that Israel would ultimately reject Him and subsequently another more general and inclusive church would be built. This took place under the ministry of Paul. However, in the Lord's time, this was still a [3]*mystery*, and although the Lord may have been aware of it, it was not going to be revealed until after Israel as a nation had been given every chance to accept Him and had then let go of its opportunity. Those who continued to believe after this formed the core of the church that was to follow, which also included gentile believers. At this present time then there is still [4]*neither Jew nor Gentile,* in [5]spiritual terms, so that until the prophetic clock starts to tick again for Israel in God's will, all of us, whether Jew and gentile, remain in this period of grace.

It is also evident, where prophecy is concerned, that of the four gospel writers it is Matthew who gives us the most information, his whole approach serving to illustrate the *kingship* of the Lord. Matthew's gospel also seems to have suffered more than its fair share from the efforts of the enemy to diminish its value, its authorship and validity having been questioned by many scholars. It has been variously accused of having been written originally in Hebrew, and/or by a much later Christian Jewish writer, and even worse, of being a mere reworking of Mark's Gospel. Suffice it to say that if Matthew wasn't an authentic book in the first place, why go to such lengths to discredit it? The fact is that similar types of accusation are levelled at the books of Daniel, Isaiah and Revelation, so it is in very good company. It seems to me that real biblical prophecy can be recognised by the continual attempts of the enemy either to completely discredit it, or failing that, to diminish its value. The truth of the matter is that we cannot prove that Matthew, the tax gatherer and apostle of the Lord, was the author, or whether or not it was written originally in Greek, any more than anyone else can disprove it. What we can do is accept that it is the inspired word of God, and as such it is worthy of our full attention. Let's leave it to others to busy themselves with pointless arguments while we concentrate on finding out what the Holy Spirit wants to show us through Matthew's gospel.

Matthew then illustrates that not only was the Lord the King who came to Israel in His day, but that He is the King who is to come in a future era. It is unique in its purpose, in the same way that the other gospels are unique in theirs. For example, Mark's writings emphasised the Lord as the perfect *servant*, while Luke described Him as the perfect *man,* and finally comes John, who of course wrote about Him as the divine *Son of God*.

Matthew, however, presents us with a problem in his description of the kingdom that is to come. His gospel, apart from the six occasions when he refers to the *kingdom of God*, is centred on the phrase the *Kingdom of Heaven*. What are we to make of his use of these different terms, for this phrase *Kingdom of Heaven* is altogether exclusive to the gospel of Matthew? The general consensus of opinion seems to be that he is talking about one and the same thing, so that when he refers to the *Kingdom of Heaven*, he really means the *kingdom of God*, as it is recorded in the other Gospels. Matthew is said to be deferring to the practice of the Jewish rabbis in restricting the use of the name of God, in order not to cheapen it by overuse, therefore substituting *Heaven* for *God*.

My problem with this explanation is that I believe that the Word of God, written in its original language of Greek in the case of the New Testament, is inspired. This necessarily means that every word or phrase used is meant to be there, and is not the particular choice of the individual writing it but is rather the work of the [6]Holy Spirit. I don't see, for example, that the Hebrew scriptures of the Old Testament have avoided the use of the various names of God, neither does the Septuagint, the Greek translation of the same scriptures, so the view of the Jewish rabbinate or others, that we should tread carefully when calling God by the proper names which scripture has given us to use, seems pedantic to me. In fact, Matthew uses *Theos,* the name for God, around fifty-six times in his gospel in various other applications. Nor does such a censorious attitude afflict the writers of the other Gospels, who happily use the term *kingdom of God* when that's what they mean. Could they be wrong in this? I don't think so.

Just imagine, for a moment, that we can be convinced that Matthew was so biased in his views regarding the Jews that he wrote in Hebrew rather than Greek, and in a manner designed not to offend the traditionalists. This would then consign the

Gospel of Matthew to mere literature, the writings of a man who is eager to please other men. If we could also be convinced that it should be delegated to the ranks of being a mere copy of Mark's gospel, which then may also need to be translated from Hebrew into Greek, as some tell us, it is easy to see just where this type of argument will lead. If we find ourselves persuaded by such reasoning, we could not take Matthew's writings as seriously as we would the gospels of Mark, Luke and John. Its prophetic message would be compromised, and therefore disregarded and lost. You, the reader, need to decide for yourself, but for me Matthew's gospel is the genuine article, and is therefore worthy of our full attention.

So what are we to make of Matthews use of the term *Kingdom of Heaven?*

Let us understand first of all that this is not the English translators' particular preference, as can be found in some instances of translation, where they have used different English words to represent the same Greek word. This sort of inconsistency can be confusing, and this is where a good concordance, such as Strong's, is invaluable, and where the original Greek text can be easily recognised and compared. In Matthew's case however, they have been consistent, and where we see the *kingdom of God* written, it is because they are looking at the original texts that read *Basilea tou Theos,* in contrast with those written *Basilea ton ouranos,* meaning *the kingdom of the heavens.*

This might seem a long-winded way to prove a simple point, which is that the two terms are not the same, but are written in such a way as to direct our attention to different things, which although closely related, are not interchangeable. Paul taught us to rightly divide the word of truth, to make a straight cut or separate between it, and so, in the original language at least, we should endeavour to do this.

What then does the *kingdom of the heavens* refer to? All languages contain rules, but it is their generally accepted usage among the people that speak them that will determine their real usefulness or meaning. Their use may change over time, but it is still their accepted use *at the time* that we should consider as giving the real meaning. In English for example we might say "I've got a blinding headache" or "it's raining cats and dogs", but what the hearer is expected to understand from this is something altogether less dramatic. This can be confusing for the stranger who is trying to learn English of course, and an ordinary dictionary is unlikely to help. Ask others who know the language what is really meant, and you will get at the true meaning, rather than an exact literal one. It is how the hearers understood the Lord's words that will indicate to us what He meant by them, and it is from the context in which these expressions were used that we will see why the Spirit differentiated between the *kingdom of God* and the *Kingdom of Heaven* in the Gospel of Matthew.

The term *Kingdom of Heaven* is first found used by John the Baptist in Matthew's gospel, where we read (Matthew 3:1-2) *In those days came John the Baptist, preaching in the wilderness of Judea, and saying, Repent ye: for the Kingdom of Heaven is at hand.*

Interestingly John is not quoted in the other gospels as referring to the *gospel of the kingdom of God* in his ministry, although the Lord Himself refers to the [7]*kingdom of God* being at hand, as well as talking about the *Kingdom of Heaven*. John's concern was solely for the *Kingdom of Heaven*, rather than the *kingdom of God*. Luke confirmed this when he quoted the Lord (Luke 16:13-17) *No servant can serve two masters: for either he will hate the one, and love the other; or else he will hold to the one, and despise the other. Ye cannot serve God and mammon. And the Pharisees also, who were covetous, heard all these things: and they derided him. And he said unto them, Ye are they which justify yourselves before men; but God knoweth your hearts: for that which is highly esteemed among men is abomination in the sight of God.* **The law and the prophets were until John: since that time the kingdom of God is preached**, *and every man presseth into it. And it is easier for heaven and earth to pass, than one tittle of the law to fail.*

Clearly the revelation that the Lord brought was going to be greater in scope than that of the Old Testament prophets, of which John was the greatest, according to the Lord's own admission. But He also said later concerning John:

Matthew 11:7-15 *And as they departed, Jesus began to say unto the multitudes concerning John, What went ye out into the wilderness to see? A reed shaken with the wind? But what went ye out for to see? A man clothed in soft raiment? behold, they that wear soft clothing are in kings' houses. But what went ye out for to see? A prophet? yea, I say unto you, and more than a prophet. For this is he, of whom it is written, Behold, I send my messenger before thy face, which shall prepare thy way before thee. Verily I say unto you, Among them that are born of women there hath not risen a greater than John the Baptist:* **notwithstanding he that is least in the Kingdom of Heaven is greater than he. And from the days of John the Baptist until now the Kingdom of Heaven suffereth violence, and the violent take it by force. For all the prophets and the law prophesied until John.** *And if ye will receive it, this is Elias, which was for to come. He that hath ears to hear, let him hear.*

John's impending demise at the hands of Herod could be what the Lord means here, the violent taking the *Kingdom of Heaven* by force in a demonically-inspired effort to prevent it happening, but clearly from this, great as John was as a prophet and the herald of the Lord's coming to earth, he was not to see that *Kingdom of Heaven*, but only preached about its coming. This must mean that the *Kingdom of Heaven* refers to the period of the Lord's rule in Israel as its *king*. The Lord's confirmation of John as being the expected [8]*Elias* also bears testimony to Himself, as the expected Messiah of the Jews. What then did John understand his own ministry to be? What was he expecting to take place once the Lord was revealed to Israel? When asked by the Pharisees who he was, John replied quoting from Isaiah, knowing he was the voice who was to cry in the wilderness, to bring Zion back to greatness:

Isaiah 40:1-9 *Comfort ye, comfort ye my people, saith your God. Speak ye comfortably to Jerusalem, and cry unto her, that her warfare is accomplished, that her iniquity is pardoned: for she hath received of the Lord's hand double for all her sins. The voice of him that crieth in the wilderness, Prepare ye the way of the Lord, make straight in the desert a highway for our God. Every valley shall be exalted, and every mountain and hill shall be made low: and the crooked shall be made straight, and the rough places plain: And the glory of the Lord shall be revealed, and all flesh shall see it together: for the mouth of the Lord hath spoken it. The voice said, Cry. And he said, What shall I cry? All flesh is grass, and all the goodliness thereof is as the flower of the field: The grass withereth, the flower fadeth: because the spirit of the Lord bloweth upon it: surely the people is grass. The grass withereth, the flower fadeth: but the word of our God shall stand forever. O Zion, that bringest good tidings, get thee up into the high mountain; O Jerusalem, that bringest good tidings, lift up thy voice with strength; lift it up, be not afraid; say unto the cities of Judah, Behold your God! Behold, the Lord God will come with strong hand, and his arm shall rule for him: behold, his reward is with him, and his work before him. He shall feed his flock like a shepherd: he shall gather the lambs with his arm, and carry them in his bosom, and shall gently lead those that are with young.*

This prophecy shows that John understood his place as the herald of good news towards Jerusalem (in its role as representing the nation Israel). It looks forward to the time of restoration of Israel as a nation under God, and as the people of God on the earth. These people are to be His representatives on the earth, and He will gather them together in His own time, for this very purpose. We can see from this that John's expectation was of the restoration of the people, reconciled to God through the Lord's ministry. The *Kingdom of Heaven* that he spoke of was actually a kingdom on the earth, subject to the Lord as their king, the Jewish nation being in their right place with God, now vindicated and justified in the open sight of other nations. When John the Baptist and the Lord spoke, according to Matthew, about the *Kingdom of Heaven,* they referred specifically to the Jewish nation being gathered together on earth, and restored as a nation for Gods purposes. John also understood the need for the nation's *repentance* before these events could become a reality, for, speaking of the Lord's appearing to establish His kingdom he said:

Matthew 3:11-12 *I indeed baptise you with water unto repentance: but He that cometh after me is mightier than I, whose shoes I am not worthy to bear: he shall baptise you with the Holy Ghost and with fire. Whose fan is in His hand, and he will thoroughly purge His floor, and gather his wheat unto the garner, but he will burn up the chaff with unquenchable fire.*

Once judgement began, it would not end until all the chaff, the wicked of Israel and elsewhere, were destroyed. John's ministry had a twofold purpose, to bring the people to repentance, thus gathering them together, and also to announce the onset of the *Kingdom of Heaven*, which would be completed by the cleansing of the nation.

We should now be aware that when John the Baptist and the Lord spoke of the *Kingdom of Heaven*, they referred to the establishment of Israel as God's people on earth subject to their king, the Lord Jesus Christ. When the Lord spoke of the *kingdom of God,* the *Kingdom of Heaven* was included within its scope, but this could not be said to be true the other way around. The term *kingdom of God* is more inclusive and not merely confined to the affairs of Israel on the earth, being farther reaching than this and referring to the whole and final purposes of God.

CHAPTER TWO

The Sermon on the Mount: teaching on the Kingdom of Heaven

Matthew 4:12-17 *Now when Jesus had heard that John was cast into prison, he departed into Galilee; And leaving Nazareth, he came and dwelt in Capernaum, which is upon the sea coast, in the borders of Zabulon and Nephthalim: That it might be fulfilled which was spoken by Esaias the prophet, saying, The land of Zabulon, and the land of Nephthalim, by the way of the sea, beyond Jordan, Galilee of the Gentiles; The people which sat in darkness saw great light; and to them which sat in the region and shadow of death light is sprung up. From that time Jesus began to preach, and to say, Repent: for the Kingdom of Heaven is at hand.*

It is interesting that the Lord does not start His own ministry concerning the *Kingdom of Heaven* until it is clear to Him that John the Baptist's own ministry is complete. We must remember that John was the last of the Old Testament prophets, who spoke under the power and anointing of God, and whose concern was for the nation Israel, under the Laws of God. The Lord had the greatest respect for John, who although he was not yet dead, was living on borrowed time because of his outspokenness concerning Herod's [9]involvement with Herodias. The Lord took John's imprisonment to indicate that He should go forward with His own particular teachings, after having recently defeated Satan in His temptation in the wilderness. He also moved away from His home town, taking up residence in Capernaum for a time.

His and John's messages are the same in that there was a need for change, repentance being the thing needed. This only means, to put it in simple terms, a turning around, the literal meaning of 'repentance' being to 'think differently or reconsider'. This change of heart was required in the light of the forthcoming appearance of the *Kingdom of Heaven*, which contained, as John had implied, both good and bad news for the nation of Israel. Good for those who were in the correct frame of mind to receive their Messiah, but not so good for the majority, who although they might consider themselves 'religious' in the sense of outwardly observing the law, were so caught up in their own concerns that in reality they were simply going through the motions under the religious leadership of the Pharisees and Sadducees, who, incidentally, did not take kindly to anyone who rocked the boat for them. Interestingly, the Pharisees did not take John on directly, even though he was openly critical of them. Their questioning of him produced nothing that they could use against him, and they stopped short of trying to set him up. John was no shrinking violet, and was more than a match for them in an open debate. No doubt had he continued they would have found some way of handing him over to the authorities, but in the event they did not need to, because he fell foul of Herod when criticising him over Herodias, his brother's wife.

John's ministry had caused quite a stir, for he had rekindled interest in the prophecies concerning the coming of the Messiah, and had readied the [10]ground for the Lord Himself to appear. Now was the time, and the message of both John and the Lord was consistent. One way in which the Lord differed from John was that He did not baptize in water, although his [11]disciples we are told, did baptize more people than John had. The Lord's baptism was contained in His words for the hearers, and so on hearing and believing Him they were effectively baptised into His name, which would later be confirmed by baptism in the Holy Spirit for those who had accepted His teaching. John's baptism was symbolic; it was the outward sign that pointed to the inward change or cleansing that had to take place in the hearts of men. The Lord had submitted Himself to it, and had in fact [12]insisted upon it, despite John's protest. Those that [13]heard the Lord then, as well as those of us who hear Him now, are changed completely, having no need of any outward demonstration of water immersion, which was in any case fulfilled by Him for us, in His act of submission to it under John's ministry.

The Lord's fame began to come from His teachings, preaching, healing of the sick, and also the casting out of devils from those possessed by them. Although He initially confined His ministry to the Galilee area, people followed him from much farther afield:

"BEHOLD, I HAVE FORETOLD YOU ALL THINGS"

Matthew 5:23-25 *And Jesus went about all Galilee, teaching in their synagogues, and preaching the gospel of the kingdom, and healing all manner of sickness and all manner of disease among the people. And his fame went throughout all Syria: and they brought unto him all sick people that were taken with divers diseases and torments, and those which were possessed with devils, and those which were lunatick, and those that had the palsy; and he healed them. And there followed him great multitudes of people from Galilee, and from Decapolis, and from Jerusalem, and from Judaea, and from beyond Jordan.*

Eventually the multitudes cause Him to seek to have some time to Himself on the mount, and then, once the disciples have come to Him, he started to teach them from what was later to become famous as the Sermon on the Mount. These teachings, as we will see, are the bedrock of the teachings of the *Kingdom of Heaven*, and contain what are probably the best known of all bible teachings, often mistakenly applied as the basis of all Christian belief. They are in fact the Lord's [14]divine interpretations of the Mosaic Law, and explain the spirit in which the Law was written, showing what the Lord will expect of the Jewish believer in His kingdom. They also stand in stark contrast to the 'rod' of the Law, with which the scribes, Pharisees and Sadducees had beaten the people into submission to themselves, ostensibly in the name of the Jewish religion, but in reality according to their own interpretations of it. Here we have the real thing, taught by the one true authority on it.

The Lord's teachings here start with what we now call the *Beatitudes*, which simply means *blessings/happiness,* of which there are eight. In order to explain them more fully, we will compare them with the eight *Woes/griefs* connected to them, and subsequently given in the light of the Lord's rejection by the leaders, which are later described in Matthew Chapter 23. At some point during this discourse, and we are not told when, both the Lord and the disciples are joined by the multitude who have come to hear Him.

This account is exclusive to Matthew, although some of the same teachings are later repeated in Luke's [15]gospel. It should be noted that the teaching in Luke takes place at a later time and under different circumstances. Here there are only four of the disciples present with the Lord, Andrew, Peter, James and John, as the others have not yet been called to the ministry. In contrast, Luke's account includes all of the disciples.

Matthew 5:1-48 *And seeing the multitudes, he went up into a mountain: and when he was set, his disciples came unto him: And he opened his mouth, and taught them, saying,*

(1) Matthew 5:3 *Blessed are the poor in spirit: for theirs is the Kingdom of Heaven.*

Remember that this instruction is primarily for the disciples, those four initially chosen to hear the Lord in fullness, and who were to play the more prominent part. The Lord is teaching them about His coming kingdom, and here he gives an indication to them of the type of person who will be in it. The word for blessed, used here and in the other beatitudes, is 'makarios', which elsewhere is translated as happy, or happier. It means to be fortunate or well off, and is put here in tandem with the *poor in spirit*, which means almost the opposite, that is having to beg. To further understand this, we are pointed at those to whom the Lord pronounced His woes in His later ministry. Compare with:

Matthew 23:13 **But woe unto you, scribes and Pharisees, hypocrites! for ye shut up the Kingdom of Heaven against men: for ye neither go in yourselves, neither suffer ye them that are entering to go in.**

The *Woe* here is an expression of basic grief, which was the future expectation of those to whom the Lord addresses His words. Here we see the fortunate in this life, the leaders of the people who should have known better, trying to prevent others, the poor, from gaining entry into the kingdom. This trait was beginning to be seen in the leadership during the latter part of the Lord's ministry, and the Lord speaks out against their rejection of Him as King and therefore their rejection of the *Kingdom of Heaven* itself. Eventually they would have Him killed because of their arrogance towards Him, and in their fear of losing their position under the Romans, to whom they would say [16]*We have no king but Caesar.* The kingdom therefore is opened to the poor in spirit but closed to the hypocrites, the actors and pretenders, found particularly amongst the religious leaders of the time, the scribes, Pharisees, and Sadducees.

(2) Matthew 5:4 *Blessed are they that mourn: for they shall be comforted.*

They that mourn, the vulnerable among the people, are typified by the *widows,* with no one to protect them from the powerful. Compare this with:

Matthew 23:14 **Woe unto you, scribes and Pharisees, hypocrites! for ye devour widows' houses, and for a pretence make long prayer: therefore ye shall receive the greater damnation.**

This devouring, or preying on the powerless, is compounded by their outward act of spirituality while they rob them of everything. People in authority will no doubt give account later for their actions, particularly for their abuse of power for their own ends. The Lord states that for those that do not have a voice in their present situation, there will be judgement and equity when He rules. Injustice carried out in His name, especially when performed under the guise of being for someone's good, will reap its own judgement eventually.

(3) Matthew 5:5 *Blessed are the meek: for they shall inherit the earth.*

The meek here, or the humble, are described as the inheritors of the earth, or in its context here, the land or the *Kingdom of Heaven*. Twice the Lord uses this word *meek* as a [17]description of Himself, and [18]once Peter uses it to extol the virtues of women who with *a meek and quiet spirit,* hold to their seat or place in dignity. Contrast this with:

Matthew 23:15 **Woe unto you, scribes and Pharisees, hypocrites! for ye compass sea and land to make one proselyte, and when he is made, ye make him twofold more the child of hell than yourselves.**

Here we see restlessness and a determination to control others by making them proselytes or converts to Judaism, then ruining them by their own empty doctrines. This attitude will not cause them to inherit anything other than woe, or grief. Their religious fanaticism is not of the Lord, nor is it the method that He chooses to use in the enlargement of His kingdom. An example of this is evident today. As Christians now we live in an age where evangelism is brought to us through every medium, with some giving the true message of the cross, whilst others preach blatant materialism in the name of 'giving to the Lord's work'. There does not seem to be any standard by which people can differentiate between what they listen to or watch, as the good and the bad are cleverly intermingled. The truth can be swamped in this overload of information, and it must be difficult for those starting out to tell the difference between what is right, and what is wrong.

God's work is neither hindered nor advanced by financial

considerations, and nor does He always choose to use the gifted orator over the stammering lips of the novice. The Holy Spirit is best placed to decide how to reach an individual for the Lord, and is well able to use any person or means that He wishes to. The true last day Jewish seeker will be shown the path through the minefield that constitutes religious society, and those that follow the truth will be recognised by their integrity and simplicity. The meek, or humble, have a witness and a peace all of their own which cannot be fabricated, and in the end to keep one's own place in peace is altogether the best option, unless given any specific ministry for others. The *Kingdom of Heaven* will be inhabited by the humble, not the brash!

(4) Matthew 5:6 *Blessed are they which do hunger and thirst after righteousness: for they shall be filled.*

The happiness contained here is in the desire for the truth of God's word, and if that is what is desired, then that is what they shall be filled with. Any other motive inevitably brings disappointment, for if we look to be found righteous, this will only be possible in the knowledge of the sacrifice of the Lord, which is a spiritual, and not a material blessing. The pull of this world may be used to convince some that the Lord's blessing is manifest in other ways, and once on that slippery path it is easy to start to look at the trappings of religion for inspiration, but it is no substitute for the real thing. Compare this with:

Matthew 23:16 ***Woe unto you, ye blind guides, which say, Whosoever shall swear by the temple, it is nothing; but whosoever shall swear by the gold of the temple, he is a debtor! Ye fools and blind: for whether is greater, the gold, or the temple that sanctifieth the gold? And, Whosoever shall swear by the altar, it is nothing; but whosoever sweareth by the gift that is upon it, he is guilty. Ye*** *fools and blind: for whether is greater, the gift, or the altar that sanctifieth the gift? Whoso therefore shall swear by the altar, sweareth by it, and by all things thereon. And whoso shall swear by the temple, sweareth by it, and by him that dwelleth therein. And he that shall swear by heaven, sweareth by the throne of God, and by him that sitteth thereon.*

This could be a particular stumbling block for the Jew who had a bona fide religion to look to, typified by the gold of the temple, the gifts on the altar etc, and he may well have become enamoured by all of these things, which are but a shadow of things to come, thus forgetting the one that is the creator of it all anyway. If we forget the Lord as the priority in our lives, then our conversation soon becomes about the world, church business, the pastor, people in the church, family, car, or pets, mortgage or whatever – in fact anything and everything but the Lord Himself, and the Word of God. We, and they, should consider the type of fellowship we have, and examine whether it adds to our mutual joy in the Word, or in the Lord. If it does not then the likely cause is that we have lost sight of our Saviour, and our spiritual life has gone flat. This is what religion is, offering things that the Lord does not require, after having neglected the things that he does. This is what the Lord points to in this instance.

(5) Matthew 5:7 *Blessed are the merciful: for they shall obtain mercy.*

The real meaning of mercy is seen below, for the weightier matters that they should have been concerned with are judgement, mercy and faith, instead of the detail that they went into regarding petty issues of no real account. The Lord's description of their narrow-minded attitude shows that they did not do what was required of them at all, and despite their outward show of spirituality, their lack was not hidden from Him. Compare this with:

Matthew 23:23-24 ***Woe unto you, scribes and Pharisees, hypocrites! for ye pay tithe of mint and anise and cummin, and have omitted the weightier matters of the law, judgment, mercy, and faith: these ought ye to have done, and not to leave the other undone. Ye blind guides, which strain at a gnat, and swallow a camel.***

(6) Matthew 5:8 *Blessed are the pure in heart: for they shall see God.*

The purity that the scribes and Pharisees tried so hard to portray for others to see was again of no account, for what was required of them was the purity of heart, which in the Lord's view was sadly lacking in them. Comparing themselves with each other and their preoccupation in outdoing one another would ultimately mean that they would become unacceptable in God's sight. Ironically, it would have taken less effort for them to concentrate on their inner cleanliness, for then they would have had no need to be concerned with how they appeared to others. The truth was that they were only really interested in extortion and excess, literally 'pillage' and 'lack of self-control.' Compare with:

Matthew 23:25-26 ***Woe unto you, scribes and Pharisees, hypocrites! For ye make clean the outside of the cup and of the platter, but within they are full of extortion and excess. Thou blind Pharisee, cleanse first that which is within the cup and platter that the outside of them may be clean also.***

The Lord's criticism of them was that they robbed the ordinary people, being self-proclaimed guides who had nothing of spiritual value to offer.

(7) Matthew 5:9 *Blessed are the peacemakers: for they shall be called the children of God.*

The *peacemakers*, those whose attitude is to pacify or bring unity, are set in contrast to the scribes and Pharisees, who although they may have appeared to have the same goal, in reality caused division and dissent through their actions. The term *whited sepulchres* referred to the practice of marking graves with whitewash so that the unwary would not defile themselves by touching anything associated with the dead. The Lord's words imply that whilst they may appear acceptable, or even perhaps better than the real thing, they are in reality likely to contaminate all those who are touched by them. This type of hypocrisy and iniquity marks the difference between the truly cleansed, and those who only appear clean. Only the truly clean will be accounted as the children of God in His kingdom. Compare this with:

Matthew 23:27-28 **Woe unto you, scribes and Pharisees, hypocrites! For ye are like unto whited sepulchres, which indeed appear beautiful outward, but are within full of dead men's bones, and of all uncleanness. Even so ye also outwardly appear righteous unto men, but within ye are full of hypocrisy and iniquity.**

(8) Matthew 5:10-12 *Blessed are they which are persecuted for righteousness' sake: for theirs is the Kingdom of Heaven. Blessed are ye, when men shall revile you, and persecute you, and shall say all manner of evil against you falsely, for my sake. Rejoice, and be exceeding glad: for great is your reward in heaven: for so persecuted they the prophets which were before you.*

The persecution here refers to being pursued or hunted down, in the same manner that Paul diligently sought out Christians to bring them into condemnation with the authorities. The righteous will always find that there are those prepared to make trouble for them for no good reason, and this may involve being *reviled* or defamed, having lies told about them, and also some saying *all manner of evil* with the intention of making their lives difficult or laborious.

The Lord's answer to these was to rejoice, inasmuch as these sufferings compare with the treatment handed out to His prophets of old. We can see that righteousness in this involved more than just being a believer, but being as the prophets of old who spoke out against the ungodly and resisted them. We have just read of John the Baptist, who rebuked Herod and suffered for it, and this is what would be involved for some here, as the disciples Peter and John were later to suffer imprisonment, and [19]James was executed. The reward of course for their persecutors was the *damnation of hell*, and the Lord told them in effect to do their worst, as He knew that they were set on doing this anyway. Interestingly, such people never consider themselves to be capable of such wickedness, but it was the very same leaders that the Lord spoke to, who were to bring Him before Pilate to be condemned! Nevertheless, the Lord counts this sort of persecution for righteousness' sake as blessing, knowing the generosity of His Father when He eventually rewards the faithful. Compare this with:

Matthew 23:29-33 ***Woe unto you, scribes and Pharisees, hypocrites! because ye build the tombs of the prophets, and garnish the sepulchres of the righteous, And say, If we had been in the days of our fathers, we would not have been partakers with them in the blood of the prophets. Wherefore ye be witnesses unto yourselves, that ye are the children of them which killed the prophets. Fill ye up then the measure of your fathers. Ye serpents, ye generation of vipers, how can ye escape the damnation of hell?***

CHAPTER TWO

The above verses cover the eight 'Beatitudes' or blessings, and what follows now are three more sets of instruction for His disciples, who are being taught in their role as guardians of the kingdom. After this comes His exposition on five of the Ten Commandments:

(1) Matthew 5:13 *Ye are the salt of the earth: but if the salt have lost his savour, wherewith shall it be salted? it is thenceforth good for nothing, but to be cast out, and to be trodden under foot of men.*

The basic thought behind this is that salt cannot be salted, or putting it another way, once it has lost its *savour* or 'saltiness' it cannot be restored. In the Lord's day, it was the way that salt was stored that caused it to become contaminated. It needed to be kept separately from other minerals and away from the ground, or it would lose its properties. If its 'saltiness' was neutralised, it was no good for anything except to be used as gravel for the roads. The disciples also needed to remain 'separate/holy' for them to remain useful to the Lord, for if they returned to the world's ideas they would soon become indistinguishable from it, and would then be contaminated, of no use to anyone either in this world or to their God.

In the Old Testament salt was added to the animal sacrifices in the burnt offerings, and this idea seems to transfer to the New Testament, where salt is considered *good*. It was used both as an offering, a preservative, and a cleansing agent, and it signified friendship or fellowship, being the additional seasoning added to make a thing acceptable and attractive. Salt could also be used as payment for services, being a valuable and marketable commodity. Our word 'salary,' a monthly payment, originates from this idea, and the covenant of salt implied that there was a contract made. All of this combines to show that the Lord expected His disciples to display the highest levels of integrity, maintaining their love for one another, in order to demonstrate His love for the world. They were not to forget their original purpose, nor should they become elitist, as the religious leaders of the day had become, but rather were to continually offer their friendship to all they came across, in their promotion of the Lord's kingdom.

(2) Matthew 5:14: *Ye are the light of the world. A city that is set on an hill cannot be hid. Neither do men light a candle, and put it under a bushel, but on a candlestick; and it giveth light unto all that are in the house. Let your light so shine before men, that they may see your good works, and glorify your Father which is in heaven.*

Again the Lord points to the responsibility that He was handing on to these disciples who were present with Him. They were to allow the light in them, i.e. of Himself and later the Holy Spirit, to be seen. This light could not be prevented from shining by men, of course, but He is instructing His disciples that they should do nothing to prevent it being seen, and were to allow it to be seen even when doing so might expose them to persecution or danger. It was pointless, in His view, to give such light to men, only for them to hide it through fear or shame. The aim was for the Father to be glorified in them, so they were to take the task to heart, and allow Him to shine through regardless of the consequences.

(3) Matthew 5:17: *Think not that I am come to destroy the law, or the prophets: I am not come to destroy, but to fulfil. For verily I say unto you, till heaven and earth pass, one jot or one tittle shall in no wise pass from the law, till all be fulfilled. Whosoever therefore shall break one of these least commandments, and shall teach men so, he shall be called the*

least in the Kingdom of Heaven: but whosoever shall do and teach them, the same shall be called great in the Kingdom of Heaven. **For I say unto you**, *That except your righteousness shall exceed the righteousness of the scribes and Pharisees, ye shall in no case enter into the Kingdom of Heaven.*

Further instruction now comes specifically for the disciples in regard to the *law, or the prophets*. This phrase is often used in scripture to denote the whole of the Old Testament writings, consisting of Moses' five books of the Pentateuch, all the prophets both major and minor, as well as the historical and poetic books, Psalms, Proverbs etc. In other words, He did not want the disciples to start any new religion or set of traditions, based on what He was now instructing them, or based on negating what had been previously written in the scriptures. Therefore He tells them He did not come to destroy, but to fulfil, as His purpose was to see these things through to their natural conclusion, not to begin something entirely different.

This is particularly relevant to the *Kingdom of Heaven*, for those things written concerning the Jews cannot be completed until that nation has recognised and accepted their Lord's teachings concerning the Mosaic law, and consequently accepted Him as their awaited Messiah. This may seem contradictory, for we know from Paul's writings that there is neither [20]*Jew nor gentile* at this present time, and all are counted as being the same where salvation is concerned, so that none are presently under Jewish law, but under grace.

However the Lord here refers to the time of the *Kingdom of Heaven*, before the period of grace that we now enjoy was revealed, and which will now also be reinstated when His purposes regarding the gentile church are [21]completed. Then there will be a return to these kingdom teachings, and the *law and the prophets* will be seen in their true context. If we are *ignorant of this mystery,* as Paul said, the scriptures will then present us with a set of contradictions that we will never unravel, truly beyond understanding. This is why we must seek to rightly divide the scriptures, and understand the different dispensations, to know how God is dealing with man at any given time.

Notice too in this passage that there will be people present in the *Kingdom of Heaven* who will be able to break and contradict these teachings, even persuading others to do the same. Also there will be those who obey and teach others properly, who will be called the greatest in the kingdom. This is a further indication that this kingdom is on earth, and exists before the great and final judgements of God where the wicked and righteous are finally separated. The standard expected of the disciples and others in this kingdom is for their righteousness to exceed that of the present religious leaders, for whom the Lord had little time, and whose integrity was questionable. He expected far more of the disciples than an outward pretence of obeying the law as a display for others, claiming to be righteous whilst at the same time robbing the people through complicated rules, such as the burdensome doctrines of the [22]oral traditions of the Pharisee. The last thing the Lord wanted was to be the instigator of a new set of traditions, so He reiterated the fact that the law as it stood written was sufficient for them, and His teachings here on what that law involved would supply the understanding which had become eroded and lost through the ages, the spirit of that same law which God gave them in the first place, to keep them in His blessing.

The Lord now turns His attention to six of the Old Testament commandments. He picks the six least, or shortest, of the commandments to illustrate His point, which is that there is far more implied in even these briefest of commandments than in their literal fulfilment. As an example of this, the Pharisee may have considered that as he had never actually killed anyone, in his view he had fulfilled this first mentioned commandment, and so could then legitimately forget about it, but the murderous heart which some of them later displayed towards the Lord, after He had pointed out their own unrighteousness, proves the point that unless obedience comes from the heart it is flawed, and so the commandment is broken. It should also be noted that the commandments that the Lord chose to use in His illustration are all concerned with ones 'neighbour,' and not to a direct relationship towards God. This is typical when the *Kingdom of Heaven* is referred to, and shows what the Lord is trying to get across to these people, is that you cannot say on the one hand that you love God, and then mistreat your brother, or anyone else. The law makes no [23]allowance for this, and nor incidentally does the Christian faith that was to follow!

We start with the sixth of the Ten Commandments:

(1) Matthew 5:21: *Ye have heard that it was said by them of old time, Thou shalt not kill; and whosoever shall kill shall be in danger of the judgment:* ***But I say unto you****, That whosoever is angry with his brother without a cause shall be in danger of the judgment: and whosoever shall say to his brother, Raca, shall be in danger of the council: but whosoever shall say, Thou fool, shall be in danger of hell fire. Therefore if thou bring thy gift to the altar, and there rememberest that thy brother hath ought against thee; Leave there thy gift before the altar, and go thy way; first be reconciled to thy brother, and then come and offer thy gift. Agree with thine adversary quickly, whiles thou art in the way with him; lest at any time the adversary deliver thee to the judge, and the judge deliver thee to the officer, and thou be cast into prison.*

Verily I say unto thee, *Thou shalt by no means come out thence, till thou hast paid the uttermost farthing.*

An interesting view on what seems a simple statement. Whilst those that kill can expect retribution under the law, it is less obvious that this law was to include being *angry,* (violent passion) for no reason, calling someone *Raca* (empty headed, hence worthless), and finally *thou fool* (dull or stupid). It is the last of these to which our attention is drawn, and though it seems just a commonplace insult, its root meaning comes from the word *musterion* or something kept quiet, and so we begin to see that this is an insult to a man's spirituality. All of the above have their consequences, but to imply to a Jew that he or she does not have the capacity to be truly spiritual, and that there were spiritual things that they were incapable of comprehending and should therefore keep quiet about, unless they were instructed by the enlightened, was, in the Lord's eyes, worthy of being cast into *gehenna,* or the continual fire of the landfill site of Jerusalem! This was His view of the doctrines of the Pharisees, who claimed that the written law could only be understood properly through the 'oral law' or traditions, of which they were self-appointed guardians. Anyone not respecting the so-called superior knowledge that they claimed to have was considered a fool. Incidentally neither the Pharisee nor Sadducee sects were in existence until after the people returned from the captivity in Babylon, and they had no long-standing biblical credentials at all. When presenting oneself to God, offerings are only acceptable when an acceptance of others around you is present. It doesn't matter how great the sacrifice is, the first requirement is an appreciation of our brothers' worth, before our own efforts are acceptable.

CHAPTER TWO

(2) Matthew 5:27 *Ye have heard that it was said by them of old time, Thou shalt not commit adultery:* **But I say unto you**, *That whosoever looketh on a woman to lust after her hath committed adultery with her already in his heart. And if thy right eye offend thee, pluck it out, and cast it from thee: for it is profitable for thee that one of thy members should perish, and not that thy whole body should be cast into hell. And if thy right hand offend thee, cut it off, and cast it from thee: for it is profitable for thee that one of thy members should perish, and not that thy whole body should be cast into hell.*

The seventh of the Ten Commandments referred to here, and again the spirit of what is said is opened out to include any that *looketh,* or more accurately, *continually looks* at a married woman to *lust after her.* If this is the case, it is as if the act itself has been committed already. Realistically men will admire women, and can be attracted to them for various reasons, including their various feminine characteristics as well as their looks. This is not what is meant here, as the Lord Himself was an admirer of women, being often found in their company, and who must have also been [24]tempted as we also are, at times. The Lord's answer to this is that it is the responsibility of the one so caught up to extricate themselves, so that it goes no further. The Lord gives a graphic illustration of the lengths to go to if necessary in order to disengage from such an event, but in reality it means to do whatever is necessary to keep the body under control. One's own will determines the outcome, and it is always possible, by some means to detach oneself from the possibility of getting involved with someone else's spouse. Pretending to others to have no such feelings whilst at the same time nurturing and developing them is not a solution.

(3) Matthew 5:31 *It hath been said, Whosoever shall put away his*

wife, let him give her a writing of divorcement: **But I say unto you,** *That whosoever shall put away his wife, saving for the cause of fornication, causeth her to commit adultery: and whosoever shall marry her that is divorced committeth adultery.*

This is a controversial and contested passage, taken out of context by many, particularly if attempting to apply it to Christian marriage and divorce. The first important point to remember is the context in which this was written, and to whom it was written. It does not apply to Christian marriage (for which we need to refer to Paul's teaching); it refers to Jewish law, and what was written originally in *Deuteronomy 24:1*. With this in mind we realise that the Lord showed what the Law intended to convey to the Jewish man who, finding that he had married someone who had misled him concerning her fitness to be married, was then entitled to give her a writing of divorcement[25] and send her away.

Deuteronomy does not specify what this uncleanness is, but the Lord demonstrates that the Law was given to apply specifically in the case of adultery or fornication (before or after marriage), and it was the man who had sole rights to initiate divorce. In this case in fact, pressure could be put on the husband to divorce and end the marriage, whether he wanted to or not. We are reminded here of Joseph, who chose to divorce Mary [26]privately, before the angel explained the situation to him. Complications arose because the rabbis, in an effort to improve on the original law, or make it fairer in their eyes, had in fact produced a whole series of doctrines regarding this issue. Divorces were allowed for pretty much any reason, and it was only comparatively recently, after Byzantium times, that the Jewish woman was given any voice at all.

In any event, the divorce consisted of two stages, the putting or sending away, and the bill of divorcement. Until the bill of divorcement or 'get' was presented to the woman, she was unable to marry again without it being considered adultery, no matter who was at fault, or how long they had been separated. This is still true under Mosaic Law, for even if a marriage has been dissolved in a civil court, the marriage is still considered valid by the more orthodox Jew until a 'get' has been issued. The 'get' does not state the reason for the divorce, but allows the woman to remarry. The Lord responds to the traditions of the rabbis here in showing that the only really acceptable reason for divorce was adultery, and apart from that, husband and wife were expected to stay together. A divorce did not negate the rights of the wife, which would have been established when the marriage contract was being discussed. The Lord simply states that without the 'bill of divorcement' the woman could not remarry without it being considered adultery, but that under the law, once divorced she could not then return to her first husband. It is interesting that the Pharisees later tried to use these teachings against the Lord to trap Him, but He [27]maintained His position that marriage should be for life, and was intended to be so by God.

(4) Matthew 5:33: *Again, ye have heard that it hath been said by them of old time, Thou shalt not forswear thyself, but shalt perform unto the Lord thine oaths:* **But I say unto you**, *Swear not at all; neither by heaven; for it is God's throne: Nor by the earth; for it is his footstool: neither by Jerusalem; for it is the city of the great King. Neither shalt thou swear by thy head, because thou canst not make one hair white or black. But let your communication be, Yea, yea; Nay, nay: for whatsoever is more than these cometh of evil.*

This refers to Leviticus 19:12: *Thou shalt not swear by my name falsely, neither shalt thou profane the name of thy God. I am the Lord,* and the idea that a promise or declaration of fidelity can be supported by an oath is a principle long established. However, the Lord in His explanation shows that where men are concerned such an oath has no power, as the things that men swear by do not belong to them anyway. We still have the practice of [28]swearing an oath on the bible to establish veracity in our English courts, the implication being that we will answer to God if we do not tell the truth. The Lord taught that this whole idea of swearing by another person or another thing is a vanity. The idea behind His teaching of course, is that a man's word should be sufficient, and if his word cannot be trusted, then no oath he swears can be trusted either. The Old Testament references to this were intended to show that a man's requests to God were heard, and that any oath would be required of him, so he should not make rash promises before God, yet the Lord shows here that such promises to God are not necessary. In the Kingdom of Heaven they are to make their requests to Him, without any sort of promise given in order to earn favour. We cannot barter with the Lord, as we have nothing to offer Him anyway.

(5) Matthew 5:38: *Ye have heard that it hath been said, An eye for an eye, and a tooth for a tooth:* **But I say unto you**, *That ye resist not evil: but whosoever shall smite thee on thy right cheek, turn to him the other also. And if any man will sue thee at the law, and take away thy coat, let him have thy cloke also. And whosoever shall compel thee to go a mile, go with him twain. Give to him that asketh thee, and from him that would borrow of thee turn not thou away.*

In our present cynical and street-wise society these teachings seem to fly in the face of common sense, and promote an attitude that guarantees we will be taken advantage of, or at the very least despised for our weakness. The Lord however talks of a society that is living under God's Laws, and so the expectation is that people will be basically honest. The Old Testament provided for retribution in kind, when wrong was done, and the Lord's teachings seem a radical departure from what the Law says. The principle here is that they *resist not evil*, literally the effects or influence of evil, and if it exists in this coming society He spoke of, it will be because the evildoer has power and authority over others.

An example of this is found in the origin of the word for *compel*, which comes from the Persian practice of forcing its citizens to help the king's messengers go about their business. They had authority to compel citizens to give up their goods, horses etc, in order to carry out their duties, with dire consequences for them if they did not comply. In this sense, the Lord does not advocate rebellion, but rather submission to the inevitable. He never, for instance, advocated open rebellion against the Roman authorities, even when [29]pressed to do so. This theme is continued into Christian [30]doctrine by Paul, and has led to Christians being seen as people that always 'turn the other cheek' as in weakness. The reality is that it takes more strength of character to be passive in such cases than to retaliate, but non-violent struggle has often succeeded where other methods have failed. The important thing for believers, whether Jewish or Christian, is that they trust the Lord in their circumstances, whatever they are, and do not look to their own strength or ability. This is the case here, and what the Lord is looking for in His kingdom.

(6) Matthew 5:43: *Ye have heard that it hath been said, Thou shalt love thy neighbour, and hate thine enemy.* ***But I say unto you****, Love*

your enemies, bless them that curse you, do good to them that hate you, and pray for them which despitefully use you, and persecute you; That ye may be the children of your Father which is in heaven: for he maketh his sun to rise on the evil and on the good, and sendeth rain on the just and on the unjust. For if ye love them which love you, what reward have ye? do not even the publicans the same? And if ye salute your brethren only, what do ye more than others? do not even the publicans so? Be ye therefore perfect, even as your Father which is in heaven is perfect.

The Lord in His interpretation of the Law reiterates what is written, whilst comparing what they had *heard*. Leviticus 19:18 states: *Thou shalt not avenge nor bear any grudge against the children of thy people, but thou shalt love thy neighbour as thyself.* Note that there is no reference here to enemies in the original text, this has been added since, so it was said that while it is not right to treat a fellow Israelite in this way, the rules did not apply to any *enemies* who can be hated etc. This is a subtle twisting of what is said, which the Lord rectifies. In His view the hearers are to *love their enemies*. This is shown to be a characteristic of God, and for those who want to be considered the children of God, it is the normal expectation. Their love was to extend not only to those from whom they could not expect any reward or return of favours, but also to the stranger, and even to those who took advantage of them. They are to do *more* than the world would. The emphasis here is on reward, and what the Lord advocates is an attitude where men look to their Father in heaven for His reward, rather than to their fellow men for compensation, or retribution. Perfection is bound up in this universal love, and is the standard that the children of God are expected to attain.

This completes the references to the law, but the Lord has more to say about this subject, and following along the same lines, shows that reward should be sought from God.

Matthew 6:1-34: *Take heed that ye do not your alms before men, to be seen of them: otherwise ye have no reward of your Father which is in heaven. Therefore when thou doest thine alms, do not sound a trumpet before thee, as the hypocrites do in the synagogues and in the streets, that they may have glory of men.* ***Verily I say unto you,*** *They have their reward. But when thou doest alms, let not thy left hand know what thy right hand doeth: That thine alms may be in secret: and thy Father which seeth in secret himself shall reward thee openly.*

The examples given are of the failures of the religious men of the time, those He considers hypocrites for their double standards. Their reward is in the admiration of men, but note that this is all they get (and probably all they want!). However the reward that the Father gives comes later on, and is a recompense for deeds that may well not have been noticed by men at all. This is not as easy to achieve as it may sound, for the temptation to tell others of one's charitable works is a strong one, and it requires a certain mindset to achieve this. The ability to give while receiving no recognition at all has to be worked on. Notice too that there is nothing missed by the Father, who sees all the secret things, whether good or bad.

Matthew 6:5-15 *And when thou prayest, thou shalt not be as the hypocrites are: for they love to pray standing in the synagogues and in the corners of the streets, that they may be seen of men.* ***Verily I say unto you****, They have their reward. But thou, when thou prayest, enter into thy closet, and when thou hast shut thy door, pray to thy Father which is in secret; and thy Father which seeth in secret shall reward thee openly. But when ye pray, use not vain repetitions, as the heathen do:*

for they think that they shall be heard for their much speaking. Be not ye therefore like unto them: for your Father knoweth what things ye have need of, before ye ask him. After this manner therefore pray ye: Our Father which art in heaven, Hallowed be thy name. Thy kingdom come. Thy will be done in earth, as it is in heaven. Give us this day our daily bread. And forgive us our debts, as we forgive our debtors. And lead us not into temptation, but deliver us from evil: For thine is the kingdom, and the power, and the glory, for ever. Amen. For if ye forgive men their trespasses, your heavenly Father will also forgive you: But if ye forgive not men their trespasses, neither will your Father forgive your trespasses.

This secretive giving also applies to one's prayer life, which ideally should be private, and will receive its own reward, but for those who simply do these things for the admiration and regard of men, there is no further recompense given, other than the knowledge that others have seen it.

Notice too that the *vain repetition* the Lord refers to can now be applied to what we now call the 'Lord's prayer' that He gives here, but this prayer merely shows the approach to God that we should take, and was never intended to be quoted verbatim or by rote. First, knowing that the things that we need are known of the Father beforehand, we can start by asking in His name for His kingdom to appear, His will to be done, our daily provision to be met and our failings to be forgotten. Recognising His power to keep us in His love and committing ourselves to His power to bring all this about is the basis for any approach to the Father, but other more immediate things can also be added to this.

This was never intended to be a vain repetition, but a guide as to how to approach the Father, as He did. We should not forget to do this in the Lord's name, or to use our everyday language. There is no need for pretence, and we do not need to add any 'thees and thous' to improve its sound, as this was merely Shakespeare's English, the language of the time in which the English King James Bible was translated and written down. It is not a 'holy' language, it's just old English, and adds no weight to our prayers, although it has to be said that most of us now do this by habit, and feel more comfortable with it. The real secret to prayers being heard, and responded to is in ones attitudes to others, which is again in keeping with the whole of His teaching about the *Kingdom of Heaven*. Despising others in our hearts, or secretly holding grudges, will cause our prayers to fall on a divinely deaf ear. We must bear in mind too, that this prayer was given as part of His kingdom teachings, and has far greater application to the Jew, who was then looking for the Kingdom of Heaven to appear on earth, than to ourselves, who are waiting for the Lord to take us up to His kingdom in heaven.

Matthew 6:16-18: *Moreover when ye fast, be not, as the hypocrites, of a sad countenance: for they disfigure their faces, that they may appear unto men to fast.* ***Verily I say unto you****, They have their reward. But thou, when thou fastest, anoint thine head, and wash thy face; That thou appear not unto men to fast, but unto thy Father which is in secret: and thy Father, which seeth in secret, shall reward thee openly.*

A different instruction now that refers to *fasting,* which the Lord connects to prayer life by the use of the word *moreover.* This was a practice more prevalent in those times, of petitioning God for a particular thing, whilst at the same time abstaining from basic needs. The Lord Himself fasted when He was [31]facing a particular trial, and His instruction here shows that it can be a voluntary feature of an experience in His kingdom. Please note that there is no commandment to do this, and common sense should always prevail, if undertaking a fast. The idea behind fasting is that it concentrates the mind on the thing being sought, and it can be used in the Christian [32]experience as well as the Jewish, but nowhere is it considered mandatory, or conversely, to be used to display one's spirituality to others. Its use is a personal thing between oneself and God, and the spirit of the Lord's instruction here shows that it was acceptable, when done privately. The practice of 'disfiguring the face' simply means to make it unattractive, such as the practice of wearing [33]sackcloth and ashes, i.e. rubbing ashes into the face to make it appear paler. The Lord's advice, (and remember that He is showing the effective way to do these things in the Kingdom) is to hide the fact from others that you are doing it at all, so that it remains a personal experience between you as the petitioner, and the Father.

Matthew 6:19-34: *Lay not up for yourselves treasures upon earth, where moth and rust doth corrupt, and where thieves break through and steal: But lay up for yourselves treasures in heaven, where neither moth nor rust doth corrupt, and where thieves do not break through nor steal: For where your treasure is, there will your heart be also. The light of the body is the eye: if therefore thine eye be single, thy whole body shall be full of light. But if thine eye be evil, thy whole body shall be full of darkness. If therefore the light that is in thee be darkness, how great is that darkness! No man can serve two masters: for either he will hate the one, and love the other; or else he will hold to the one, and despise the other. Ye cannot serve God and mammon.* **Therefore I say unto you,** *Take no thought for your life, what ye shall eat, or what ye shall drink; nor yet for your body, what ye shall put on. Is not the life more than meat, and the body than raiment? Behold the fowls of the air: for they sow not,*

CHAPTER TWO

neither do they reap, nor gather into barns; yet your heavenly Father feedeth them. Are ye not much better than they? Which of you by taking thought can add one cubit unto his stature? And why take ye thought for raiment? Consider the lilies of the field, how they grow; they toil not, neither do they spin: **And yet I say unto you,** *That even Solomon in all his glory was not arrayed like one of these. Wherefore, if God so clothe the grass of the field, which to day is, and to morrow is cast into the oven, shall he not much more clothe you, O ye of little faith? Therefore take no thought, saying, What shall we eat? or, What shall we drink? or, Wherewithal shall we be clothed? (For after all these things do the Gentiles seek:) for your heavenly Father knoweth that ye have need of all these things. But seek ye first the kingdom of God, and his righteousness; and all these things shall be added unto you. Take therefore no thought for the morrow: for the morrow shall take thought for the things of itself. Sufficient unto the day is the evil thereof.*

Next, instruction on possessions, and more particularly one's attitude toward riches. Nowhere in the scriptures is striving towards poverty advocated, and the circumstances of each of us will differ according to the path along which the Lord has led us. His instruction here is about the heart displayed towards riches, or more accurately the priority given to one's material possessions. Speaking specifically of His Kingdom, it is the amassing of 'treasure', and having abundant reserves, that is spoken against. In effect concentrating on laying aside large amounts as a security buffer against the uncertainties of the future. We get down to the fundamental fact here of deciding on who we are dependent. Is it in our own ability to gather and protect ourselves, to the detriment of spiritual blessing eternally, or are we reliant daily on God to take care of both our present and future needs, thus leaving ourselves free to concentrate on finding out what is His best for us? The Lord clearly wants His hearers to let God take care of their daily needs, the provision of which is built-in to any walk of faith. We do not need to set out to prove or try Him in this, but our every physical need, down to basic health and well-being, is accommodated within His will. Yes, we do need to take care of ourselves by using the means at our disposal, such as doctors and hospitals, and yes, of course we need to eat and drink in moderation, but there is no need to occupy ourselves to distraction with these things, for in everything we have the Father's protection.

In His kingdom, to those whom He particularly addresses here, there would be no need to ensure their own safety, for all of these things are included when concentrating single-mindedly on seeking *FIRST the kingdom of God,* that is, by letting this be the priority even before the consideration of the other things! If they are worried, or under stress about the future, or having a particularly difficult time, that is a good time to remember the Lord's words here, and ensure they take things one day at a time, finishing each day in His Grace.

Matthew Chapter 7:1-29: *Judge not, that ye be not judged. For with what judgment ye judge, ye shall be judged: and with what measure ye mete, it shall be measured to you again. And why beholdest thou the mote that is in thy brother's eye, but considerest not the beam that is in thine own eye? Or how wilt thou say to thy brother, Let me pull out the mote out of thine eye; and, behold, a beam is in thine own eye? Thou hypocrite, first cast out the beam out of thine own eye; and then shalt thou see clearly to cast out the mote out of thy brother's eye.*

This is perhaps one of the more difficult of the instructions to follow, because of human nature when living within any community. When we are close to one another we can begin to find the smallest things irritating, and this can lead to our judging, or literally 'pronouncing an opinion' on the doings of others. From the Lord's words here it is clear that He is talking about minor things, *the mote that is in your brother's eye,* those things about others that we consider imperfections, things that we might not do or think ourselves. The heart has a wonderful way of both [34]condemning us wrongly and [35]accusing others falsely, whilst at the same time justifying our own actions. This dual contradictory nature is called the 'flesh', and it is what we have to deal with daily, as our own hearts are basically [36]deceitful and corrupt!

The Lord here is showing how to deal with pettiness amongst brethren, and not with real sin, or wicked actions, which He goes on to talk about later. They were not expected to be blind to the enemy's ways, and were in fact required to be vigilant. However within His kingdom it is expected that people will be tolerant of the foibles and differences that are manifest in any given group of individuals. If there is no tolerance for others, then it need not take too long for the Lord to show us our own weaknesses, exposing to us those traits that are glaringly obvious to others, but perhaps not so clear to ourselves.

Matthew 7:6: *Give not that which is holy unto the dogs, neither cast ye your pearls before swine, lest they trample them under their feet, and turn again and rend you.*

The essential truth here is that all dogs and swine are interested in is food, and whatever is not of use to them is going to be trodden on and not considered for a moment. The spiritual things that are available, the knowledge of The Son, the Father, the Spirit, and in the Word of God are precious in the Lord's sight. They are hard earned and come to us through the Lord's death, and so are not given out lightly. Consequently the hearers should treat them with respect, and hold them as valuable. The Lord does not advocate total secrecy when revelations are manifested, but when despised by others, they should not be put on display for ridicule. In the Lord's time, dogs were not pampered pets or part of the family; they were for the most part tolerated as a nuisance, and needed to be kept under control. Nor are swine, unclean animals to the Jew, considered of any status. These terms were as derogatory then, as they are now. These animals were of limited use, and in the light of the Lord's words dogs and swine can be identified by their lack of appreciation of the things of God. They were kept 'without', or outside, the camp. Interestingly, it was the Lord who gave the real meaning of this later in Matthew when dealing with the Woman of Canaan, saying)Matthew 15:26): *It is not meet to take the children's bread, and to cast it to the dogs,* but He changed His mind when seeing her persistence, and her appreciation of who He was. The things of God are not generally going to be considered of any value by those outside of His kingdom, and so they are not to be distributed without thought.

Matthew 7:7-12: *Ask, and it shall be given you; seek, and ye shall find; knock, and it shall be opened unto you: For every one that asketh receiveth; and he that seeketh findeth; and to him that knocketh it shall be opened. Or what man is there of you, whom if his son ask bread, will he give him a stone? Or if he ask a fish, will he give him a serpent? If ye then, being evil, know how to give good gifts unto your children, how much more shall your Father which is in heaven give good things to them that ask him? Therefore all things whatsoever ye would that men should do to you, do ye even so to them: for this is the law and the prophets.*

By way of contrast, the hearer and earnest inquirer is to be met with an abundance, and we notice that this is in stages, for those that ask are given, the seekers will find, and the knocker, the persistent and cheeky one that hammers on the door finds that it is opened up to him. The more one puts into it, the greater the reward. All these efforts are met by gifts of increasing nutritional value, and as the Father knows what is best to give His children, so any spiritual reward is not to our detriment, but rather contributes to [37]growth, and spiritual health.

The Lord here related this to His kingdom, insomuch as they are exhorted to be of the same mind towards others, and thereby also to fulfil the Law. This is set in contrast with the above verses concerning dogs, and they are now encouraged to give to those that asked them, in the same way that their Father had given to them. Again this is illustrated by the Lord's actions towards the woman of Canaan, and shows the openness of the Kingdom towards others, other than Jews, who make the effort to seek and approach the Lord. What is also seen in these few words is a wonderful summing up of what the Law really was, being the channel of God's righteousness towards men, advocating fairness amongst themselves, and thus enabling the Jewish believer to be a partaker of the divine nature, through obedience to His Word.

What follows by way of conclusion to these sayings are three sets of instruction to ensure that the believer will complete his path, and enter in to the Kingdom in its fullness:

Matthew 7:13-20: *Enter ye in at the strait gate: for wide is the gate, and broad is the way, that leadeth to destruction, and many there be which go in thereat: Because strait is the gate, and narrow is the way, which leadeth unto life, and few there be that find it. Beware of false prophets, which come to you in sheep's clothing, but inwardly they are ravening wolves. Ye shall know them by their fruits. Do men gather grapes of thorns, or figs of thistles? Even so every good tree bringeth forth good fruit; but a corrupt tree bringeth forth evil fruit. A good tree cannot bring forth evil fruit, neither can a corrupt tree bring forth good fruit. Every tree that bringeth not forth good fruit is hewn down, and cast into the fire. Wherefore by their fruits ye shall know them.*

The strait gate, from the Greek *stenos,* always denotes narrow, as contrasted with broad, and yet in its root meaning, *hystemi*, it also means established, appointed or standing. The Lord clearly explains that there are many possible ways to take, but that there is only one way that is going to lead the believer to his home and eternal life, and that is the one way that God has established. Inevitably, along the way lurk the false prophets, who *come to you* in the guise of being guides along the same path having the same end in view, but who are in reality following a very different agenda, and who as ravening wolves are intent on stealing whatever they can from the unwary. They cannot be known from their appearance, for they appear the same, or perhaps better, but they are known from their *fruits*. This means it is what they DO that reveals what they are, and watching carefully the acts and words they produce, reveals their intentions.

The prime motivator for such fleshly men is money and increase, but they may also be there as sexual predators, seeking to have power and influence over people to further their lust. The danger is in the confusion and mistrust they sow, for once they have done their work their victims are left mistrusting and vulnerable, and unsure of how to regain the 'right ways' again. Pastors of course, are appointed as protectors of the flock, and if they do their job properly such false prophets should be identified and removed. However, if the pastor is himself a false prophet, as many are, the congregation will then have a difficult choice to make, as the *fruit* a man produces does not lie, even if his appearance and words look admirable.

Matthew 7:21-23: *Not every one that saith unto me, Lord, Lord, shall enter into the Kingdom of Heaven; but he that doeth the will of my Father which is in heaven. Many will say to me in that day, Lord, Lord, have we not prophesied in thy name? and in thy name have cast out devils? and in thy name done many wonderful works? And then will I profess unto them, I never knew you: depart from me, ye that work iniquity.*

Another warning for those whose motivation is not to serve the Lord but themselves. Even their claiming to know the Lord and producing miracles to back such claims will not deceive the Lord, who knows our hearts. Lots of things are done ostensibly in the Lord's name that are nothing to do with Him, but which are in reality the works of *iniquity*. The acceptable works are those done in the *will of my father which is in heaven* and these are not easily gained or fabricated. It takes a lifetime to even begin to understand the Father's will, and He will not give His intended glory in these works to anyone else. The faithful servant will remain in the background, ready to do His Lord's bidding, conscious of his own place and lowliness. Beware of the man who proclaims and promotes his own goodness!

Matthew 7:24-27: *Therefore whosoever heareth these sayings of mine, and doeth them, I will liken him unto a wise man, which built his house upon a rock: And the rain descended, and the floods came, and the winds blew, and beat upon that house; and it fell not: for it was founded upon a rock. And every one that heareth these sayings of mine, and doeth them not, shall be likened unto a foolish man, which built his house upon the sand: And the rain descended, and the floods came, and the winds blew, and beat upon that house; and it fell: and great was the fall of it.*

Finally the Lord gave the simplest of instructions for the potential follower. It is not enough to hear only, for everyone hears, but not all DO what they hear. To hear and to walk away carrying on in the same way is going to mean that the foundation is not laid, and when the opposition comes, which it surely will, being attracted by the Word given, it will search and try the true hearers but destroy those who have done nothing with what they heard. In the Lord's eyes this is the only difference between the wise and the foolish; those that hear and follow up on it, compared with those that hear only but do nothing.

Matthew 7:28: *And it came to pass, when Jesus had ended these sayings, the people were astonished at his doctrine: For he taught them as one having authority, and not as the scribes.*

The Lord's words to these people cause them to be astounded, or speechless, as they had never been taught as clearly as this by anyone. Suffice it to say that the teachings of the scribes did not carry the same weight as the Lord's did, their manner being to quote from other teachers, as well as from their own traditions, as evidence for their thoughts. The Lord only ever quoted from Hebrew scripture, and being the Word of God Himself, was the real authority behind it.

CHAPTER THREE

The Parables, *The mysteries of the Kingdom of Heaven*

Matthew 10:1-23: *And when he had called unto him his twelve disciples, he gave them power against unclean spirits, to cast them out, and to heal all manner of sickness and all manner of disease. Now the names of the twelve apostles are these; The first, Simon, who is called Peter, and Andrew his brother; James the son of Zebedee, and John his brother; Philip, and Bartholomew; Thomas, and Matthew the publican; James the son of Alphaeus, and Lebbaeus, whose surname was Thaddaeus Simon the Canaanite, and Judas Iscariot, who also betrayed him. These twelve Jesus sent forth, and commanded them, saying, Go not into the way of the Gentiles, and into any city of the Samaritans enter ye not: But go rather to the lost sheep of the house of Israel. And as ye go, preach, saying, The Kingdom of Heaven is at hand. Heal the sick, cleanse the lepers, raise the dead, cast out devils: freely ye have*

received, freely give. Provide neither gold, nor silver, nor brass in your purses, Nor scrip for your journey, neither two coats, neither shoes, nor yet staves: for the workman is worthy of his meat. And into whatsoever city or town ye shall enter, enquire who in it is worthy; and there abide till ye go thence. And when ye come into an house, salute it. And if the house be worthy, let your peace come upon it: but if it be not worthy, let your peace return to you. And whosoever shall not receive you, nor hear your words, when ye depart out of that house or city, shake off the dust of your feet. Verily I say unto you, It shall be more tolerable for the land of Sodom and Gomorrha in the day of judgment, than for that city. Behold, I send you forth as sheep in the midst of wolves: be ye therefore wise as serpents, and harmless as doves. But beware of men: for they will deliver you up to the councils, and they will scourge you in their synagogues; And ye shall be brought before governors and kings for my sake, for a testimony against them and the Gentiles. But when they deliver you up, take no thought how or what ye shall speak: for it shall be given you in that same hour what ye shall speak. For it is not ye that speak, but the Spirit of your Father which speaketh in you. And the brother shall deliver up the brother to death, and the father the child: and the children shall rise up against their parents, and cause them to be put to death. And ye shall be hated of all men for my name's sake: but he that endureth to the end shall be saved. But when they persecute you in this city, flee ye into another: for verily I say unto you, Ye shall not have gone over the cities of Israel, till the Son of man be come.

Shortly after the Lord gave the Sermon on the Mount, He commissioned His disciples to preach the same message that He and John the Baptist gave. Again it concerns the Kingdom of Heaven, and we should take note that this message is limited to the *lost sheep of Israel*, and concerned neither the gentile nations nor the Samaritans who occupied Northern Israel. With this commission the disciples were also given a measure of supernatural power as a sign or testament to the ministry, and this was to be dispensed freely, without charge to others. Nor were they to worry about providing for themselves, as their gospel work was to be subsidised in kind by those who heard it. Notice too that the preaching of the Kingdom of Heaven would be contested, and that while the consequences for the disciples in the short term might be unpleasant, the consequence for those who rejected it was certain judgement, which although delayed, would be severe. These circumstances would continue for the whole time until the Son of Man came, which shows us that the Kingdom of Heaven is to contain its fair share of detractors, who will be tolerated within the kingdom for a time, until the Lord returns to claim it all for His Father.

Too often these words, which were specifically spoken to the apostles, are appropriated by well-meaning Christians to apply to themselves, and believing that the Lord was speaking in general terms to all believers, they miss the point here. This commission was to the twelve apostles, its scope was limited to that time and place and to those particular circumstances, and any future ministries would be different and operate under different conditions. The Lord does not guild the lily here or anywhere else, laying out plainly just what the apostles could expect, so that from the very start they are under no illusion about what this work involves. He expands on this further:

Matthew 10:24-42: *The disciple is not above his master, nor the servant above his Lord. It is enough for the disciple that he be as his master, and the servant as his Lord. If they have called the master of the house Beelzebub, how much more shall they call them of his household? Fear them not therefore: for there is nothing covered, that shall not be revealed; and hid, that shall not be known. What I tell you in darkness, that speak ye in light: and what ye hear in the ear, that preach ye upon the housetops. And fear not them which kill the body, but are not able to kill the soul: but rather fear him which is able to destroy both soul and body in hell. Are not two sparrows sold for a farthing? and one of them shall not fall on the ground without your Father. But the very hairs of your head are all numbered. Fear ye not therefore, ye are of more value than many sparrows. Whosoever therefore shall confess me before men, him will I confess also before my Father which is in heaven. But whosoever shall deny me before men, him will I also deny before my Father which is in heaven. Think not that I am come to send peace on earth: I came not to send peace, but a sword. For I am come to set a man at variance against his father, and the daughter against her mother, and the daughter in law against her mother in law. And a man's foes shall be they of his own household. He that loveth father or mother more than me is not worthy of me: and he that loveth son or daughter more than me is not worthy of me. And he that taketh not his cross, and followeth after me, is not worthy of me. He that findeth his life shall lose it: and he that loseth his life for my sake shall find it. He that receiveth you receiveth me, and he that receiveth me receiveth him that sent me. He that receiveth a prophet in the name of a prophet shall receive a prophet's reward; and he that receiveth a righteous man in the name of a righteous man shall receive a righteous man's reward. And whosoever shall give to drink unto one of these little ones a cup of cold water only in the name of a disciple, verily I say unto you, he shall in no wise lose his reward.*

A wonderful insight into what true discipleship can involve, for the disciples were not expected to go beyond the Lord in anything, but rather to be partakers in a measure of the Lord's own experience. The measure given to each will vary according to their calling and commitment, but it is rare that any are called on to be martyred for the cause in the same way He was, although let it be said, some seem determined to act this way in their Christian lives, believing that this is what is expected of them and is what the Christian life involves. Where sufferings are self-inflicted because of others' reaction to being provoked by a holier-than-thou attitude, this neither glorifies God nor is respected by men. Sadly this is how the Jews and other religions, Christianity included, are often perceived. It is enough for us to be partakers in the Lord. We don't need to outdo Him, and we certainly cannot improve on what He has achieved through His sacrifice, which has already been freely offered.

The Lord does not rule out the death of any of His followers here, and although He explains the Father's care for the individual, this does not guarantee that they will not fall as men, but this can only happen when it is according to His will, and in His full knowledge. In the Acts period for example, Stephen was stoned to death, whilst Peter, who was earmarked by the Romans for death, was delivered from prison to carry on his ministry! It remains that the Kingdom of Heaven is fraught with difficulties, and its preaching can in extreme circumstances divide families, especially where some members seek to interfere with another's spiritual choice. The Lord Himself came under pressure from His family to conform to the acceptable standards of the time, and needed to handle the situation carefully in order not to compromise Himself, or offend them. This is not always possible and can lead, in some cases, us to hard decisions. Ultimatums can be given to that will leave us no choice, and then the Lord's 'Lordship' will be tried and proved, as we are bound to follow Him regardless of what others think, or would prefer we do.

To return to the narrative though, we see that The Lord gave His backing to His servants, and those in Israel who readily received the apostles and their teaching were deemed to have accepted the Lord Himself, so that even in the most basic act of hospitality, they were acknowledged, and rewarded.

Matthew 13:1-23: *The same day went Jesus out of the house, and sat by the sea side. And great multitudes were gathered together unto him, so that he went into a ship, and sat; and the whole multitude stood on the shore. And he spake many things unto them in parables, saying, Behold, a sower went forth to sow; And when he sowed, some seeds fell by the way side, and the fowls came and devoured them up: Some fell upon stony places, where they had not much earth: and forthwith they sprung up, because they had no deepness of earth: And when the sun was up, they were scorched; and because they had no root, they withered away. And some fell among thorns; and the thorns sprung up, and choked them: But other fell into good ground, and brought forth fruit, some an hundredfold, some sixtyfold, some thirtyfold. Who hath ears to hear, let him hear. And the disciples came, and said unto him, Why speakest thou unto them in parables? He answered and said unto them, Because it is given unto you to know the mysteries of the Kingdom of Heaven, but to them it is not given. For whosoever hath, to him shall be given, and he shall have more abundance: but whosoever hath not, from him shall be taken away even that he hath. Therefore speak I to them in parables: because they seeing see not; and hearing they hear not, neither do they understand. And in them is fulfilled the prophecy of Esaias, which saith, By hearing ye shall hear, and shall not understand; and seeing ye shall see, and shall not perceive. For this people's heart is waxed gross, and their ears are dull of hearing, and their eyes they have closed; lest at any time they should see with their eyes, and hear with their ears, and should understand with their heart, and should be converted, and I should heal them. But blessed are your eyes, for they see: and your ears, for they hear. For verily I say unto you, That many prophets and righteous men have desired to see those things which ye see, and have not seen them; and to hear those things which ye hear, and have not heard them.*

CHAPTER THREE

A word here about what a parable is. The Greek word *parabole* comes from a root meaning to 'throw alongside' or a similitude, where a fictitious story is given to illustrate a real-life situation. The parable was never automatically given with an explanation, and it required a key or solution, which the Lord normally provided to the disciples but not always to others. This effectively means that although the Lord was imparting real spiritual truths, the *mysteries of the Kingdom of Heaven,* through these illustrations, the real meaning could not be arrived at without the explanation being given by Him.

In another place the Lord said (Mark 4:13): *know ye not this parable, how then will ye know all parables?* And the explanation and way of interpreting the particular parable of the sower must therefore apply to all the others. If they had shown no curiosity about these things, the disciples might well have lost the truths contained here, showing that where the *mysteries of the kingdom* are concerned, it is only those with enough interest to ask the Lord for an explanation who will gain any understanding at all. It is up to the individual to seek for understanding, and it requires some effort on the hearer's part.

What strikes me, looking through this, is the almost casual acceptance of the Lord, confirmed by His quote from Isaiah, that for the majority, no understanding will be given at all. In fact it is only those that *have* to which more shall be given, and for others any cursory knowledge of these truths will be lost in the general confusion of information that goes through all of our heads. The sower sows his seed in a methodical manner; he doesn't break his routine when he comes across rocky or dry ground, nor is he concerned about the thorny patches or pathways. The seed is uniformly distributed throughout, accepting the fact that a significant percentage of it will be lost.

The Sower knows through his experience that in this way, enough of the seed will be successful to make up for what is lost, and what at first glance seems an inefficient waste of seed actually ensures that the whole of the ground is covered, and its success is then left to the elements. When the fowls of the air and the lack of depth of earth have taken their toll of it, it leaves the good ground to do its work. This may give us a clue as to the Lord's attitude to the opposition He faced, and His advice to His disciples to preach the word whether or not it was accepted. When it was not accepted, they were simply to move on without regret as the sower does, without breaking his rhythm. The Lord's time was limited, and where there was no reaction or acceptance of His words He did not linger. This was also true when He performed miracles, where for the most part He made Himself scarce as soon as he could after performing a miraculous event. He did not take time out to bask in the glory of men. He didn't want that, and there was too much else to achieve in the limited time He had.

Also notice here that although the disciples questioned the Lord as to why he addressed the crowd by means of parables, knowing that even while He was giving them information He was withholding the understanding from them, they did not grasp these truths themselves, until they asked and were given the missing explanations. As the Lord said, they were privileged as His chosen disciples to receive these things. This shows that the effort to find out is not nearly as difficult as we might imagine. We just need to show some interest, as His own disciples did, simply putting our questions back to Him and then letting Him impart His understanding back to us. Those that *have* will be given more, but to blithely hear these things without showing any interest will mean the opportunity is lost, perhaps forever. How we hear what is given determines whether we are good ground or not, and if the word is allowed to be lost, stolen, trampled underfoot or whatever, it is ultimately the hearer's responsibility. When it is nurtured, appreciated and generally given some degree of attention, it will produce fruit, and continuing to seek and ask could well then produce the full 100-fold growth that is possible. It rests with the hearer to react, for as we have seen, the word 'sown' is impartial and covers all of the ground.

This is the first mystery of the Kingdom of Heaven revealed, that anyone can become as the *good ground*, regardless of where they are when the word comes to them. We may be passers-by, or have no depth, or be troubled and overtaken by the things of the world when the word is heard, but it is still possible to change, once we have heard. The word is sown everywhere, giving everyone an equal opportunity to respond to it, and then seek the Lord and get more if they want to. This is explained further:

Matthew 13:18: *Hear ye therefore the parable of the sower. When any one heareth the word of the kingdom, and understandeth it not, then cometh the wicked one, and catcheth away that which was sown in his heart. This is he which received seed by the way side.*

Those on the wayside are people who are travelling from one place to another and just happen to come across where the word is being sown. They are not particularly seeking it, but hear it anyway. If at this point their attention remains on where they are going, then almost immediately, because the word has no priority in their schedule, the wicked one, personified in the fowls of the air, swoops down, takes it away, and it is gone out of mind.

Matthew 13:23: *But he that received the seed into stony places, the same is he that heareth the word, and anon with joy receiveth it; Yet hath he not root in himself, but dureth for a while: for when tribulation or persecution ariseth because of the word, by and by he is offended.*

Those in the stony places have some outward chance of growth in the short term, but as it requires a certain depth of earth to maintain it through the dry spells, there is not enough moisture to keep it going for long. The initial joy that it brings is soon replaced by offence when the word begins to effect a real change, and is consequently opposed. Tribulation or persecutions follow the word of God when it begins to show fruit, and this will cause some to give up, which is its real intention and purpose. Without depth, or a real desire, those that are on the fringes will not survive, and they will soon backtrack to something a bit easier, a compromise that does not cause them offence, which seems to satisfy, but is in reality a spiritual wasteland. In this case the opposition has succeeded by making it difficult.

Matthew 13:22: *He also that received seed among the thorns is he that heareth the word; and the care of this world, and the deceitfulness of riches, choke the word, and he becometh unfruitful.*

Here the opposition succeeds by providing an alternative, which seems to make life easier. Amongst the thorns is the place where there is a struggle for light, where growth is challenged through the multitude of other things that are going on around. Almost invariably, when the word starts to develop in any believer's life, other interests are soon introduced. The world's attractions, in whatever form they take, are presented in glorious Technicolor, and there is consequently strong competition for the believers time. These things are not necessarily what we would call wicked activities, they don't need to be, but are just sufficiently attractive to draw away a person from spending any amount of time in pursuing their spiritual growth. Those who previously had little in the way of social life may find they are suddenly more popular, and secular pursuits are now available to them. Old friends may reappear, doors can open up career-wise, and generally the world seems a more attractive place. For the unwary, this may appear to represent blessing, but any worldly involvement at this point should be considered in the light of what it costs in real spiritual terms. For those whose real interest at this point is not focused on the spiritual, this is a critical time, when he or she may lose the blessing. The opposition has succeeded if he can make you *unfruitful* as it means that you will never get very far, and at the very best, you will stay at basic levels of understanding. In these cases it is more likely that the word will be forgotten altogether, or relegated to the back of the cupboard, and any real faith is lost.

Matthew 13:23: *But he that received seed into the good ground is he that heareth the word, and understandeth it; which also beareth fruit, and bringeth forth, some an hundredfold, some sixty, some thirty.*

Here we see the fruitful hearer, who both hears the word and understands it. This understanding comes in the same way that the key to the parable does, by seeking and asking. The development of this can vary too, for some according to their desire can achieve a fuller reward, whilst others less so, but all are considered acceptable. We are able to set our own goals in this to a degree, and the fact is that we may all, from time to time, change what sort of hearers we are, through personal circumstances. We may start out as good ground, but for one reason or another become distracted, afraid or overcome by persecution before we realise what is happening and then climb back into a fruitful state. We may also, before hearing the word, be totally uninterested in it, but then find ourselves caught up in the word of God, so that we forget wherever else it was that we intended to go, and so change our course entirely. In this parable we should focus on what the Lord shows, which is that hearing the word only is not enough, as we must hear it and also pursue it, seeking for more until it comes to its fruition. The danger is always present in all of us to fall short, and neglect our own salvation for whatever reason, but the seed that is sown in good ground will in time, shoot forth and prosper if we stick with it.

After this come the parables of the tares, of the mustard seed, and the parable of the leaven. The Lord only gives an explanation of the tares here, so we will consider the mustard seed, and the leaven first, and then the tares.

Matthew 13:31-32: *Another parable put he forth unto them, saying, The Kingdom of Heaven is like to a grain of mustard seed, which a man took, and sowed in his field: Which indeed is the least of all seeds: but when it is grown, it is the greatest among herbs, and becometh a tree, so that the birds of the air come and lodge in the branches thereof.*

There is no explanation of these two parables either offered or requested, and while they also appear in the other gospels, they are there related to the kingdom of God, and must therefore also apply in a broader sense, referring to both the Kingdom of Heaven here, and also the kingdom of God in Mark and Luke's gospel accounts. [38]

The grain of mustard seed is referred to elsewhere in scripture, and always in relation to its small size, in comparison with other seeds of herbs. The Lord contrasts its beginning as a seed with its later development as a herb, greater than all herbs, then becoming a tree, strong enough to support birds and their nests. This fact would be known to the hearers, for the wild mustard is said to grow to some ten feet when left alone, and domestic mustard trees to something more like six feet. It would be unusual for a farmer to grow mustard only, and the Lord seems here to refer to a single grain, a tree planted for personal use. Few would argue that the difference in the initial size of the seed, compared to its possible eventual growth is the meaning that the Lord intended for the hearers, and it may well be that He was looking at real mustard trees around Him, when He said this. Certainly the mustard seed was not the smallest seed ever, nor was it the greatest of trees when it grew wild, but the Lord is simply making a comparison here with the fact that the kingdom, when it started, did not look like it was going to produce much, or indeed last very long.

Perhaps He was trying to open their eyes to the fact that it was not what they could see by sight they should look towards, but at who was behind the Kingdom of Heaven, and who had the power to make it grow, i.e. Himself. Later on he [39]compares having a little faith to a mustard seed, and also of being of great power, and we can conclude that walking by faith is nothing more than believing without sight. If we were to make such a comparison I would say that the Lord was comparing the mustard seed to himself, although the fowls of the air mentioned along with it do suggest the opposition of the enemy (that devours the seed sown) is also involved, which makes the point that the opposition will also grow, at the same time as the kingdom does. This theme is also suggested in the next verses, which are equally ambiguous.

Matthew 13:33-35: *Another parable spake he unto them; The Kingdom of Heaven is like unto leaven, which a woman took, and hid in three measures of meal, till the whole was leavened. All these things spake Jesus unto the multitude in parables; and without a parable spake he not unto them: That it might be fulfilled which was spoken by the prophet, saying, I will open my mouth in parables; I will utter things which have been kept secret from the foundation of the world.*

Here it is leaven, and a woman who produces it, both suggesting to the Jew symbols of corruption in a bad sense. It is unlikely that the Lord is using examples that they could not interpret by using typology in such a way that is against the accepted 'types', for the parables were not meant to baffle the hearers, merely to hide the real truths from the disinterested. The true hearer should be able to work it out with some spiritual help. We must therefore assume that the corruption, or leavening, here is wicked, and does not refer to the general claim that the gospel is spread throughout the world, and has a beneficial effect eventually in reaching and saving all, but rather I suggest, the Lord refers to wickedness coming to its fullness during this time. This runs in line with other facts we are given about the Kingdom of Heaven, as we also know that corruption will continue to exist in the kingdom until the Lord returns to cleanse it. We should remember that the Kingdom of Heaven is a period of trial and cleansing for Israel, until the Kingdom of God, being of the Father, appears to replace it. What is hidden in the Kingdom of Heaven therefore, any wickedness that still exists within it, will be allowed to do its full work throughout the period of the kingdom, before being dealt with by the Lord at the very [40]end.

Matthew 13:24-30 *Another parable put he forth unto them, saying, The Kingdom of Heaven is likened unto a man which sowed good seed in his field: But while men slept, his enemy came and sowed tares among the wheat, and went his way. But when the blade was sprung up, and brought forth fruit, then appeared the tares also. So the servants of the householder came and said unto him, Sir, didst not thou sow good seed in thy field? from whence then hath it tares? He said*

CHAPTER THREE

unto them, An enemy hath done this. The servants said unto him, Wilt thou then that we go and gather them up? But he said, Nay; lest while ye gather up the tares, ye root up also the wheat with them. Let both grow together until the harvest: and in the time of harvest I will say to the reapers, Gather ye together first the tares, and bind them in bundles to burn them: but gather the wheat into my barn.

Matthew 13:36-43: *Then Jesus sent the multitude away, and went into the house; and His disciples came unto Him saying, declare unto us the parable of the tares of the field. He answered and said unto them, He that soweth the good seed is the son of man. The field is the world; the good seed are the children of the kingdom; but the tares are the children of the wicked one; the enemy that sowed them is the devil; the harvest is the end of the world; and the reapers are the angels. As therefore the tares are gathered and burned in the fire; so shall it be in the end of this world. The Son of man shall send forth his angels, and they shall gather out of his kingdom all things that offend, and them which do iniquity; And shall cast them into a furnace of fire: there shall be wailing and gnashing of teeth. Then shall the righteous shine forth as the sun in the kingdom of their Father. Who hath ears to hear, let him hear.*

The parable of the tares is given in the hearing of the multitude, after that of the parable of the sower, but it is not until the people are sent away and the disciples are back in the house and remember what was said about seeking an explanation that they ask Him about the parable of the tares. Notice that they do not ask about the 'mustard seed' or the 'leaven' and consequently no explanation is given for those.

However the explanation given regarding the tares is complete, and again relates to natural events that could be illustrated by things around them. The main point is that the work of the Lord in sowing the seed is opposed by means of laying [41]false seed among the wheat, which is not apparent until the time of the harvest. These are allowed to grow amongst the wheat until the time of the end, when they shall be dealt with first. The wisdom in this shows the intertwining of both plants, so that in pulling up the one, in the early stages, the other would be affected, and so we must accept that in this case it is better that the wicked are left, for the sake of the others. Again we see that in His Kingdom, the Kingdom of Heaven, are those who offend and commit iniquity, and they are hidden amongst the real believers. This is of course more relevant to Israel's last day experience showing that a part of their problems at least, are going to come from some within their own ranks, until the angels are sent to separate the wicked from amongst the believers that remain. After this of course, the kingdom becomes the Kingdom of the Father, passing from the Lord's Kingdom on Earth, the Kingdom of Heaven, to the Kingdom of God. Notice that none of this is a surprise to the Lord, and we are reminded of Jeremiah's writings, where He is quoted as saying:

Jeremiah chapter 23:28-29: *What is the chaff to the wheat? Is not my word like as a fire? saith the Lord; and like a hammer that breaketh the rock in pieces?*

He ends this with the statement *He that hath ears to hear, let him hear* and as this is not for general knowledge, but spoken within the confines of the house with His disciples, it shows that they were expected to pay attention individually, especially when He was talking about such momentous future events for Israel. The *hearers* among them would be given more in time, providing they tuned in to what He was telling them. As we have seen, some of the disciples were more astute in this than others, and consequently the revelation was not equally divided amongst them, although the opportunity to hear usually was. It is a wise strategy to put oneself in the place of blessing, and to be around those that are blessed in fellowship, so that nothing is missed, and this is what Peter, James, John and Andrew generally did, as they made sure they were close to the Lord.

There follow three further parables, none of which came with an explanation, but the Lord does ask at the end whether they have been understood, to which they answer *Yes*, so we must assume that they were:

Matthew 13:44: *Again, the Kingdom of Heaven is like unto treasure hid in a field; the which when a man hath found, he hideth, and for joy thereof goeth and selleth all that he hath, and buyeth that field.*

Matthew 13:45-46: *Again, the Kingdom of Heaven is like unto a merchant man, seeking goodly pearls: Who, when he had found one pearl of great price, went and sold all that he had, and bought it.*

The first two show that to benefit from the teachings of the Kingdom, it is necessary to commit entirely to it, but in the first instance the finder keeps it to himself until he is sure of its possession, leaving nothing to chance and not giving another the opportunity to jump in first. In the second parable there is a similar message of commitment, where all other possessions are forsaken for the one prize. In the final analysis there is no room for holding anything in the world to be of value when compared with the things of God. This was the attitude that the Lord felt necessary for His disciples to adopt in order to survive spiritually, in what He knew was coming for them. Remember, at the time the Lord was speaking, the Kingdom of Heaven was imminent, as the Jews had not yet rejected Him nationally.

Matthew 13:47-50 *Again, the Kingdom of Heaven is like unto a net, that was cast into the sea, and gathered of every kind: Which, when it was full, they drew to shore, and sat down, and gathered the good into vessels, but cast the bad away. So shall it be at the end of the world: the angels shall come forth, and sever the wicked from among the just, And shall cast them into the furnace of fire: there shall be wailing and gnashing of teeth.*

The final parable here shows that the net that was cast on Israel would pull in all sorts of people, who had all sorts of motives for following Him. There would be some wicked among the just, for this was not the final Kingdom, but the one that would precede judgement under His righteousness. There would be no argument at the end, people would either be accepted or rejected according to their acceptance of Him, and His words.

Matthew 13:51-52: *Jesus saith unto them, Have ye understood all these things? They say unto him, Yea, Lord. Then said he unto them, Therefore every scribe which is instructed unto the Kingdom of Heaven is like unto a man that is an householder, which bringeth forth out of his treasure things new and old.*

The disciples here are compared to the scribes that are instructed, and shows that in the coming Kingdom of Heaven, men needed to be trained for this role, just as they would in any other field. These men were to be the ones intended to lead others through the tribulations that were to shortly come on Israel. Some of the things He taught were new, some were from the familiar Law and Prophets, but all things were shown in new light through His teaching.

Matthew 22:1-14: *And Jesus answered and spake unto them again by parables, and said, The Kingdom of Heaven is like unto a certain king, which made a marriage for his son, And sent forth his servants to call them that were bidden to the wedding: and they would not come. Again, he sent forth other servants, saying, Tell them which are bidden, Behold, I have prepared my dinner: my oxen and my fatlings are killed, and all things are ready: come unto the marriage. But they*

CHAPTER THREE

made light of it, and went their ways, one to his farm, another to his merchandise: And the remnant took his servants, and entreated them spitefully, and slew them. But when the king heard thereof, he was wroth: and he sent forth his armies, and destroyed those murderers, and burned up their city. Then saith he to his servants, The wedding is ready, but they which were bidden were not worthy. Go ye therefore into the highways, and as many as ye shall find, bid to the marriage. So those servants went out into the highways, and gathered together all as many as they found, both bad and good: and the wedding was furnished with guests. And when the king came in to see the guests, he saw there a man which had not on a wedding garment: And he saith unto him, Friend, how camest thou in hither not having a wedding garment? And he was speechless. Then said the king to the servants, Bind him hand and foot, and take him away, and cast him into outer darkness; there shall be weeping and gnashing of teeth. For many are called, but few are chosen.

The last parable the Lord gives before talking about the End Times begins to show His own recognition and acceptance of His rejection by the leaders of the people, the Israelites who were the called, but not necessarily the chosen ones, as they liked to think. The marriage celebration remains an important institution, and refusal to come on the slightest pretext would be unacceptable in any society. Certainly to finally kill the servants sent by the king is a provocation that no powerful king could afford to ignore, and most would agree that such a response is justified. The marriage still has to take place however, so servants are sent again, this time to invite anyone they find to be a guest of the king, so that the marriage can proceed. It is on seeing a guest without the wedding garment that has been provided that the King's anger is finally stirred, and on finding there is no reason at all for it, and no answer offered, He is enraged. Another insult, from someone who has made no effort, even though everything has been provided for him.

The Lord offers no explanation for this parable, but it is clear that the Pharisees take this personally, and assume that He is condemning them for their constant refusal to submit themselves to God's Laws, preferring their own ways and traditions rather than His teachings.

Matthew 22:15-22: *Then went the Pharisees, and took counsel how they might entangle him in his talk. And they sent out unto him their disciples with the Herodians, saying, Master, we know that thou art true, and teachest the way of God in truth, neither carest thou for any man: for thou regardest not the person of men. Tell us therefore, What thinkest thou? Is it lawful to give tribute unto Caesar, or not? But Jesus perceived their wickedness, and said, Why tempt ye me, ye hypocrites? Shew me the tribute money. And they brought unto him a penny. And he saith unto them, Whose is this image and superscription? They say unto him, Caesar's. Then saith he unto them, Render therefore unto Caesar the things which are Caesar's; and unto God the things that are God's. When they had heard these words, they marvelled, and left him, and went their way.*

From this point on their intention is to kill him, and while they try to hide this fact, they give up on any pretence of listening to Him without prejudice. In this last parable the Lord touches on the unthinkable, which is that the Jewish nation might lose the place of blessing or uniqueness with God that they had always enjoyed. The parable shows that it is the bad and the good, the *hoi polloi*, the general population who will enjoy the benefits of the King's celebration, and not the well to do, the affluent or the deserving, as the Pharisees would have no doubt considered themselves to be! Even so, there were rules in the marriage ceremony, and anyone not properly dressed would have to give account of their presence there, and this rule would apply regardless of any class distinction.

CHAPTER THREE

Let us be clear on what is written here, for this is not the Lord talking about the later inclusion of gentiles into the nation Israel (although this was always possible under the law anyway), nor is He referring to the church which came about after Israel's total rejection of the Gospel message of the Apostles, and later Paul. For this was a *mystery* until Paul revealed it. What we see here is that provision is made in the event of some refusing what was originally their right and privilege as Jews, and the Lord shows that their actions would not affect God's will in the long term. A consistent refusal to listen or change could mean that many would lose their salvation, despite feeling [42]secure in the knowledge that they were the Children of Israel. In the event the present leaders of that people were soon to demonstrate their true heart towards God in their rejection and murder of His Son, and in their rejection of His call in their purely selfish and unacceptable excuses, they would prove the truth of His words here.

CHAPTER FOUR

The Mount of Olives, *When shall these things be?*

Matthew 24:1-3: *And Jesus went out, and departed from the temple: and his disciples came to him for to shew him the buildings of the temple. And Jesus said unto them, See ye not all these things? verily I say unto you, There shall not be left here one stone upon another, that shall not be thrown down. And as he sat upon the Mount of Olives, the disciples came unto him privately, saying, Tell us, when shall these things be? And what shall be the sign of thy coming, and of the end of the world?*

We should not be too surprised at the disciple's enthusiasm concerning the temple buildings, as to them it would be inconceivable that any introduction of the Lord's Kingdom on Earth would not be associated with that present Temple. This was not the original temple that Solomon built under the Lord's instruction, but what is known as Herod's temple, the second temple, incomplete at that time and not to be finished till 64AD. Herod ostensibly rebuilt this to demonstrate his magnanimous attitude towards the Jews, but in reality it was built to impress them and stand as a monument to his own greatness.

The future of this temple was of course, known to the Lord beforehand, as was His imminent rejection and crucifixion at the hands of the leaders of the people, as this discourse was only given about three days before He was taken. What the future of the Temple would have been if in fact He had been accepted as Messiah we cannot tell, but its destruction at the hands of the Romans in AD70 certainly marked the end, for the foreseeable future, of any Jewish hopes of independent worship as the morning and evening, or daily, sacrifices could no longer be made there. Jewish religion after this was without a point of focus, and the orthodox Jews' 'Wailing or Western Wall', which they [43]believe is part of the outer wall of Herod's temple, is the only tangible object left for them to associate with what was once a marvel to all who saw it. It is worth noting that while He spoke of the destruction of this temple, nowhere does He mention it being rebuilt, and we have to look further to unearth what is to happen to Jewish worship, under the Law. We will consider this in due course.

Later of course, when the disciples are with Him on the Mount of Olives that overlooked the temple, they ask Him what He meant by this, and they were concerned about three things. They ask *'When shall these things be?'* mainly referring to the destruction of the temple, and two other questions seemingly in one, *what shall be the sign of thy coming, and of the end of the world?* It is reasonable to suppose that they considered that all three of these events would come at the same time, and as He had spoken of the temple's destruction, they may have also assumed this would happen at His coming, and that He would be the one to destroy it.

They needed some proper teaching on this, so He began to show them that the period of the *End* is rather more complicated, and would take place over an extended period of time.

Notice that He does not answer their first question, as the destruction of the temple is not now relevant to the end days, although it is an interesting exercise to consider how it might have turned out if Israel had accepted Him at the time. Of course it might not have been destroyed at all in the event of His acceptance; we cannot be sure, although the Lord's words, combined with Ezekiel's earlier prophecy, suggest that it must be levelled at some point to make way for the third Temple!

The study of End Day Prophecy as a whole is a complex undertaking, going beyond the scope of this present [44]book, which is centred on the Kingdom and Millennial prophecies for Israel. For this reason I will confine myself here to what the Lord says in Matthew as being the Gospel of the King. As it happens, Matthew's gospel gives far more detail than either Mark or Luke's, with John being remarkably silent on the subject until he later writes his book of Revelation.

Matthew 24:4-5: *And Jesus answered and said unto them, Take heed that no man deceive you. For many shall come in my name, saying, I am Christ; and shall deceive many.*

Interestingly, the first thing that the Lord warns of is not the destruction of the Temple, or of any other dramatic event that the Jews of the End Times should be watching for, but rather a resurgence of deceivers, to the extent that some would even claim to be the long-awaited Messiah. This, from its place at the beginning, shows the danger, for it is extremely important for the latter-day Jews that they know what to expect and are properly grounded in the doctrines of their own times, so that they can be discerning as to what they accept, and recognise what is likely to come next. Should they lose their perspective, and be swayed by these deceivers, the game is over for them, as they will neither be in the right place to receive the truth, nor recognise the lies when they come. This has to be a real possibility at the beginnings of these troubled times.

Matthew 24:6-7: *And ye shall hear of wars and rumours of wars: see that ye be not troubled: for all these things must come to pass, but the end is not yet. For nation shall rise against nation, and kingdom against kingdom...*

Again, the signs of the times are both actual wars and the rumour and threat of wars, both between nations and within nations, which is a present reality. Although these are not yet in Israel itself, they do indirectly affect its security, as modern Israel is very much aware. Certainly at this present time we can point to countless wars as indicators of the End Times, and news of internal disputes in particular regularly graces our media, along with countless border disputes. Many of these are in areas close to Israel, for example Syria, Palestine, Egypt, Turkey, Iraq, Iran, Libya, and Yemen are all current hot spots, problem areas with no real hope of resolution. The Lord's advice is for the Jews in this instance, that they should not to be troubled, seems strange advice, until we realise the context this is set in, for they are asking about His coming, and wars are only one of the several early indicators that this is getting nearer.

Matthew 24:7-8: *and there shall be famines, and pestilences, and earthquakes, in divers places. All these are the beginning of sorrows.*

Alongside these wars and rumours are famine, pestilence and earthquakes, and the Lord gives this period a title, the *beginnings of sorrows*, as distinguished from the *End*. Wars of course, bring famine and disease in their wake, and the consequences for populations are far reaching, but at the same time the world will experience natural disaster in the form of earthquakes, which are not only unpredictable but also extremely destructive despite man's best efforts to monitor and control them. All of these events will cause the world's nations to be preoccupied with their own particular difficulties, and some things may go unnoticed, when the concern of individual nations is focused on finding solutions to their own problems. Even world powers such as America are subject to public opinion, and any disasters closer to home must take priority, so the normal balance of policing or monitoring world affairs can be altered very quickly at such times.

Matthew 24:9-10: *Then shall they deliver you up to be afflicted, and shall kill you: and ye shall be hated of all nations for my name's sake. And then shall many be offended, and shall betray one another, and shall hate one another.*

In this same period, we are told that the Jews become a persecuted people, this time hated of all nations, not just one, to the extent that they are delivered up to be tortured and killed This is also done internally by those, presumably other Jews, who become offended. We might wonder what will happen to make the world suddenly blame the Jews for its troubles, especially when we remember the lessons of the previous holocaust, and its aftermath of blame and guilt, but there is a clue in the Lord's next words: *And this gospel of the kingdom shall be preached in all the world for a witness unto all nations.* This might well be the core of the offence that causes such an adverse reaction, even amongst the Jews themselves. This is the Gospel Kingdom being proclaimed again, the later preaching of the *Kingdom of Heaven* that has been delayed up until this point. We can see that the world is bound to be offended at this new Israel, which in recent history has gained a reputation for its supposed arrogance and heavy-handed treatment of its Arab neighbours, and has subsequently lost support from its traditional allies. Imagine the world's chagrin when the Jews, or some of them at least, start to proclaim that their Messiah is about to return, and that they, the Jewish people, are about to become reinstated as God's chosen people on earth. They may also legitimately [45]claim that the world's calamities are a sign of this, so there is bound to be a backlash against them.

This may also cause problems amongst the more orthodox of the Jewish people, as well as the more secular, who will see this as bringing unwanted negative attention towards Israel, and themselves. The Lord never claimed that preaching the gospel would be problem free, and the truth being proclaimed at this time will undoubtedly cause the same divisions as it has in the past.

Matthew 24:11-14: *And many false prophets shall rise, and shall deceive many. And because iniquity shall abound, the love of many shall wax cold. But he that shall endure unto the end, the same shall be saved. And this gospel of the kingdom shall be preached in all the world for a witness unto all nations; and then shall the end come.*

The other effect of the gospel being preached is that it will bring forth many more false prophets, who will once again *deceive many* who will themselves, once deceived, become enemies of the gospel. Others may just give up hope altogether. Notice that this is the second warning about being deceived, but not the last, in this discourse. Their only option at this time is to look to the Word of God, to find out what He has said about this period, and to know and stick to the instruction, the

Lord's words gave here, which are specific to this [46]time. It would be far better for them not to leave it too late though, and to consider these things before they are come upon them.

Matthew 24:15-20: *When ye therefore shall see the abomination of desolation, spoken of by Daniel the prophet, stand in the holy place, (whoso readeth, let him understand:) Then let them which be in Judae flee into the mountains: Let him which is on the housetop not come down to take any thing out of his house: Neither let him which is in the field return back to take his clothes. And woe unto them that are with child, and to them that give suck in those days! But pray ye that your flight be not in the winter, neither on the sabbath day...*

This is a significant change in the narrative, and begins the period the Lord calls the Great Tribulation, or the End, as the disciples described it earlier. Now is the time for the believing Jew to get out of Judea, for this is the fulfilment of the prophecy of [47]Daniel (and also later of John in the book of Revelation) concerning this *Abomination of Desolation*, the image of the *Beast* that the *False prophet* causes to be set up on the Temple site at Jerusalem.

The onus here is on the reader to understand, and shows that the Lord expects His followers to be diligent and aware of scriptural prophecy concerning these times. Those in Israel who despise or neglect their own scriptures, are the ones most likely to become victims at this time, for this is the greatest test of faith that the nation will ever face.

Whilst [48]detail here is beyond the scope of this book, this abomination will be set up in the *Holy place*, the Temple [49]site, in the middle of the last prophetic week, or seven years period at the end, and its appearance divides the last prophetic week, so that it is safe to say that the first three and a half years can be entitled *the beginnings of sorrows,* and the period after the

Abomination of desolation, is set up, the final three and a half years, is named the *Great tribulation*. This is the time of the *End*, as the Lord describes it, and is the period the disciples initially questioned Him about. But this is not necessarily the time of the Lord's return and nor does it complete the *End* period, as we shall see.

Matthew 24:21-23: *For then shall be great tribulation, such as was not since the beginning of the world to this time, no, nor ever shall be. And except those days should be shortened, there should no flesh be saved: but for the elect's sake those days shall be shortened. Then if any man shall say unto you, Lo, here is Christ, or there; believe it not. For there shall arise false Christs, and false prophets, and shall shew great signs and wonders; insomuch that, if it were possible, they shall deceive the very elect. Behold, I have told you before.*

The *elect*, the Jewish believers at this time, some of whom will survive these experiences, will find some relief from the troubles, but there is yet another warning in addition to the first two, regarding both *False Christs and False prophets,* who display miraculous powers to back up their claims. Nowhere does the Lord name the *Anti-Christ* or the *False prophet* of Revelation as individuals, but He does warn here of several such characters being around during this latter half of the week, who would, except for the Lord's assistance, deceive even the faithful by their miraculous signs. Clearly everyone must be spiritually alert at this time, constantly referring back to what the Lord taught in scripture, rather than heeding the views of any other self-proclaimed but false *teachers*. There will be a lot of confusion at this time, and in times of such uncertainty and persecution believers will be desperate to see the Lord appear to restore order and safety. He is the only hope here, but His appearance will be unmistakeable, and no one will be able to counterfeit it by any sleight of hand. Attempts will be made to draw his followers from their places of refuge, and the actual *Beast* will be at the height of his powers at this time, but they are to await the sign of his coming, which appears in the heavens.

Matthew 24:26-28: *Wherefore if they shall say unto you, Behold, he is in the desert; go not forth: behold, he is in the secret chambers; believe it not. For as the lightning cometh out of the east, and shineth even unto the west; so shall also the coming of the Son of man be. For wheresoever the carcase is, there will the eagles be gathered together.*

The strong message for the latter-day Jewish believer is to hold fast to his scriptures and wait for the conclusion of these tragedies, disregarding the claim of any to be the Messiah. The period of the *Great tribulation* is limited to three and a half years, or twelve hundred and sixty days, but it would be a mistake to think that this is the end of the matter, although after this the Jew is relatively safe in his homeland.

What is completed though is the [50]*Seventy years of Jeremiah*, the period of the *Desolations* that Daniel had written about. This marks the end of the Lord's prophesied anger towards the nation Israel, the final week, and the nation can now look forward to their renaissance as His people. In dispensational terms they are entering into the period of the Millennium reign, the thousand-year period spoken of by [51]John in the book of Revelation, and the period of Israel's earthly rule under their king in heaven. This is nothing other than the *Kingdom of Heaven*, as it would have appeared had the Jewish people accepted their saviour, either during His lifetime, or soon after His resurrection under the testimony of the disciples.

Matthew 24:29-31: *Immediately after the tribulation of those days shall the sun be darkened, and the moon shall not give her light, and the stars shall fall from heaven, and the powers of the heavens shall be shaken: And then shall appear the sign of the Son of man in heaven: and then shall all the tribes of the earth mourn, and they shall see the Son of man coming in the clouds of heaven with power and great glory. And he shall send his angels with a great sound of a trumpet, and they shall gather together his elect from the four winds, from one end of heaven to the other.*

Notice how this new period commences, with darkness. What the powers of the heavens are is a matter of conjecture, but we know that Satan, who is now on earth, is yet to be dealt with, and so this is the likely time his of his temporary [52]confinement. The *Great tribulation* has finished, but their darkest hour precedes the appearing of the *sign of the son of man in heaven*. The immediate assumption might be that this is a gigantic cross in the skies, but this is unlikely, as the cross indicates His humiliation at the hands of men. Here is His appearing in triumph over Satan and the world, and as Paul talks of the wicked one being destroyed with the [53]*brightness of His coming,* this is the more likely explanation of what the sign is – His light appearing through the darkness. There is also a move at this time to bring home the Jews that are scattered abroad, for the danger is past in Israel, and this trumpet heralds a new beginning for this earth. At the same time, the earth mourns with the realisation that they had backed the wrong 'Messiah', recognising belatedly who the Son of God really is, and who His people are. Perhaps they can now appreciate that they should have given the Jews better treatment through these times, and done what they could to protect them?

What is remarkable in Matthew's narrative is that the Lord offers more parables, and these clearly relate to a period following that of the great tribulation. This suggests a further time of trial or waiting for the Lord's appearance, and yet there is no timescale indicated. We have the *sign of His coming*, but no Lord as yet. These parables must therefore be further teachings about the Kingdom, and what the people are expected to do whilst waiting for His actual coming. Taking into account that during this time Satan has been bound, the people are now responsible for their own actions, and cannot use the spiritual opposition once ranged against them as an excuse. In theory at least it should be a lot easier for them to get things right from now on, and there is no reason why they shouldn't.

Matthew 24:32-36: *Now learn a parable of the fig tree; When his branch is yet tender, and putteth forth leaves, ye know that summer is nigh: So likewise ye, when ye shall see all these things, know that it is near, even at the doors. Verily I say unto you, This generation shall not pass, till all these things be fulfilled. Heaven and earth shall pass away, but my words shall not pass away. But of that day and hour knoweth no man, no, not the angels of heaven, but my Father only.*

The Lord in establishing the certainty of His words also shows *that day and hour is known to no man*, only of course His Father, and we should consider here what He means by this.

I have heard these words misquoted as referring to the Gentile church and its rapture, and that He is talking here about His coming to take us to Himself in the clouds. We have already established that the Lord is talking to Israel here, and specifically to His disciples who were the ones chosen to lead the people into the *Kingdom of Heaven,* should it have appeared at that time. Although the actual time of the *parousia* or gathering together of the church is not known, it is specifically referred to by Paul in 1 and 2 Thessalonians, where we are taught to be ready at any time for this event. Compare Paul's words, firstly to the church:

1 Thessalonians Chapter 4:16-18: *For the Lord Himself shall descend from heaven with a shout, with the voice of the arch-angel, and*

with the trump of God, and the dead in Christ shall rise first: then we which are alive and remain shall be caught up together with them in the clouds, to meet the Lord in the air, and so shall we ever be with the Lord. Wherefore comfort one another with these words.

And then to the same people about the Jewish expectation:

1 Thessalonians Chapter 5:1-6: *But of the times and seasons brethren, ye have no need that I write unto you. For yourselves know perfectly that the day of the Lord so cometh as a thief in the night. For when they shall say peace and safety; then sudden destruction cometh upon them, as travail upon a woman with child; and they shall not escape. But ye brethren are not in darkness that that day should overtake you as a thief. Ye are all the children of light, and the children of the day; we are not of the night, nor of darkness. Therefore let us not sleep as do others, but let us watch and be sober.*

Paul's comparison shows that the church is to be comforted by the fact that the Lord is coming for them, and so should wait for Him, being in the light, and completely aware of the times whilst watching for these events to take place. There is no indication of any time given, it could literally be at any time, as there are no conditions set for this, unlike for the *Day of the Lord* which not only *cometh as a thief in the night*, but will not come, unless as 2 Thessalonians 2:3 shows:

[54]*that day shall not come, except there come a falling away first, and that man of sin be revealed, the son of perdition, who opposeth and exalteth himself above all that is called God, or is worshipped.*

We see, from Paul's instruction to the church, that there are differences between the two events, and in actual fact the *Day of the Lord*, which is the same as the [55]*times and seasons* that the Jews spoke of, will not commence until after the appearance of the *beast*. This appearance is subject to his establishing, or ratifying, a seven-year covenant or contract with the Jewish people regarding the daily sacrifice, as we have discussed. He is properly revealed when he breaks this covenant in the middle of the week, or seven-year period, and then turns on the Jews in his full fury. This is when some see him for who he really is, but by this time it is too late to stop him.

The point I want to make here is that when the Lord is talking about His coming for the Jews, the *Day of the Lord*, it is not altogether unexpected, as it has to fit in to a particular timescale. The Lord's crucifixion date completed the sixty-nine weeks of Daniel's prophecy, and there is an indeterminate middle period, of which we are a part, where the *Gospel of Grace* is preached to both Jew and Gentile alike. However, once the covenant is signed with Israel, we know that there is going to be a defined seven-year period, the first half being roughly what the Lord called the *beginning of sorrows*, the middle, where the covenant is broken and the *abomination of desolation* is set up, and then the final three and a half years consisting of the *Great Tribulation* period. These timings are not too much of a mystery, and once into the last seven years must take their course, but the Lord's coming for Israel is a mystery, as no one knows that day. If He was to come as many suppose, straight after the tribulation, to reign over Israel, then the expression *as a thief in the night* would not really apply, for as soon as His sign appears in the sky, He will be expected. What He is telling His people in these parables is that He expects faithfulness beyond the period of the tribulation, as they really have no idea, and neither does He, when He will come. They have the sign of His coming, but when He actually will come is not shown. If we look at the following parables in this light, they begin to make more sense:

Matthew 24:37-44: *But as the days of Noe were, so shall also the coming of the Son of man be. For as in the days that were before the flood they were eating and drinking, marrying and giving in marriage, until the day that Noe entered into the ark, And knew not until the flood came, and took them all away; so shall also the coming of the Son of man be. Then shall two be in the field; the one shall be taken, and the other left. Two women shall be grinding at the mill; the one shall be taken, and the other left. Watch therefore: for ye know not what hour your Lord doth come. But know this, that if the goodman of the house had known in what watch the thief would come, he would have watched, and would not have suffered his house to be broken up. Therefore be ye also ready: for in such an hour as ye think not the Son of man cometh.*

The above scenario is not of a people in the midst of tribulation and dangers but of peace, prosperity and carrying out normal activities. The warning here is of spiritual complacency in the absence of anything greater to worry about than marriage and feasting. This is the time when the Lord will come, in their prosperity, when things look good, and all dangers have past. His appearance will catch the unwary by surprise, and the idea here is that they should be vigilant at all times.

Matthew Chapter 24:45-51: *Who then is a faithful and wise servant, whom his Lord hath made ruler over his household, to give them meat in due season? Blessed is that servant, whom his Lord when he cometh shall find so doing. Verily I say unto you, That he shall make him ruler over all his goods. But and if that evil servant shall say in his heart, My Lord delayeth his coming; And shall begin to smite his fellowservants, and to eat and drink with the drunken; The Lord of that servant shall come in a day when he looketh not for him, and in an hour that he is not aware of, And shall cut him asunder, and appoint him his portion with the hypocrites: there shall be weeping and gnashing of teeth.*

Again the message here is of continued faithfulness in the temporary absence of the Lord. The reward is for those who maintain their responsibilities, in particular towards their fellow servants, but the temptation is to revert to more selfish ways, and in their drunken state to forget that there will eventually be a reckoning, which comes *in a day that he looketh not for him,* when the faithful will find reward, but the slothful and wicked, judgement. Notice the language here is of *servants and fellow servants,* which are the terms used to describe the Israelites under the law, and not the [56]gentile or Jewish believers in the church. These sayings apply to the Jewish nation, who are now once again become His servants on the earth.

Matthew Chapter 25:1-13: *Then shall the Kingdom of Heaven be likened unto ten virgins, which took their lamps, and went forth to meet the bridegroom. And five of them were wise, and five were foolish. They that were foolish took their lamps, and took no oil with them: But the wise took oil in their vessels with their lamps. While the bridegroom tarried, they all slumbered and slept. And at midnight there was a cry made, Behold, the bridegroom cometh; go ye out to meet him. Then all those virgins arose, and trimmed their lamps. And the foolish said unto the wise, Give us of your oil; for our lamps are gone out. But the wise answered, saying, Not so; lest there be not enough for us and you: but go ye rather to them that sell, and buy for yourselves. And while they went to buy, the bridegroom came; and they that were ready went in with him to the marriage: and the door was shut. Afterward came also the other virgins, saying, Lord, Lord, open to us. But he answered and said, Verily I say unto you, I know you not. Watch therefore, for ye know neither the day nor the hour wherein the Son of man cometh.*

Here is a similar warning that defines how the Lord views the difference between wisdom and folly. We are reminded here of the calling to the marriage supper that is to take place at the end of days, described in the Book of [57]Revelation. The difference between the two groups, the wise and the foolish, is clear in that the wise have prepared for the eventuality that the groom may delay his coming, and they have made sure that should this happen, they will be ready anyway. They have made no assumptions, and know that they will only get one chance at this. They are not heartless where the foolish are concerned, and tell them exactly what they need to do, but they will not compromise themselves because of the others' lack of foresight. Because the groom can come at any time (which depends on the father of the bridegroom being satisfied that everything is ready) in this parable the foolish miss their chance, and it is only the ones who are ready who are let in. The Lord is fair in this, as He is in all of His dealings with them, and is giving fair warning to the nation that they should be ready at any time for Him, whether His coming is delayed or not.

Matthew Chapter 25:14-30: *For the Kingdom of Heaven is as a man travelling into a far country, who called his own servants, and delivered unto them his goods. And unto one he gave five talents, to another two, and to another one; to every man according to his several ability; and straightway took his journey. Then he that had received the five talents went and traded with the same, and made them other five talents. And likewise he that had received two, he also gained other two. But he that had received one went and digged in the earth, and hid his Lord's money. After a long time the Lord of those servants cometh, and reckoneth with them. And so he that had received five talents came and brought other five talents, saying, Lord, thou deliveredst unto me five talents: behold, I have gained beside them five talents more. His Lord said unto him, Well done, thou good and faithful servant: thou hast been faithful over a few things, I will make thee ruler over many things: enter thou into the joy of thy Lord. He also that had received two talents came and said, Lord, thou deliveredst unto me two talents: behold, I have gained two other talents beside them. His Lord said unto him, Well done, good and faithful servant; thou hast been faithful over a few things, I will make thee ruler over many things: enter thou into the joy of thy Lord. Then he which had received the one talent came and said, Lord, I knew thee that thou art an hard man, reaping where thou hast not sown, and gathering where thou hast not strawed: And I was afraid, and went and hid thy talent in the earth: lo, there thou hast that is thine. His Lord answered and said unto him, Thou wicked and slothful servant, thou knewest that I reap where I sowed not, and gather where I have not strawed: Thou oughtest therefore to have put my money to the exchangers, and then at my coming I should have received mine own with usury. Take therefore the talent from him, and give it unto him which hath ten talents. For unto every one that hath shall be given, and he shall have abundance: but from him that hath not shall be taken away even that which he hath. And cast ye the unprofitable servant into outer darkness: there shall be weeping and gnashing of teeth.*

Another misquoted parable, often said to mean that we should use our 'talents' in the churches for the kingdom's sake. The Lord is neither speaking to the church here nor is a 'talent' in its original translation a gift or skill but a weight or equivalent in coinage. He is again speaking regarding the kingdom, and the fact that for a while it will be expected to manage without its king. In the parable, instructions are left, and the servants are expected to be faithful according to their ability in the eyes of the Lord. This means that the expectation from each is different, but each knows what he has to do and is capable of doing it. It is on the Lord's assessment that judgement and reward are given out, but this time given should be viewed as an opportunity for the nation to show its faithfulness towards its God, and maintain its position spiritually. This includes the expectation of reward, as Paul showed in Hebrews 11:6: *But without faith it is impossible to please him: for he that cometh to God must believe that he is, and*

CHAPTER FOUR

that he is a rewarder of them that diligently seek him.

This shows that there is nothing wrong in believing that our efforts will be rewarded eternally, but this will be when He is ready to judge, and not necessarily in this life. The believing Jew at this time must also bear in mind that when the Lord returns there will be both reward and judgement, which for him will be dependent on his works, or what he has done as a servant within the level of trust imparted to him. The unprofitable servant can look forward to darkness, so again we understand that the Kingdom of Heaven contains both the faithful and the unfaithful, in these times of trial.

Matthew 25:31-46: *When the Son of man shall come in his glory, and all the holy angels with him, then shall he sit upon the throne of his glory: And before him shall be gathered all nations: and he shall separate them one from another, as a shepherd divideth his sheep from the goats: And he shall set the sheep on his right hand, but the goats on the left. Then shall the King say unto them on his right hand, Come, ye blessed of my Father, inherit the kingdom prepared for you from the foundation of the world: For I was an hungred, and ye gave me meat: I was thirsty, and ye gave me drink: I was a stranger, and ye took me in: Naked, and ye clothed me: I was sick, and ye visited me: I was in prison, and ye came unto me. Then shall the righteous answer him, saying, Lord, when saw we thee an hungred, and fed thee? or thirsty, and gave thee drink? When saw we thee a stranger, and took thee in? or naked, and clothed thee? Or when saw we thee sick, or in prison, and came unto thee? And the King shall answer and say unto them, Verily I say unto you, Inasmuch as ye have done it unto one of the least of these my brethren, ye have done it unto me. Then shall he say also unto them on the left hand, Depart from me, ye cursed, into everlasting fire, prepared for the devil and his angels: For I was an hungred, and ye gave me no meat: I was thirsty, and ye gave me no drink: I was a stranger, and ye took me not in: naked, and ye clothed me not: sick, and in prison, and ye visited me not. Then shall they also answer him, saying, Lord, when saw we thee an hungred, or athirst, or a stranger, or naked, or sick, or in prison, and did not minister unto thee? Then shall he answer them, saying, Verily I say unto you, Inasmuch as ye did it not to one of the least of these, ye did it not to me. And these shall go away into everlasting punishment: but the righteous into life eternal.*

Finally, here we see how that both nations and individuals will be judged at the very end. There will be no arguments or excuses accepted at this time, but there may be some surprises, for notice the reactions of both the righteous and the cursed who find that it is in their treatment of others, specifically the brethren of the Lord, on which they have been subject to the Lord's particular scrutiny.

The contrast made between sheep and goats here is interesting, for the goat is an inquisitive animal, hard to confine in one place and independently minded, whereas sheep tend to be more gregarious, and are happy to be led. In fact, the Middle Eastern shepherd often uses the goats to go before the flock and lead them. The lesson here though is that those nations who consider the laws of God restrictive, and refuse them, will eventually be separated from the faithful nations who do accept His rule.

We must accept here that as this is the final or eternal judgement, the brethren referred to must include believers in the both the Christian and Jewish churches, who will eventually be included together in blessing, when the Jewish church shall also have been tried and found faithful. As Paul said:

Romans 10:10-14: *But why dost thou judge thy brother? or why dost thou set at nought thy brother? for we shall all stand before the judgment seat of Christ. For it is written, As I live, saith the Lord, every knee shall bow to me, and every tongue shall confess to God. So then every one of us shall give account of himself to God. Let us not therefore judge one another any more: but judge this rather, that no man put a stumblingblock or an occasion to fall in his brother's way.*

CHAPTER FIVE

The book of Isaiah: Israel in God's blessing

The authorship of the book of Isaiah has been questioned since around the beginning of the nineteenth century, with some claiming that there is a distinct division between the end of Chapter 39 and the remainder of the book. They discuss the former and latter parts as if the first part was written by the original Isaiah and then as if there were other so-called Isaiahs, up to three or more, who completed the prophecy after the death of the original. To confirm this they offer the fact that different Hebrew words are used in each section, then state that these are exclusive to either the first or second part. But there is no internal evidence for such theories, and as scripture is silent regarding other authors, we can reasonably suppose that the Lord, John the Baptist, Matthew, Mark, John, James, and the apostle Paul accepted just one Isaiah, as they all freely [58]quote in the New Testament from both of the supposed divisions of the book, without reference to any other authors. In fact Isaiah is quoted in twenty out of the twenty-seven books of the New Testament without there being a single reference to any dual authorship.

Isaiah began as a prophet during the latter part of the reign of King Uzziah, whose reign initially started out well enough but who towards the end of his life exceeded his place as king when attempting to offer incense in the temple. For this act he contracted leprosy, eventually dying separated from both his kingdom and the temple. Isaiah's period of prophesy spanned about 61 years, making him a contemporary of both Hosea and Micah, but at what age he died we cannot be sure, except that he must have been in his eighties, from the historical evidence. From the wording of Isaiah 6:1, it is likely that his commission to prophecy commenced in the last year of Uzziah, but as Uzziah's son Jotham was a good king, it was probably not until the reign of Jotham's successor, Ahaz, under whose influence the people were turned away from the Lord, that this prophecy became relevant.

From the beginning Isaiah's words are directed towards the future state of Judah, being written not only as a warning but as a confirmation of the promise of blessing, should the people listen. For this reason the prophecy is far reaching, extending to the time when Israel would be blessed. Sadly, because of their conduct, blessing would be delayed for a very long time. It is held by tradition that Isaiah was the one referred to in Hebrews 11:37 as being 'sawn asunder' during the persecutions in the reign of Manasseh the son of Hezekiah, after having hid himself in a hollow tree trunk, but my own view is that a man of his experience and calibre would have accepted his own fate with more dignity. However, it is a good story.

Isaiah's writings concern the nation Israel typified in Judah and Jerusalem, but the difficulty we face when studying his prophecies (and those of others) is that many of them refer to historical events which although future to Isaiah at the time when they were given, are now long past and fulfilled. Like many prophecies in scripture however, they were elastic in their scope, and it is clear that in many instances the Holy Spirit was also speaking about events far into the future. Prophecy takes account of the fickleness of men allowing them space to do the right thing, to change their ways and therefore avoid any judgements uttered against them. This truly is the main purpose of God in using men of God to speak on His behalf, in order that others might hear, consider their ways, and change. If it was not so, then why would God bother to communicate with man at all? He could just as easily allow him to carry on in his own destructive ways, and then judge him, if He was so inclined.

One example of this is Jonah, who when he went to speak to the men of Nineveh, [59]recognised the mercy of God, and knew that if they did change and listen, this would not bode well for Israel later. This was why he ran away from his commission initially, and why God saved him and sent him back. We do not always allow God the liberty of changing His own mind, although we continually expect to be able to do this ourselves!

To consider the book of Isaiah:

Isaiah 1:9-20: *Except the Lord of hosts had left unto us a very [60]small remnant, we should have been as Sodom, and we should have been like unto Gomorrah. Hear the word of the Lord, ye rulers of Sodom; give ear unto the law of our God, ye people of Gomorrah. To what purpose is the multitude of your sacrifices unto me? saith the Lord : I am full of the burnt offerings of rams, and the fat of fed beasts; and I delight not in the blood of bullocks, or of lambs, or of he goats. When ye come to appear before me, who hath required this at your hand, to tread my courts? Bring no more vain oblations; incense is an abomination unto me; the new moons and sabbaths, the calling of assemblies, I cannot away with; it is iniquity, even the solemn meeting. Your new moons and your appointed feasts my soul hateth: they are a trouble unto me; I am weary to bear them. And when ye spread forth your hands, I will hide mine eyes from you: yea, when ye make many prayers, I will not hear: your hands are full of blood. Wash you, make you clean; put away the evil of your doings from before mine eyes; cease to do evil; Learn to do well; seek judgment, relieve the oppressed, judge the fatherless, plead for the widow. Come now, and let us reason together, saith the Lord: though your sins be as scarlet, they shall be as white as snow; though they be red like crimson, they shall be as wool. If ye be willing and obedient, ye shall eat the good of the land: But if ye refuse and rebel, ye shall be devoured with the sword: for the mouth of the Lord hath spoken it.*

From the beginning of Isaiah's vision we learn that Israel, typified now by Judah and Jerusalem, will survive, despite the worst excesses of some of its kings and leaders and their followers. Because of the promises first given to Abraham and others that they would not be destroyed completely, God remained faithful and has kept His word. This was not the case for others such as Sodom and Gomorrah, who are given here as examples of His power and ability to bring extreme judgement if necessary. God's anger against His people was due mainly to the fact that they had despised the revelation and heritage that was exclusively theirs. He had warned them from the beginning that He was a jealous God, and in their turning to the ways and gods of the nations around them, they were about to provoke

His anger. He showed in effect that they were just as bad as Sodom, and from this point on were in danger of suffering similar consequences. Although this did not take place immediately, eventually this is what happened, and throughout its history Israel has been at odds with its God, and has suffered the consequences of it. However, in the very end, through a small remnant of the faithful, He will have His way, and Israel will finally be held up as His representatives, His people on earth, both glorifying Him and justifying His faithfulness and patience towards them.

The rulers here are compared to the Sodomites and the people to Gomorrah, both towns having been [61]destroyed for their complacency and wickedness. Judah's religious observance, whilst still in place, had now also turned into an abomination to the Lord, because their real heart was against Him. Going through the motions was not good enough for Him, nor was He fooled by their outward pretence. Even their keeping the law, to which obedience was a requirement, meant nothing to Him at this point, as everything was being done in the wrong spirit. Their sacrifices meant nothing, for they neglected what He really wanted from them. Notice from the above passage what they were really required to do was: *'Wash you, make you clean; put away the evil of your doings from before mine eyes; cease to do evil; Learn to do well; seek judgment, relieve the oppressed, judge the fatherless, plead for the widow'*.

It was the poor people who were suffering the most, and had the majority listened to the solution offered at this stage, there would have been an opportunity for them to renew their fellowship with the Lord. The change of heart required is reminiscent of the Lord's words on the Sermon on the Mount, showing how basically simple the nature and requirements of

CHAPTER FIVE

His laws are. Looking out for the less fortunate is one thing He is looking for in His followers.

Here is one prophecy that has definitely never been fulfilled:

Isaiah 2:1-22: *The word that Isaiah the son of Amoz saw concerning Judah and Jerusalem. And it shall come to pass in the last days, that the mountain of the Lord 's house shall be established in the top of the mountains, and shall be exalted above the hills; and all nations shall flow unto it. And many people shall go and say, Come ye, and let us go up to the mountain of the Lord, to the house of the God of Jacob; and he will teach us of his ways, and we will walk in his paths: for out of Zion shall go forth the law, and the word of the Lord from Jerusalem. And he shall judge among the nations, and shall rebuke many people: and they shall beat their swords into plowshares, and their spears into pruninghooks: nation shall not lift up sword against nation, neither shall they learn war any more. O house of Jacob, come ye, and let us walk in the light of the Lord. Therefore thou hast forsaken thy people the house of Jacob, because they be replenished from the east, and are soothsayers like the Philistines, and they please themselves in the children of strangers. Their land also is full of silver and gold, neither is there any end of their treasures; their land is also full of horses, neither is there any end of their chariots: Their land also is full of idols; they worship the work of their own hands, that which their own fingers have made: And the mean man boweth down, and the great man humbleth himself: therefore forgive them not. Enter into the rock, and hide thee in the dust, for fear of the Lord, and for the glory of his majesty. The lofty looks of man shall be humbled, and the haughtiness of men shall be bowed down, and the Lord alone shall be exalted in that day. For the day of the Lord of hosts shall be upon every one that is proud and lofty, and upon every one that is lifted up; and he shall be brought low: And upon all the cedars of Lebanon, that are high and lifted up, and upon all the oaks of Bashan, And upon all the high mountains, and upon all the hills that are lifted up, And upon every high tower, and upon every fenced wall, And upon all the ships of Tarshish, and upon all pleasant pictures. And the loftiness of man shall be bowed down, and the haughtiness of men shall be made low: and the Lord alone shall be exalted in that day.*

The narrative above jumps to a future time, one of many instances in the book of Isaiah where this happens. Notice that the ministry is confined to Judah and Jerusalem, and mentions the period of the *last days*. From the description, we can see that Isaiah is talking about a future period of prosperity and righteousness for Judah for which the conditions have not yet been met. That is not to say it was impossible for it to be achieved, and certainly, the Lord's appearance in Jerusalem was intended to herald this time of prosperity, yet the Jews rejection of both Him and the subsequent ministry of the Holy Spirit, through the apostles, meant that the promises have been left unfulfilled, and kept in abeyance until the time when the Jews show a change of heart.

This passage shows some interesting aspects of the coming kingdom:

The mountain of the Lord 's house shall be established in the top of the mountains, and shall be exalted above the hills; and all nations shall flow unto it. And many people shall go and say, Come ye, and let us go up to the mountain of the Lord, to the house of the God of Jacob; and he will teach us of his ways, and we will walk in his paths: for out of Zion shall go forth the law, and the word of the Lord from Jerusalem.

In the previous chapter we learned of the destruction of Herod's temple, yet here the Lord's house is again established and respected by the nations around Israel who go there to learn of *His ways and His paths, through the Law, and His word.* As a result there is no more war, or the need to train for war, as many of the surrounding nations are now walking in the light of the

Lord. This truly is an idyllic situation, previously unknown on the earth, being the peace that everyone claims they want but have been unable to achieve, despite their best efforts. The world considers that religion is the cause of most wars, yet here *His ways* are plainly stated, that bring an end to all violence and war. Of course the suggestion to the world that they should allow the Jews to build a new Temple on the Holy site in Jerusalem, and then themselves be expected to go there to find the answers to its problems, will raise a few eyebrows, especially in the current climate. It does look like a far-fetched idea, but scripture is consistent with itself throughout on this matter, and what we cannot presently see by sight we are going to have to learn to accept by faith. It is a fact that there is presently a growing movement in Israel, with some financial backing from the government, to prepare for and build what is known as the Third Temple.

Sadly, in Isaiah's time, the real condition of the people is described:

…because they be replenished from the east, and are soothsayers like the Philistines, and they please themselves in the children of strangers. Their land also is full of silver and gold, neither is there any end of their treasures; their land is also full of horses, neither is there any end of their chariots: Their land also is full of idols; they worship the work of their own hands, that which their own fingers have made: And the mean man boweth down, and the great man humbleth himself: therefore forgive them not.

In their rejection of the Lord, and their decision to involve themselves with the nations around them, they had lost their opportunity to be pre-eminent amongst the nations as God's chosen people, and instead had placed themselves in line for the same judgments that all those who deny God will face. We should be careful to differentiate between the immediate fulfilling of these prophecies given to that generation, against the more far-reaching judgments that the world will face, which is what is described in this passage. Judah itself was later to be carried away to Babylon, and many consider this historical fact enough to satisfy this prophecy. But Israel has never yet become a place of worship drawing all nations to itself to seek God, so that while there may be some partial fulfilment, there remain aspects of this yet to be revealed, particularly in regard to Israel's blessing. To this present day we see only war and bloodshed in the earth, and so should realistically accept that we are looking at a yet future time described in this passage, both for the judgments to come on Israel and the world, but also in the blessing that is to be found in Israel when it is finally restored as God's people. Notice too, that these judgments were targeted towards specific people:

The lofty looks of man shall be humbled, and the haughtiness of men shall be bowed down, and the Lord alone shall be exalted in that day. For the day of the Lord of hosts shall be upon every one that is proud and lofty, and upon every one that is lifted up; and he shall be brought low: And upon all the cedars of Lebanon, that are high and lifted up, and upon all the oaks of Bashan, And upon all the high mountains, and upon all the hills that are lifted up, And upon every high tower, and upon every fenced wall, And upon all the ships of Tarshish, and upon all pleasant pictures. And the loftiness of man shall be bowed down, and the haughtiness of men shall be made low. And the Lord alone shall be exalted in that day.

This should give some encouragement to those who are aware of the coming judgment on the earth, and yet remain faithful to their Lord!

We now jump forward in Isaiah to a prophecy concerning

the Lord's appearance, which had they accepted Him, would have heralded the appearance of the Kingdom of Heaven:

Isaiah 11:1-13: *And there shall come forth a rod out of the stem of Jesse, and a [62]Branch shall grow out of his roots: And the spirit of the Lord shall rest upon him, the spirit of wisdom and understanding, the spirit of counsel and might, the spirit of knowledge and of the fear of the Lord; And shall make him of quick understanding in the fear of the Lord: and he shall not judge after the sight of his eyes, neither reprove after the hearing of his ears: But with righteousness shall he judge the poor, and reprove with equity for the meek of the earth: and he shall smite the earth with the rod of his mouth, and with the breath of his lips shall he slay the wicked. And righteousness shall be the girdle of his loins, and faithfulness the girdle of his reins.*

It is apparent here that there would have been a judgement in some form on the nations that oppressed Israel, but how this would have materialised is difficult to know now. If we refer to the Lord's words to the disciples, many of the events prophesied in Daniel concerning the end days could have found their fulfilment in the early Acts period, and characters such as the Roman Emperor Caligula, for example, may have fulfilled the role of the anti-Christ at the time. He certainly demanded worship, as was common under the Emperor cult, and just before he died had made a statue of himself, to be displayed in Herod's temple, which in other circumstances might have served as the *abomination of desolation*, which is now yet to appear. We may also have found that the destruction of the temple and Jerusalem in 70AD would have served to fulfil other aspects of the prophecy, for these events are certainly shadows or types, and could have been used to expedite events surrounding the End Times for Israel. John the Baptist himself fulfilled the role of [63]Elijah who was to come before the Day of the Lord, a similar role being now taken by the two witnesses of Revelation. However, by the time the Lord spoke to the disciples about the *End days* in depth, it was clear to Him that He was going to be rejected, and so the fulfilment of some of these prophecies would have to wait until other events had unfolded. It is an interesting exercise to ponder on what might have been, but things changed with the Jewish response and rejection of Him, and what the Lord discussed with the disciples at the Mount of Olives concerning the End Times will be the true and definitive fulfilment of events that the believing Jew should expect to take place. What is certain from His words is that His Kingdom will be set up on this earth eventually, and that it will centre on Jerusalem.

Isaiah gives us a further remarkable insight into changes that are to take place not only in man, but also in nature. There is a growing tendency today to spiritualize plain statement in scripture and to relegate some scriptures to the realms of quaint stories, supposedly given to explain away misunderstood or difficult events, to the unsophisticated and simple. It is then implied that in these enlightened times we should not take such stories too literally. This is often done under the guise of supporting scriptural truth, when in reality it undermines God's written word, consigning away the miraculous to the natural world. Sadly, a lot of the time this is done by ministers in churches, who, when attempting to present themselves as modern thinkers, discredit the very scriptures they are paid to uphold. Of course at times God did use natural events to further His will, but we should not forget that He is perfectly capable of performing the miraculous without being obliged to provide a natural explanation for it.

We should not be persuaded that in this day and age we are

too sophisticated to be expected to believe such things, and should we be offered alternative explanations more fitted to our modern times, we ought to be rightly suspicious, as believers. This type of thinking does no credit to past generations of believers both Jewish and Christian, who in their simplicity have accepted the truths of scripture as being the plain Word of God, and in some cases have died in order for these truths to be heard and published. Below we have a case in point, described by some as being too far-fetched for the modern mind to tolerate, but which is in reality is no effort for a creator God. In my view getting nations to live together in harmony is the greater of the two miracles, given the present climate in the Middle East!

The wolf also shall dwell with the lamb, and the leopard shall lie down with the kid; and the calf and the young lion and the fatling together; and a little child shall lead them. And the cow and the bear shall feed; their young ones shall lie down together: and the lion shall eat straw like the ox. And the sucking child shall play on the hole of the asp, and the weaned child shall put his hand on the cockatrice' den. They shall not hurt nor destroy in all my holy mountain: for the earth shall be full of the knowledge of the Lord, as the waters cover the sea.

However literally we choose to interpret the above, it is clear that the natural order of things must change for this to take place, for the inherent fear and antagonism between man and animals will disappear. This may suggest a vegetarian diet being introduced once more, as it was before the flood, but any such changes are only possible through the *knowledge of the Lord* being in all the earth. It may also be that this is confined to His *Holy Mountain*, but it does seem that the holy mountain is to extend over all the earth in its influence, making such things normal in these times. In Isaiah 65:25 we see another reference to these changes, where they are clearly associated with the *Kingdom of*

God, the period where the new heaven and new earth are created, so it may be that these supernatural phenomena are not initially a part of the *Kingdom of heaven*, the millennial reign, but belong to the later period of the *Kingdom of God*, the new heavens and new earth.

And in that day there shall be a root of Jesse, which shall stand for an ensign of the people; to it shall the [64]Gentiles seek: and his rest shall be glorious. And it shall come to pass in that day, that the Lord shall set his hand again the second time to recover the remnant of his people, which shall be left, from Assyria, and from Egypt, and from Pathros, and from Cush, and from Elam, and from Shinar, and from Hamath, and from the islands of the sea. And he shall set up an ensign for the nations, and shall assemble the outcasts of Israel, and gather together the dispersed of Judah from the four corners of the earth. The envy also of Ephraim shall depart, and the adversaries of Judah shall be cut off: Ephraim shall not envy Judah, and Judah shall not vex Ephraim.

This passage seems to reflect the Lord's words in Matthew concerning His people's physical gathering together in Israel, but this blessing is not exclusive to Jews, as it also applies to any non-Jewish nations or individuals that seek Him.

This does not only include the dispersal of Judah (including Benjamin, as the tribe that continued with it after the Northern tribes had been taken into captivity) but also Ephraim, one of the ten northern tribes that were dispersed amongst the Assyrian Empire. When they are finally gathered together, previous differences amongst the Jews are resolved and they will then act in unison regardless of past tensions, whether real or imagined. The tribes will also be identifiable, which shows that there are still some remnants left to represent them. From what the Lord said in Matthew, this gathering together comes after the *Great Tribulation* period, being a feature of the new Israel, the *Kingdom of Heaven.* We should be careful not to include the Gentile church (as distinguished from the Jewish Church) in these verses, for this period is the beginning of the millennial reign, by which time the Gentile church will have gone to be with the Lord. By this time, any non-Jews wishing to seek God will need to conform to the Jewish Laws of the time, and seek Him under the same conditions as the Jew, under an altogether different dispensation to the one we have now.

Moving on:

Isaiah 14:12-25: *How art thou fallen from heaven, O Lucifer, son of the morning! how art thou cut down to the ground, which didst weaken the nations! For thou hast said in thine heart, I will ascend into heaven, I will exalt my throne above the stars of God: I will sit also upon the mount of the congregation, in the sides of the north: I will ascend above the heights of the clouds; I will be like the most High. Yet thou shalt be brought down to hell, to the sides of the pit. They that see thee shall narrowly look upon thee, and consider thee, saying, Is this the man that made the earth to tremble, that did shake kingdoms; That made the world as a wilderness, and destroyed the cities thereof; that opened not the house of his prisoners? All the kings of the nations, even all of them, lie in glory, every one in his own house. But thou art cast out of thy grave like an abominable branch, and as the raiment of those that are slain, thrust through with a sword, that go down to the stones of the pit; as a carcase trodden under feet. Thou shalt not be joined with them in burial, because thou hast destroyed thy land, and slain thy people: the seed of evildoers shall never be renowned. Prepare slaughter for his children for the iniquity of their fathers; that they do not rise, nor possess the land, nor fill the face of the world with cities. For I will rise up against them, saith the Lord of hosts, and cut off from Babylon the name, and remnant, and son, and nephew, saith the Lord. I will also make it a possession for the bittern, and pools of water: and I will sweep it with the besom of destruction, saith the Lord of hosts. The Lord of hosts hath sworn, saying, Surely as I have thought, so shall it come to pass; and as I have purposed, so shall it stand: That I will break the Assyrian in my land, and upon my mountains tread him under foot: then shall his yoke depart from off them, and his burden depart from off their shoulders.*

We find another informative section of Isaiah's prophecy, which in the first instance relates to Babylon's destruction after it had been used to punish Israel but also extends to the *End Times*, and shows that the real inspiration behind Babylon is Satan himself, who is mentioned as its king! The narrative switches to Lucifer, another of his names, and his impending destruction, the beginning of which can be compared to John's writings in the book of Revelation:

Revelation 12:6-9: *And the woman fled into the wilderness, where she hath a place prepared of God, that they should feed her there a thousand two hundred and threescore days. And there was war in heaven: Michael and his angels fought against the dragon; and the dragon fought and his angels, And prevailed not; neither was their place found any more in heaven. And the great dragon was cast out, that old serpent, called the Devil, and Satan, which deceiveth the whole world: he was cast out into the earth, and his angels were cast out with him.*

It is at this time, during the middle of the last week, that Satan is cast out of heaven and promptly empowers his man on earth, the *beast,* to *weaken the nations* and set about destroying Israel. Clearly the nation Babylon is involved with this, as Satan is associated with Babylon as its king, but there is another character in Isaiah named as the *Assyrian* to whom our attention is directed. Assyria, whilst it included a part of Babylon, was an earlier empire, and roughly covered the area now inhabited by the Kurds, consisting of parts of Syria, Turkey Iraq, and Iran. This

CHAPTER FIVE

is now a fiercely contested area, sometimes called Kurdistan, which the Kurds are attempting to claim for their homeland. It is also the present base of operations for the Islamic state organisation, or Isil, who have the stated intention of making this area their Caliphate. In any event, this character the *Assyrian* seems to come from this area, and I would suggest that he is the person whom Satan uses and empowers in these last times. Satan himself is bound for a thousand years after the *Great Tribulation* has finished, to be freed later but by then the [65]*beast* and his *false prophet* have already been cast into the lake of fire, from which there is no return.

Our interest is then drawn to Isaiah 19:18-25:

In that day shall five cities in the land of Egypt speak the language of Canaan, and swear to the Lord of hosts; one shall be called, The city of destruction. In that day shall there be an altar to the Lord in the midst of the land of Egypt, and a pillar at the border thereof to the Lord. And it shall be for a sign and for a witness unto the Lord of hosts in the land of Egypt: for they shall cry unto the Lord because of the oppressors, and he shall send them a saviour, and a great one, and he shall deliver them. And the Lord shall be known to Egypt, and the Egyptians shall know the Lord in that day, and shall do sacrifice and oblation; yea, they shall vow a vow unto the Lord, and perform it. And the Lord shall smite Egypt: he shall smite and heal it: and they shall return even to the Lord, and he shall be intreated of them, and shall heal them. In that day shall there be a highway out of Egypt to Assyria, and the Assyrian shall come into Egypt, and the Egyptian into Assyria, and the Egyptians shall serve with the Assyrian. In that day shall Israel be the third with Egypt and with Assyria, even a blessing in the midst of the land. Whom the Lord of hosts shall bless, saying, Blessed be Egypt my people, and Assyria the work of my hands, and Israel mine inheritance.

Another prophecy, interesting in its scope as it concerns the final status of both Egypt and Assyria (or part of modern Syria). This shows that the borders of Israel will extend far into these countries, and subsequently the people there will be included in the blessing for the whole region, under Israel's umbrella. Notice that their inclusion also involves sacrifice and oblation, or freewill offerings, which are acceptable in this new dispensation. There is no suggestion here that this is forced upon them, but is rather a voluntary submission to the God of Israel, all of which the Lord states is the work of His hands. This will also provide living space for the many thousands of Jews who are to return to their homeland, and will herald the real solution to the Palestinian problem. After the destruction of the nations who fight against Israel, the restoration of the land begins, as described below:

Isaiah 35:1-10: *The wilderness and the solitary place shall be glad for them; and the desert shall rejoice, and blossom as the rose. It shall blossom abundantly, and rejoice even with joy and singing: the glory of Lebanon shall be given unto it, the excellency of Carmel and*

Sharon, they shall see the glory of the Lord, and the excellency of our God. Strengthen ye the weak hands, and confirm the feeble knees. Say to them that are of a fearful heart, Be strong, fear not: behold, your God will come with vengeance, even God with a recompence; he will come and save you. Then the eyes of the blind shall be opened, and the ears of the deaf shall be unstopped. Then shall the lame man leap as an hart, and the tongue of the dumb sing: for in the wilderness shall waters break out, and streams in the desert. And the parched ground shall become a pool, and the thirsty land springs of water: in the habitation of dragons, where each lay, shall be grass with reeds and rushes. And an highway shall be there, and a way, and it shall be called The way of holiness; the unclean shall not pass over it; but it shall be for those: the wayfaring men, though fools, shall not err therein. No lion shall be there, nor any ravenous beast shall go up thereon, it shall not be found there; but the redeemed shall walk there: And the ransomed of the Lord shall return, and come to Zion with songs and everlasting joy upon their heads: they shall obtain joy and gladness, and sorrow and sighing shall flee away.

The Lord's intention for this land is not only for it to be fruitful and well-watered, as opposed to the desert it presently is, but that it should also be accessible to the nations that remain, and so this highway, *the way of holiness*, will provide a means for them to access it. This is not for the *unclean* or *fools*, but for the *redeemed, and the ransomed* of the Lord to return by. This may refer to refugees from other places, or those who have been forced out of Israel by the previous *tribulations*, but in any event seems to refer to any who want to seek the Lord in these times, which is now possible through access to the restored religion of Israel.

Isaiah 40:1-31: *Comfort ye, comfort ye my people, saith your God. Speak ye comfortably to Jerusalem, and cry unto her, that her warfare is accomplished, that her iniquity is pardoned: for she hath received of the Lord's hand double for all her sins. The voice of him that crieth in the wilderness, Prepare ye the way of the Lord, make straight in the desert a highway for our God. Every valley shall be exalted, and every mountain and hill shall be made low: and the crooked shall be made straight, and the rough places plain: And the glory of the Lord shall be revealed, and all flesh shall see it together: for the mouth of the Lord hath spoken it. The voice said, Cry. And he said, What shall I cry? All flesh is grass, and all the goodliness thereof is as the flower of the field: The grass withereth, the flower fadeth: because the spirit of the Lord bloweth upon it: surely the people is grass. The grass withereth, the flower fadeth: but the word of our God shall stand forever. O Zion, that bringest good tidings, get thee up into the high mountain; O Jerusalem, that bringest good tidings, lift up thy voice with strength; lift it up, be not afraid; say unto the cities of Judah, Behold your God! Behold, the Lord God will come with strong hand, and his arm shall rule for him: behold, his reward is with him, and his work before him. He shall feed his flock like a shepherd: he shall gather the lambs with his arm, and carry them in his bosom, and shall gently lead those that are with young. Who hath measured the waters in the hollow of his hand, and meted out heaven with the span, and comprehended the dust of the earth in a measure, and weighed the mountains in scales, and the hills in a balance? Who hath directed the Spirit of the Lord, or being his counsellor hath taught him? With whom took he counsel, and who instructed him, and taught him in the path of judgment, and taught him knowledge, and shewed to him the way of understanding? Behold, the nations are as a drop of a bucket, and are counted as the small dust of the balance: behold, he taketh up the isles as a very little thing. And Lebanon is not sufficient to burn, nor the beasts thereof sufficient for a burnt offering. All nations before him are as nothing; and they are counted to him less than nothing, and vanity. To whom then will ye liken God? or what likeness will ye compare unto him? The workman melteth a graven image, and the goldsmith spreadeth it over with gold, and casteth silver chains. He that is so impoverished that he hath no oblation chooseth a tree that will not rot; he seeketh unto him a cunning workman to prepare a graven image, that shall not be moved. Have ye not known? have ye not heard? hath it not been told you from the beginning? have ye not understood from the foundations of the earth? It is he that sitteth upon the circle of the earth, and the inhabitants thereof are as grasshoppers; that stretcheth out the heavens as a curtain, and spreadeth them out as a tent to dwell in: That bringeth the princes to nothing; he maketh the judges of the earth as vanity. Yea, they shall not be planted; yea, they shall not be sown: yea, their stock shall not take root in the earth: and he shall also blow upon them, and they shall wither, and the whirlwind shall take them away as stubble. To whom then will ye liken me, or shall I be equal? saith the Holy One. Lift up your eyes on high, and behold who hath created these things, that bringeth out their host by number: he calleth them all by names by the greatness of his might, for that he is strong in power; not one faileth. Why sayest thou, O Jacob, and speakest, O Israel, My way is hid from the Lord , and my judgment is passed over from my God? Hast thou not known? hast thou not heard, that the everlasting God, the Lord , the Creator of the ends of the earth, fainteth not, neither is weary? there is no searching of his understanding. He giveth power to the faint; and to them that have no might he increaseth strength. Even the youths shall faint and be weary, and the young men shall utterly fall: But they that wait upon the Lord shall renew their strength; they shall mount up with wings as eagles; they shall run, and not be weary; and they shall walk, and not faint.*

The above verses can be said to refer to the coming of John the Baptist, whose mission was to:

Prepare ye the way of the Lord, make straight in the desert a highway for our God. Every valley shall be exalted, and every mountain and hill shall be made low: and the crooked shall be made straight, and the rough places plain: And the glory of the Lord shall be revealed, and all flesh shall see it together: for the mouth of the Lord hath spoken it.

We again notice a highway mentioned, and whilst we may understand this as being symbolic in describing John's work, it is closely related to the very real road of access, the *way of holiness* in the new Israel. In all road construction this process of levelling, building up and straightening of all things takes place, and such is the case with the Lord's dealings with Israel in the *End Times*. The people, both through Isaiah and later through John the Baptist, were being prepared for such changes, which were evidently due after the Lord's first appearing. The people are reminded of His great power here, and the *nations,* who at the time seem all powerful as conquerors, are shown to be merely tools, a means to an end, in the grand purpose of the Father's will. However unlikely it would seem, the people of God, once they demonstrate the right spirit towards Him, are to be exalted above the nations around them. In the Lord's time the great Empire was of course Rome, and for a time His Jewish followers were expecting their Messiah to be a great military leader who would bring them out from subjection to other nations. This will be the case in the last days, for Israel will once again be subject to a power physically greater than themselves, and will look for deliverance. For believers in any age there is strength available to them to overcome, which they will surely need in Israel whilst waiting patiently to see His purposes worked out. This in fact is the very thing that the Lord is looking for in His people: a complete reliance on Him, glorifying Him as they overcome any adversities presented to them. This must be achieved in His strength and not their own, and only then will their deliverance come, after they have accepted the Lord and proved themselves to Him, and not after He has first proved Himself to them.

Moreover, despite Israel's several failures, the scriptures consistently support His choosing them as His servants and although other nations may be incensed at this, it remains a fact that their eventual victory is assured. The land will be restored to a people who now trust their God for their strength, and the reason is shown at the end of this chapter:

That they may see, and know, and consider, and understand together, that the hand of the Lord hath done this, and the Holy One of Israel hath created it.

Israel's very existence and survival as a nation stands as a testimony to God's power, and their raising up at the end of

CHAPTER FIVE

times will an unmistakable testament to His handiwork.

Isaiah 41:8-20: *But thou, Israel, art my servant, Jacob whom I have chosen, the seed of Abraham my friend. Thou whom I have taken from the ends of the earth, and called thee from the chief men thereof, and said unto thee, Thou art my servant; I have chosen thee, and not cast thee away. Fear thou not; for I am with thee: be not dismayed; for I am thy God: I will strengthen thee; yea, I will help thee; yea, I will uphold thee with the right hand of my righteousness. Behold, all they that were incensed against thee shall be ashamed and confounded: they shall be as nothing; and they that strive with thee shall perish. Thou shalt seek them, and shalt not find them, even them that contended with thee: they that war against thee shall be as nothing, and as a thing of nought. For I the Lord thy God will hold thy right hand, saying unto thee, Fear not; I will help thee. Fear not, thou worm Jacob, and ye men of Israel; I will help thee, saith the Lord, and thy redeemer, the Holy One of Israel. Behold, I will make thee a new sharp threshing instrument having teeth: thou shalt thresh the mountains, and beat them small, and shalt make the hills as chaff. Thou shalt fan them, and the wind shall carry them away, and the whirlwind shall scatter them: and thou shalt rejoice in the Lord, and shalt glory in the Holy One of Israel. When the poor and needy seek water, and there is none, and their tongue faileth for thirst, I the Lord will hear them, I the God of Israel will not forsake them. I will open rivers in high places, and fountains in the midst of the valleys: I will make the wilderness a pool of water, and the dry land springs of water. I will plant in the wilderness the cedar, the shittah tree, and the myrtle, and the oil tree; I will set in the desert the fir tree, and the pine, and the box tree together: That they may see, and know, and consider, and understand together, that the hand of the Lord hath done this, and the Holy One of Israel hath created it.*

Here we see the wilderness and the waste places planted and prosperous through the abundance of water, and so it must seem there is a change in the topography of Israel to allow such variety of trees to grow, its prosperity is in itself a sign to the world of Gods favour towards Israel.

Isaiah 49:17-26: *Thy children shall make haste; thy destroyers and they that made thee waste shall go forth of thee. Lift up thine eyes round about, and behold: all these gather themselves together, and come to thee. As I live, saith the Lord, thou shalt surely clothe thee with them all, as with an ornament, and bind them on thee, as a bride doeth. For thy waste and thy desolate places, and the land of thy destruction, shall even now be too narrow by reason of the inhabitants, and they that swallowed thee up shall be far away. The children which thou shalt have, after thou hast lost the other, shall say again in thine ears, The place is too strait for me: give place to me that I may dwell. Then shalt thou say in thine heart, Who hath begotten me these, seeing I have lost my children, and am desolate, a captive, and removing to and fro? and who hath brought up these? Behold, I was left alone; these, where had they been? Thus saith the Lord God, Behold, I will lift up mine hand to the Gentiles, and set up my standard to the people: and they shall bring thy sons in their arms, and thy daughters shall be carried upon their shoulders. And kings shall be thy nursing fathers, and their queens thy nursing mothers: they shall bow down to thee with their face toward the earth, and lick up the dust of thy feet; and thou shalt know that I am the Lord: for they shall not be ashamed that wait for me. Shall the prey be taken from the mighty, or the lawful captive delivered? But thus saith the Lord, Even the captives of the mighty shall be taken away, and the prey of the terrible shall be delivered: for I will contend with him that contendeth with thee, and I will save thy children. And I will feed them that oppress thee with their own flesh; and they shall be drunken with their own blood, as with sweet wine: and all flesh shall know that I the Lord am thy Saviour and thy Redeemer, the mighty One of Jacob.*

Again referring to the end times it is seen that two things

happen: that the oppressors of Israel are dispersed, and that Israel itself is repopulated to the extent that more land is needed to accommodate the new arrivals. The *children* here are likely to consist of the *many people* spoken of earlier, of all nations, but who are seeking God in this reconstituted Israel, We must remember that a large number of the original population will have been killed in the *tribulations*, as well as many others leaving to save their own lives, most of these will now return to their homeland.

Isaiah 54:1-17: *Sing, O barren, thou that didst not bear; break forth into singing, and cry aloud, thou that didst not travail with child: for more are the children of the desolate than the children of the married wife, saith the Lord. Enlarge the place of thy tent, and let them stretch forth the curtains of thine habitations: spare not, lengthen thy cords, and strengthen thy stakes; For thou shalt break forth on the right hand and on the left; and thy seed shall inherit the Gentiles, and make the desolate cities to be inhabited. Fear not; for thou shalt not be ashamed: neither be thou confounded; for thou shalt not be put to shame: for thou shalt forget the shame of thy youth, and shalt not remember the reproach of thy widowhood any more. For thy Maker is thine husband; the Lord of hosts is his name; and thy Redeemer the Holy One of Israel; The God of the whole earth shall he be called. For the Lord hath called thee as a woman forsaken and grieved in spirit, and a wife of youth, when thou wast refused, saith thy God. For a small moment have I forsaken thee; but with great mercies will I gather thee. In a little wrath I hid my face from thee for a moment; but with everlasting kindness will I have mercy on thee, saith the Lord thy Redeemer. For this is as the waters of Noah unto me: for as I have sworn that the waters of Noah should no more go over the earth; so have I sworn that I would not be wroth with thee, nor rebuke thee. For the mountains shall depart, and the hills be removed; but my kindness shall not depart from thee, neither shall the covenant of my peace be removed, saith the Lord that hath mercy on thee. O thou afflicted, tossed with tempest, and not comforted, behold, I will lay thy stones with fair colours, and lay thy foundations with sapphires. And I will make thy windows of agates, and thy gates of carbuncles, and all thy borders of pleasant stones. And all thy children shall be taught of the Lord; and great shall be the peace of thy children. In righteousness shalt thou be established: thou shalt be far from oppression; for thou shalt not fear: and from terror; for it shall not come near thee.*

Behold, they shall surely gather together, but not by me: whosoever shall gather together against thee shall fall for thy sake. Behold, I have created the smith that bloweth the coals in the fire, and that bringeth forth an instrument for his work; and I have created the waster to destroy. No weapon that is formed against thee shall prosper; and every tongue that shall rise against thee in judgment thou shalt condemn. This is the heritage of the servants of the Lord, and their righteousness is of me, saith the Lord.

The desolations do not just extend to Israel, but the Lord talks here of the restoration of other nations under Israel's blessing, comparing Israel here to the forsaken and refused wife, and Himself as the husband. Those who believe that the church is now the bride take note here, for although Israel is the forsaken wife, it is only for *a small moment*. This type of language is significant, for the Lord talks about Himself as being the husband and redeemer, the one who created Israel in the first place and the one who will eventually be joined to it, as a man and wife are joined. The insistence of translators and interpreters over the years on placing the gentile church in this position, quoting passages that Paul gave, which were really just given as illustrations of other things, should be measured against the truth of scripture in Isaiah that His *bride* is, and always will be, the nation Israel, when it finally becomes subject to its Lord. Attempting to shoehorn the church into a position where it does not belong has led to doctrinal confusion, shared by many branches of the church, which is quite unnecessary. The gentile church loses none of its glory in the Lord's eyes in its place as His body, nor does it have to compete with His own nation Israel, when it is reinstated. It is for this reason that the Apostle Paul wrote at great length in the Book of Romans to impart to believers, both there and elsewhere, a full understanding of the church's own dispensational nature, to make them realise that its formation came about in the period immediately after Israel's temporary rejection of the Lord, the culmination of which is described at the end of the Book of Acts. It has never replaced the nation Israel in the promises and will of God, nor will it ever become the expected *bride* in Israel's place as the modern 'replacement theologies' claim. If these theories had been true then Paul would surely have written about them, but he wrote instead that Israel's position is that of God's people on this earth, called to be a demonstration of His grace to be seen by those on earth, and that the (gentile) church is a demonstration to angels and others of His grace eternally in the [66]heavens. The real gentile church will never be, nor was ever intended to be, visible in this world as a united physical body, in the way that Israel undoubtedly will be. There is no question that we in the church are witnesses of Him in a measure whilst Israel waits in the wings, but we will be taken up to fulfil our heavenly role, when the time comes for Israel to take up its own right and proper place on the Earth.

Notice that for the children, all those in subjection to the Lord, is this promise:

And all thy children shall be taught of the Lord; and great shall be the peace of thy children. In righteousness shalt thou be established: thou shalt be far from oppression; for thou shalt not fear: and from terror; for it shall not come near thee.

This is set in contrast to the previous unrest and tribulation of this present world, yet this does not exclude the fact that there are still nations around who will not submit themselves, even in these times when the Lord rules on the earth through His people:

Behold, they shall surely gather together, but not by me: whosoever shall gather together against thee shall fall for thy sake. Behold, I have created the smith that bloweth the coals in the fire, and that bringeth forth an instrument for his work; and I have created the waster to destroy. No weapon that is formed against thee shall prosper; and every tongue that shall rise against thee in judgment thou shalt condemn. This is the heritage of the servants of the Lord, and their righteousness is of me, saith the Lord.

This is in perfect accord with what is written in the Revelation about the nations Gog and Magog:

Revelation 20:7-10: *And when the thousand years are expired, Satan shall be loosed out of his prison, And shall go out to deceive the nations which are in the four quarters of the earth, Gog and Magog, to gather them together to battle: the number of whom is as the sand of the sea. And they went up on the breadth of the earth, and compassed the camp of the saints about, and the beloved city: and fire came down from God out of heaven, and devoured them. And the devil that deceived them was cast into the lake of fire and brimstone, where the beast and the false prophet are, and shall be tormented day and night forever and ever.*

We should not confuse this event with the previous attempts of Satan through the *beast* and the *false prophet* to overcome Israel, for this is clearly after the Millennium or thousand-year reign spoken of here, after which Satan is freed from the bottomless pit, to stir up strife once more against Israel. This time it is the nations Gog and Magog, together with those that have been incited to come against Israel, that lend themselves to his purpose, rather than the Empires of Babylon, Persia, Greece and Rome, or their modern-day equivalents. This is Satan's final attempt to undo Israel and thereby avoid his own judgement, this time using northern tribes, who cannot be positively identified but are most likely those we would describe as Russian nations, or possibly those of Anatolia or Turkey, who see an opportunity to take advantage of Israel's [67]peaceful co-existence. This attack is doomed to failure, and is defeated by God Himself, Israel not having the means to defend itself at this time.

The really interesting thing to note about the [68]*Millennium reign* is that its mention is exclusive to John's writings in the book of Revelation. Whilst clearly there is a gap between the Lord's coming after the *Great tribulation* ends, it does not seem to me that it was initially intended to last for a thousand years. This theory is strengthened when we consider that in the other gospels, apart from Matthew's, the emphasis is clearly on the Kingdom of God appearing, so that the people should also be preparing themselves for this. It would seem that the length of time that the Kingdom of Heaven was to be in place, was originally far shorter than a thousand years. In the book of Revelation, when we read Revelation chapter 1:1 we see:

The Revelation of Jesus Christ, which God gave unto Him, to shew unto His servants things that must shortly come to pass, and He sent and signified it by His angel unto His servant John.

My impression from these words is that this new Revelation from God now given covers and includes all of the events up to that point, such as the Jewish rejection and the formation of the church. These were things that were passed on to John probably at the same time as they were revealed to the Lord, and they were new to everyone. This would be roughly in 96AD. This contains the revised and final conclusion of God's plan for Earth, which had been altered from the original intention, to draw events to a close shortly after the Lord's death and resurrection. The book of Revelation closes the canon of the bible, and completes what can be known in the Word of God about the will of the Father for this earth. It is the last Word we hear, revealed by the Alpha and Omega, Himself the Last Word, the Beginning and the End.

This makes it likely that originally there would have been no Millennium reign planned at all, but a much shorter period, yet having the same aim, which was to cause Israel to rely totally on their God before His kingdom is established. How long this would have taken is mere conjecture, but there is evidence to suggest that it would have been expected in the lifetime of the majority present when the Lord was ministering. The wonderful thing, to my mind, is how the prophecies given concerning these events, such as those written by Daniel and Isaiah, not to mention the Lord's own words, are so in step as to allow for the flexibility that was needed to cover every eventuality, and yet still be true for each case. This is nothing less than the inspired work of the Holy Spirit in giving the exact words to the prophets to speak or write in the first place.

Isaiah 55:1-13 *Ho, every one that thirsteth, come ye to the waters, and he that hath no money; come ye, buy, and eat; yea, come, buy wine and milk without money and without price. Wherefore do ye spend money for that which is not bread? and your labour for that which satisfieth not? hearken diligently unto me, and eat ye that which is good, and let your soul delight itself in fatness. Incline your ear, and come unto me: hear, and your soul shall live; and I will make an everlasting covenant with you, even the sure mercies of David. Behold, I have given him for a witness to the people, a leader and commander to the people. Behold, thou shalt call a nation that thou knowest not, and nations that knew not thee shall run unto thee because of the Lord thy God, and for the Holy One of Israel; for he hath glorified thee. Seek ye the Lord while he may be found, call ye upon him while he is near: Let the wicked forsake his way, and the unrighteous man his thoughts: and let him return unto the Lord, and he will have mercy upon him; and to our God, for he will abundantly pardon. For my thoughts are not your thoughts, neither are your ways my ways, saith the Lord. For as the heavens are higher than the earth, so are my ways higher than your ways, and my thoughts than your thoughts. For as the rain cometh down, and the snow from heaven, and returneth not thither, but watereth the earth, and maketh it bring forth and bud, that it may give seed to the sower, and bread to the eater: So shall my word be that goeth forth out of my mouth: it shall not return unto me void, but it shall accomplish that which I please, and it shall prosper in the thing whereto I sent it. For ye shall go out with joy, and be led forth with peace: the mountains and the hills shall break forth before you into singing, and all the trees of the field shall clap their hands. Instead of the thorn shall come up the fir tree, and instead of the brier shall come up the myrtle tree: and it shall be to the Lord for a name, for an everlasting sign that shall not be cut off.*

Israel is again shown that in its own acceptance of the Lord who was to come (*Incline your ear, and come unto me: hear, and your soul shall live; and I will make an everlasting covenant with you, even the sure mercies of David. Behold, I have given him for a witness to the people, a leader and commander to the people*) their blessing would be extended towards other nations, even those that Israel has not yet known of or considered. While we acknowledge that some of these words applied to the time in which they were written, we should also accept that these words have yet to be completely fulfilled, for although their Messiah did come as promised, a large part of this prophecy remains future as the conditions for it have not yet been met.

For example: *Let the wicked forsake his way, and the unrighteous man his thoughts: and let him return unto the Lord, and he will have mercy upon him; and to our God, for he will abundantly pardon.* The national repentance of Israel will occur before its national blessing, and only then will the purpose of God be seen in all of His doings, when they finally realise that:

My thoughts are not your thoughts, neither are your ways my ways, saith the Lord. For as the heavens are higher than the earth, so are my ways higher than your ways, and my thoughts than your thoughts. For as the rain cometh down, and the snow from heaven, and returneth not thither, but watereth the earth, and maketh it bring forth and bud, that it may give seed to the sower, and bread to the eater: So shall my word be that goeth forth out of my mouth: it shall not return unto me void, but it shall accomplish that which I please, and it shall prosper in the thing whereto I sent it.

The effects of the words of God, even in this prophecy, are deeper and further reaching than most who hear them can appreciate, and even when they are not fulfilled as we might imagine they should be they are nevertheless still valid, and will yet cause this work to come to fruition. The worlds many efforts to diminish Israel, and consign it to the history books because of its previous failures, does not then give it the right to proclaim the Word of God null and void.

So we find that whilst God has delayed the performing of His word, He has neither abandoned Israel nor its place in His will as regards the world. Admittedly to date, Israel has produced little but *thorns and briars* to the nations around it, being self-interested and difficult to deal with, and altogether proving the truth of being described as a *stiff-necked people*. This attitude can be understood to some extent because of the continual and real threat they are under from their neighbours. However, under His word they are to become the *fir tree and myrtle tree*, the symbols of blessing that He will use to glorify Himself. His control in this is such that once He has bound Satan for a thousand years, He intends to let him out again to rally his forces against Israel, giving him free rein to do his worst, even to the extent of being allowed to incite other nations to join him. This is because of the Lord's confidence that when this time comes His people will have learned to trust Him, and so He permits this one final trial for them.

Isaiah 56:6-8: *Also the sons of the stranger, that join themselves to the Lord, to serve him, and to love the name of the Lord, to be his servants, every one that keepeth the sabbath from polluting it, and taketh hold of my covenant; Even them will I bring to my holy mountain, and make them joyful in my house of prayer: their burnt offerings and their sacrifices shall be accepted upon mine altar; for mine house shall be called an house of prayer for all people. The Lord God which gathereth the outcasts of Israel saith, Yet will I gather others to him, beside those that are gathered unto him.*

The Jews over the years have tended to forget that their blessing from the start was to extend to other nations, who were also intended to come under the same covenant that they enjoyed themselves. This is built in to their very temple itself, which included the 'court of the gentiles' in its construction. Paul explains this when talking to the Galatians:

Galatians 3:6-9: *Even as Abraham believed God, and it was*

accounted to him for righteousness. Know ye therefore that they which are of faith, the same are the children of Abraham. And the scripture, foreseeing that God would justify the heathen through faith, preached before the gospel unto Abraham, saying, In thee shall all nations be blessed. So then they which be of faith are blessed with faithful Abraham.

The Jews, as custodians of the scriptures, tended to overemphasize their own importance, eventually becoming superior in their attitude towards other nations. Even Peter, the chosen apostle, whose loyalty and zeal for God was greater than most, had to be strongly reminded by means of a vision of the inclusion of non-Jews in God's plan. In Peter's mind, others had to first become proselytes, or converts to the Jewish faith, before they could be offered salvation. He held to this belief far longer than he should have done, even [69]falling foul of Paul later on when he became indecisive, having become too close to the doctrines of the church organisation of the time, which was by then pulling back towards a more orthodox view. Paul, who could once have claimed to be the strictest of law-observing Jews, being expert in both the law and its traditions, could plainly see that the Jewish nation was intended to be a conduit of blessing for the whole world. You would think that Peter, a genuinely *unlearned and ignorant* fisherman, would have eagerly embraced the simplicity of a gospel that welcomed all comers, but it was Paul in fact, who having been schooled in the Jewish religion from a child, could grasp the concept of the inclusion of other peoples and nations, and welcome them. Perhaps it was these very prophecies of Isaiah that helped convince him? For Paul, keeping the good news to themselves was not an option, for in his own mind he knew that the Jews were the custodians of God's Word but not the owners of it, and nor were they the final authority on its scope!

CHAPTER FIVE

Isaiah 57:13-18: *When thou criest, let thy companies deliver thee; but the wind shall carry them all away; vanity shall take them: but he that putteth his trust in me shall possess the land, and shall inherit my holy mountain; And shall say, Cast ye up, cast ye up, prepare the way, take up the stumblingblock out of the way of my people. For thus saith the high and lofty One that inhabiteth eternity, whose name is Holy; I dwell in the high and holy place, with him also that is of a contrite and humble spirit, to revive the spirit of the humble, and to revive the heart of the contrite ones. For I will not contend forever, neither will I be always wroth: for the spirit should fail before me, and the souls which I have made. For the iniquity of his covetousness was I wroth, and smote him: I hid me, and was wroth, and he went on frowardly in the way of his heart. I have seen his ways, and will heal him: I will lead him also, and restore comforts unto him and to his mourners.*

In spite of the continued refusal of the people to listen, Isaiah's message to them is consistently optimistic in its tone, almost as if the will of the people was irrelevant to the final outcome, which in a way, it was! Eventually it would be seen that there were a few that would put their trust in God, and it is those few that would make the difference. The *holy mountain* is put in contrast with the high places where idolatrous sacrifice was made, and is not a figurative or allegorical term but the real place of fellowship in Israel, more particularly Jerusalem, where the faithful will meet with their God.

From the earliest times, when the Lord walked with Adam in the garden of Eden, and again when the Tabernacle was set up in the wilderness, we have been shown God's willingness to dwell with man, being present with him so as to have fellowship. We find such a concept difficult to accept, and being flesh, we are naturally afraid of becoming too close to God. We naturally prefer to hide behind religion with the rituals and mysticism that encourage us to keep a safe distance, at the same time convincing us of our unworthiness to approach. The natural man is more comfortable appointing a priest to go in his place to perform the ceremonial duties, thereby relieving him of any further responsibilities. This, of course, is horrifying to us as believers, for we know that the only priest we need is already in heaven, having performed all that is necessary once and for all. My point here is that it takes a certain amount of courage to keep one's nerve while the Lord is trying to draw us closer to Himself, as every natural fibre in us opposes such closeness. For the person with a *contrite and humble* heart however, there is an abundance of grace, and Israel, when it finally reaches this place, will find the fellowship and closeness that it could never have achieved through its religion alone. There is an end to the contention between God and His people, but it is yet to arrive.

Isaiah 58:1-14: *Cry aloud, spare not, lift up thy voice like a trumpet, and shew my people their transgression, and the house of Jacob their sins. Yet they seek me daily, and delight to know my ways, as a nation that did righteousness, and forsook not the ordinance of their God: they ask of me the ordinances of justice; they take delight in approaching to God. Wherefore have we fasted, say they, and thou seest not? wherefore have we afflicted our soul, and thou takest no knowledge? Behold, in the day of your fast ye find pleasure, and exact all your labours. Behold, ye fast for strife and debate, and to smite with the fist of wickedness: ye shall not fast as ye do this day, to make your voice to be heard on high. Is it such a fast that I have chosen? a day for a man to afflict his soul? is it to bow down his head as a bulrush, and to spread sackcloth and ashes under him? wilt thou call this a fast, and an acceptable day to the Lord?*

The Lord again gives Isaiah His servant the message that would bring the people into their place of blessing, and shows that while they may have imagined that they were in that place already, there was in fact no hint of any blessing with God, either in their lives or in the status of the nation. Here is the problem; they outwardly sought for knowledge, and to all intents and purposes appeared to be the people of God spending time and effort in keeping up the outward display. All their sacrifices, fasting, and seeking knowledge were done for the praises of men. They wondered why their efforts came to nothing, but they did everything in order to debate, or argue with others, pushing their own spirituality to prove they were better than others. The Lord nailed their hypocrisy here, and explained their motives in one verse: *Behold, in the day of your fast ye find pleasure, and exact all your labours.* They got what they wanted from all this effort, at the very time they did it, every act they did was broadcast so that all of their good words or works were seen and acknowledged by others. They did it for themselves and for their own glorification. There was no further reward from the Lord, as they had already received it from their contemporaries.

Sadly this attitude is accepted as the norm today, for while people are generous to a fault (and most can afford to be), they ruin it straight away in the Lord's sight by telling everyone who is prepared to listen, how charitable they are. This is now an accepted way of life, but the only reward for these things is in the present, through the admiration of men. Paul himself could say without irony in 1 Corinthians chapter 13:3 *and though I bestow all my goods to feed the poor, and though I give my body to be burned, and have not charity, it profiteth me nothing.* Paul considered the accolades of men, who undoubtedly would applaud such sacrifices, as nothing. He knew that if these things were not performed in the right spirit, then the only profit was in the here and now, when people said 'well done you'. If it did not please God then in Paul's view it was a waste of time. Being 'charitable' is not the same thing as having charity. Sadly in my view at least, such are most of the charitable works that are performed today. They are only done in order to gain the approval of our contemporaries, and profit nothing eternally. The Lord goes on to show what he really wanted from Israel, which was the very opposite of the religious show that these people were presenting Him with:

Is not this the fast that I have chosen? to loose the bands of wickedness, to undo the heavy burdens, and to let the oppressed go free, and that ye break every yoke? Is it not to deal thy bread to the hungry, and that thou bring the poor that are cast out to thy house? when thou seest the naked, that thou cover him; and that thou hide not thyself from thine own flesh? Then shall thy light break forth as the morning, and thine health shall spring forth speedily: and thy righteousness shall go before thee; the glory of the Lord shall be thy rereward. Then shalt thou call, and the Lord shall answer; thou shalt cry, and he shall say, Here I am. If thou take away from the midst of thee the yoke, the putting forth of the finger, and speaking vanity; And if thou draw out thy soul to the hungry, and satisfy the afflicted soul; then shall thy light rise in obscurity, and thy darkness be as the noonday:

Once again the Lord spells it out for them that he did not want any acts of spirituality, knowledge or pretence, but rather for the poor of the people to be regarded in society, and for the leaders of the people to extend their care equally to one and all. Their interpretation of the law were the heavy burdens, the poor were cast out and no one cared, because the poor were insignificant, and their thanks were worth nothing, it is their own contemporaries that the leaders wanted to impress, for they could in turn, be of use to them. The Law made provision for equality, but it was the very experts (as they considered themselves) in the Law, who were the ones that despised the poor, interpreting it to their own advantage. Real spirituality was to care for those that no one else wanted, and whilst there was no shortage of knowledge about the law, there was a huge gap between hearing its message, and its practical application. Here is the promise though, to those who were prepared to hear the prophecy and take it to heart:

And the Lord shall guide thee continually, and satisfy thy soul in drought, and make fat thy bones: and thou shalt be like a watered garden, and like a spring of water, whose waters fail not. And they that shall be of thee shall build the old waste places: thou shalt raise up the foundations of many generations; and thou shalt be called, The repairer of the breach, The restorer of paths to dwell in. If thou turn away thy foot from the sabbath, from doing thy pleasure on my holy day; and call the sabbath a delight, the holy of the Lord, honourable; and shalt honour him, not doing thine own ways, nor finding thine own pleasure, nor speaking thine own words: Then shalt thou delight thyself in the Lord; and I will cause thee to ride upon the high places of the earth, and feed thee with the heritage of Jacob thy father: for the mouth of the Lord hath spoken it.

What was sadly lacking in these people, for all of their public effort, was the *delight in the Lord* that He required of them in His first commandment. They didn't love Him, and so everything from that point was done for their own glory and not His. This is what will need to change in the End Days before Israel will become established before Him, and shows the reasons why this nation has taken so long, and has still not taken its rightful place.

Isaiah 59:19-21: *So shall they fear the name of the Lord from the west, and his glory from the rising of the sun. When the enemy shall come in like a flood, the Spirit of the Lord shall lift up a standard against him. And the Redeemer shall come to Zion, and unto them that turn from transgression in Jacob, saith the Lord. As for me, this is my covenant with them, saith the Lord; My spirit that is upon thee, and my words which I have put in thy mouth, shall not depart out of thy mouth, nor out of the mouth of thy seed, nor out of the mouth of thy seed's seed, saith the Lord, from henceforth and for ever.*

Isaiah jumps forward here to a time after the judgement of Israel for its rebellion, when the nations present themselves to fight against Israel. It is at this time that the Lord appears to fight for Israel, and is finally joined with them.

Isaiah 60:1-22: *Arise, shine; for thy light is come, and the glory of the Lord is risen upon thee. For, behold, the darkness shall cover the earth, and gross darkness the people: but the Lord shall arise upon thee, and his glory shall be seen upon thee. And the Gentiles shall come to thy light, and kings to the brightness of thy rising.*

These verses tie in very nicely with the description given both by the Lord, and later by John in Revelation.

Matthew 24:29-31 tells us:

Immediately after the tribulation of those days shall the sun be darkened, and the moon shall not give her light, and the stars shall fall from heaven, and the powers of the heavens shall be shaken: And then shall appear the sign of the Son of man in heaven: and then shall all the tribes of the earth mourn, and they shall see the Son of man coming in the clouds of heaven with power and great glory. And he shall send his angels with a great sound of a trumpet, and they shall gather together his elect from the four winds, from one end of heaven to the other.

Whilst in Revelation 6:12-7:17 we read:

And I beheld when he had opened the sixth seal, and, lo, there was a great earthquake; and the sun became black as sackcloth of hair, and the moon became as blood; And the stars of heaven fell unto the earth, even as a fig tree casteth her untimely figs, when she is shaken of a mighty wind. And the heaven departed as a scroll when it is rolled together; and every mountain and island were moved out of their places. And the kings of the earth, and the great men, and the rich men, and the chief captains, and the mighty men, and every bondman, and every free man, hid themselves in the dens and in the rocks of the mountains; And said to the mountains and rocks, Fall on us, and hide us from the face of him that sitteth on the throne, and from the wrath of the Lamb: For the great day of his wrath is come; and who shall be able to stand?

And after these things I saw four angels standing on the four corners of the earth, holding the four winds of the earth, that the wind should not blow on the earth, nor on the sea, nor on any tree. And I saw another angel ascending from the east, having the seal of the living God: and he cried with a loud voice to the four angels, to whom it was given to hurt the earth and the sea, Saying, Hurt not the earth, neither the sea, nor the trees, till we have sealed the servants of our God in their foreheads. And I heard the number of them which were sealed: and there were sealed an hundred and forty and four thousand of all the tribes of the children of Israel. Of the tribe of Juda were sealed twelve thousand. Of the tribe of Reuben were sealed twelve thousand. Of the tribe of Gad were sealed twelve thousand. Of the tribe of Aser were sealed twelve thousand. Of the tribe of Nepthalim were sealed twelve thousand. Of the tribe of Manasses were sealed twelve thousand. Of the tribe of Simeon were sealed twelve thousand. Of the tribe of Levi were sealed twelve thousand. Of the tribe of Issachar were sealed twelve thousand. Of the tribe of Zabulon were sealed twelve thousand. Of the tribe of Joseph were sealed twelve thousand. Of the tribe of Benjamin were sealed twelve thousand. After this I beheld, and, lo, a great multitude, which no man could number, of all nations, and kindreds, and people, and tongues, stood before the throne, and before the Lamb, clothed with white robes, and palms in their hands; And cried with a loud voice, saying, Salvation to our God which sitteth upon the throne, and unto the Lamb. And all the angels stood round about the throne, and about the elders and the four beasts, and fell before the throne on their faces, and worshipped God, Saying, Amen: Blessing, and glory, and wisdom, and thanksgiving, and honour, and power, and might, be unto our God for ever and ever. Amen. And one of the elders answered, saying unto me, What are these which are arrayed in white robes? and whence came they? And I said unto him, Sir, thou knowest. And he said to me, These are they which came out of great tribulation, and have washed their robes, and made them white in the blood of the Lamb. Therefore are they before the throne of God, and serve him day and night in his temple: and he that sitteth on the throne shall dwell among them. They shall hunger no more, neither thirst any more; neither shall the sun light on them, nor any heat. For the Lamb which is in the midst of the throne shall feed them, and shall lead them unto living fountains of waters: and God shall wipe away all tears from their eyes.

These verses combine to show that it is after the end of the *great tribulation* that the 144,000 chosen Jews are established in Israel, and that others, of all nations Jewish or otherwise are also gathered with them to form this new community consisting of those who have washed their robes in the blood of the lamb, and have therefore accepted his offer of salvation in these times. Whilst we read that they are before the throne, this does not mean they are in heaven, for as the Lord says, *he that sitteth on the throne shall dwell among them,* and not they with Him. Therefore I would take this to mean that they are on Earth, in Israel, and that He is their spiritual ruler there, as He is ours (we too stand before the throne in our present state, we have not yet sat down in heavenly places). They are eventually to be led to the *living waters*, the kingdom of God when it is established on the new earth. The rest of the world is terrified at these new signs, knowing that judgement is coming, but not having the security of knowing the Lord. These events are described in the

Book of Revelation as taking place after the [70]sixth seal is opened, which is the culmination of the events described in the former five seals. At the opening of the seventh seal, we are shown the commencement of the events that begin with the seven trumpets. The wrath of the Lamb, and the wrath of God follow as these trumpets sound, and as the vials are poured out respectively. As these things occur in scripture we are shown more detail of what is to take place. Returning to Isaiah:

Isaiah Chapter 60:4-22: *Lift up thine eyes round about, and see: all they gather themselves together, they come to thee: thy sons shall come from far, and thy daughters shall be nursed at thy side. Then thou shalt see, and flow together, and thine heart shall fear, and be enlarged; because the abundance of the sea shall be converted unto thee, the forces of the Gentiles shall come unto thee. The multitude of camels shall cover thee, the dromedaries of Midian and Ephah; all they from Sheba shall come: they shall bring gold and incense; and they shall shew forth the praises of the Lord. All the flocks of Kedar shall be gathered together unto thee, the rams of Nebaioth shall minister unto thee: they shall come up with acceptance on mine altar, and I will glorify the house of my glory. Who are these that fly as a cloud, and as the doves to their windows? Surely the isles shall wait for me, and the ships of Tarshish first, to bring thy sons from far, their silver and their gold with them, unto the name of the Lord thy God, and to the Holy One of Israel, because he hath glorified thee. And the sons of strangers shall build up thy walls, and their kings shall minister unto thee: for in my wrath I smote thee, but in my favour have I had mercy on thee. Therefore thy gates shall be open continually; they shall not be shut day nor night; that men may bring unto thee the forces of the Gentiles, and that their kings may be brought. For the nation and kingdom that will not serve thee shall perish; yea, those nations shall be utterly wasted. The glory of Lebanon shall come unto thee, the fir tree, the pine tree, and the box together, to beautify the place of my sanctuary; and I will make the place of my feet glorious. The sons also of them that afflicted thee shall come bending unto thee; and all they that despised thee shall bow themselves down at the soles of thy feet; and they shall call thee, The city of the Lord, The Zion of the Holy One of Israel.*

Whereas thou hast been forsaken and hated, so that no man went through thee, I will make thee an eternal excellency, a joy of many generations. Thou shalt also suck the milk of the Gentiles, and shalt suck the breast of kings: and thou shalt know that I the Lord am thy Saviour and thy Redeemer, the mighty One of Jacob. For brass I will bring gold, and for iron I will bring silver, and for wood brass, and for stones iron: I will also make thy officers peace, and thine exactors righteousness. Violence shall no more be heard in thy land, wasting nor destruction within thy borders; but thou shalt call thy walls Salvation, and thy gates Praise. The sun shall be no more thy light by day; neither for brightness shall the moon give light unto thee: but the Lord shall be unto thee an everlasting light, and thy God thy glory. Thy sun shall no more go down; neither shall thy moon withdraw itself: for the Lord shall be thine everlasting light, and the days of thy mourning shall be ended. Thy people also shall be all righteous: they shall inherit the land forever, the branch of my planting, the work of my hands, that I may be glorified. A little one shall become a thousand, and a small one a strong nation: I the Lord will hasten it in his time.

Whilst there is no doubt that these words were written in Isaiah's time to his own generation, it would be foolish to claim that there has ever been a complete fulfilment of them. This would mean a time of such recognition for Israel as to put them in a position of safety to the extent they could relax their borders because of their closeness to their God. Whatever these words were intended to achieve in Isaiah's time, they have not found their complete fulfilment to this day, yet they remain as certain promises to the faithful for a future time. We notice too that in these times, there is an *altar*, and the *house of my glory*, as well as *the place of my sanctuary* and these things are situated in *The city of the Lord, The Zion of the Holy One of Israel*. I find it strange that any can consider, in the weight of the evidence in scripture, that this can mean anywhere except the real city Jerusalem that is situated in Israel.

Isaiah 61:1-11: *The Spirit of the Lord God is upon me; because the Lord hath anointed me to preach good tidings unto the meek; he hath sent me to bind up the brokenhearted, to proclaim liberty to the captives, and the opening of the prison to them that are bound; To proclaim the acceptable year of the Lord…*

It is well [71]known that the Lord quoted from this passage when He preached at Nazareth, and that He stopped at this point, just before the rest of the message, which goes on to talk of judgement. It is my belief that the *day of vengeance* described here could have been a far less traumatic affair for Israel had they accepted His teachings, at the very least about who He was. They rejected Him for His claim to be the awaited Messiah, the Son of God, and then worse, hung Him up for blasphemy. With some exceptions this was with the consent of the people, although technically it took place at the hands of the leaders through the Roman occupiers. At the time there were relatively few who believed in Him. Where He stopped in this passage was at the *acceptable year of the Lord*, this being the time when all could have been restored, being what God was hoping for and expected from His people. In the event, the *Day of vengeance* is yet to appear, and when it does the consequence for Israel is the stuff of nightmares. If we consider the slaughter that took place when the Romans finally captured the city, and compare this to the time when:

Matthew 24:21: *For then shall be great tribulation, such as was not since the beginning of the world to this time, no, nor ever shall be. And except those days should be shortened, there should no flesh be saved: but for the elect's sake those days shall be shortened.*

We realise that the Lord stopped short, to allow the people the chance to do things right, but the inevitable result of their failure, was to face God's vengeance later. As we continue to read: *...and the day of vengeance of our God;* However what follows afterwards in Isaiah is as a result of the end of their chastisement:

...to comfort all that mourn; To appoint unto them that mourn in Zion, to give unto them beauty for ashes, the oil of joy for mourning, the garment of praise for the spirit of heaviness; that they might be called trees of righteousness, the planting of the Lord, that he might be glorified. And they shall build the old wastes, they shall raise up the former desolations, and they shall repair the waste cities, the desolations of many generations. And strangers shall stand and feed your flocks, and the sons of the alien shall be your plowmen and your vinedressers.

But ye shall be named the Priests of the Lord: men shall call you the Ministers of our God: ye shall eat the riches of the Gentiles, and in their glory shall ye boast yourselves. For your shame ye shall have double; and for confusion they shall rejoice in their portion: therefore in their land they shall possess the double: everlasting joy shall be unto them.

And here is the reason for this: the Laws that He gave them, and the Scriptures that were theirs as a record of His good intentions towards them, had been discarded in favour of their envy of and desire to emulate the completely godless peoples around them, to whom they looked for an example. It is no wonder that this incurred God's displeasure, which is later compounded by their rejection of His Son when He was sent to restore them to Himself. Even after being given time to reconsider, at the end of the ministry of the Apostles, it is not until the Revelation of the End (given in 95AD as I believe, through John) that God finally accepts that there is no alternative other than to bring down the judgements that He had first warned them of when they entered the promised land, at which time they should have begun what was intended to be an uninterrupted period of blessing:

Deuteronomy 11:26-29: *Behold, I set before you this day a blessing and a curse; A blessing, if ye obey the commandments of the Lord your God, which I command you this day: And a curse, if ye will not obey the commandments of the Lord your God, but turn aside out of the way which I command you this day, to go after other gods, which ye have not known. And it shall come to pass, when the Lord thy God hath brought thee in unto the land whither thou goest to possess it, that thou shalt put the blessing upon mount Gerizim, and the curse upon mount Ebal.*

So the choice of whether to obey or disobey was a matter for the Israelites to decide for themselves, but their choice was anticipated by the Lord, and in His overriding grace, their rescue at the end is a matter of [72]record. To continue with the passage:

For I the Lord love judgment, I hate robbery for burnt offering; and I will direct their work in truth, and I will make an everlasting covenant with them. And their seed shall be known among the Gentiles, and their offspring among the people: all that see them shall acknowledge them, that they are the seed which the Lord hath blessed.

Isaiah is greatly encouraged by this, both for himself and for his people, and he now says:

I will greatly rejoice in the Lord, my soul shall be joyful in my God; for he hath clothed me with the garments of salvation, he hath covered me with the robe of righteousness, as a bridegroom decketh himself with ornaments, and as a bride adorneth herself with her jewels. For as the earth bringeth forth her bud, and as the garden causeth the things that are sown in it to spring forth; so the Lord God will cause righteousness and praise to spring forth before all the nations.

Recognising by these words that, come what may, the Lord is determined to save His people and eventually produce a nation that would truly reflect His glory, as was His intention for them from the beginning. This theme is continued in the following chapters:

Isaiah 62:1-12: *For Zion's sake will I not hold my peace, and for Jerusalem's sake I will not rest, until the righteousness thereof go forth as brightness, and the salvation thereof as a lamp that burneth. And the Gentiles shall see thy righteousness, and all kings thy glory: and thou shalt be called by a new name, which the mouth of the Lord shall name. Thou shalt also be a crown of glory in the hand of the Lord, and a royal diadem in the hand of thy God. Thou shalt no more be termed Forsaken; neither shall thy land any more be termed Desolate: but thou shalt be called Hephzibah, and thy land Beulah: for the Lord delighteth in thee, and thy land shall be married. For as a young man marrieth a virgin, so shall thy sons marry thee: and as the bridegroom rejoiceth over the bride, so shall thy God rejoice over thee. I have set watchmen upon thy walls, O Jerusalem, which shall never hold their peace day nor night: ye that make mention of the Lord, keep not silence, And give him no rest, till he establish, and till he make Jerusalem a praise in the earth. The Lord hath sworn by his right hand, and by the arm of his strength, Surely I will no more give thy corn to be meat for thine enemies; and the sons of the stranger shall not drink thy wine, for the which thou hast laboured: But they that have gathered it shall eat it, and praise the Lord; and they that have brought it together shall drink it in the courts of my holiness. Go through, go through the gates; prepare ye the way of the people; cast up, cast up the highway; gather out the stones; lift up a standard for the people. Behold, the Lord hath proclaimed unto the end of the world, Say ye to the daughter of Zion, Behold, thy salvation cometh; behold, his reward is with him, and his work before him. And they shall call them, The holy people, The redeemed of the Lord: and thou shalt be called, Sought out, A city not forsaken.*

Again in these passages we see the recurring theme that a part of the blessing, for Israel at least, is their justification and acceptance in the eyes of the Gentiles. This is conditional perhaps on their willingness to accept these same Gentiles into their own blessing, enjoying the same fellowship with God through His Son. In contrast to Israel being forsaken by the world, it is now considered both *Hephzibah*, which means 'my delight is in her', and *Beulah,* or married, both wonderfully descriptive names for the future bride of the Lamb, joined together with the believing Gentiles of the time, all of whom will later combine with the present church, which will by then have been taken up to be with The Lord to make up His completed body. The appointment of the watchman shows that the Lord continually looks for His bride, or Israel, to be ready for Him, anxious almost for that time to appear, but knowing that this will only happen when the right conditions are met. We recall in this that traditionally in Israel, the groom's father is the one who decides when all things are ready, after having reviewed all of the arrangements for the marriage.

When the Lord finally does come, as He did at His first appearing, He brings these gifts with him, the reward for Israel, which is the work they would have achieved in this world, had they not rejected Him, being now presented again. This necessarily means that in grace, the time has been extended, and what this reward really entails, is yet to be seen. At the present though, we have the situation described below, where it is simply that it is the *Love and pity of the Lord* that keeps them from total destruction, until He comes again for them.

In the meantime we see that He is waiting for them to ask *Where is he that brought them up out of the sea with the shepherd of his flock?* Until they start to seek for Him in their affliction, they will not see Him.

Isaiah 63:7-14: *According to his mercies, and according to the multitude of his lovingkindnesses. For he said, Surely they are my people, children that will not lie: so he was their Saviour. In all their affliction he was afflicted, and the angel of his presence saved them: in his love and in his pity he redeemed them; and he bare them, and carried them all the days of old. But they rebelled, and vexed his holy Spirit: therefore he was turned to be their enemy, and he fought against them. Then he remembered the days of old, Moses, and his people, saying, Where is he that brought them up out of the sea with the shepherd of his flock? Where is he that put his holy Spirit within him? That led them by the right hand of Moses with his glorious arm, dividing the water before them, to make himself an everlasting name? That led them through the deep, as an horse in the wilderness, that they should not stumble? As a beast goeth down into the valley, the Spirit of the Lord caused him to rest: so didst thou lead thy people, to make thyself a glorious name.*

We can see something of what the Lord is looking for to accompany such a change of heart in what follows:

Isaiah 64:4-5: *For since the beginning of the world men have not heard, nor perceived by the ear, neither hath the eye seen, O God, beside thee, what he hath prepared for him that waiteth for him. Thou meetest him that rejoiceth and worketh righteousness, those that remember thee in thy ways.*

In their waiting for Him, they should be both *rejoicing* and *working righteousness*, the very same attributes of the wedding party waiting for the groom. This is what He was trying to convey to them in the parables that we have considered in Matthew when He spoke to them in the Sermon on the Mount. He was not, and is still not, looking for a begrudging form of keeping the Law, which causes the same type of oppression found under the teachings of the Pharisees, Sadducees and scribes of His day. He wants to find the nation Israel rejoicing in their king's appearance as the merciful saviour that He is. The problems that Israel face are essentially a result of their own doings, and until they realise this, they are in for difficult and dangerous times. Neither will all the nation Israel accept Him at this time, but there are some who He has reserved to Himself who will, and for them the blessings are assured, they are to be the *inheritor of my mountains*:

Isaiah 65:8-14: *Thus saith the Lord, as the new wine is found in the cluster, and one saith, Destroy it not; for a blessing is in it: so will I do for my servants' sakes, that I may not destroy them all. And I will bring forth a seed out of Jacob, and out of Judah an inheritor of my mountains: and mine elect shall inherit it, and my servants shall dwell there. And Sharon shall be a fold of flocks, and the valley of Achor a place for the herds to lie down in, for my people that have sought me. But ye are they that forsake the Lord, that forget my holy mountain, that prepare a table for that troop, and that furnish the drink offering unto that number. Therefore will I number you to the sword, and ye shall all bow down to the slaughter: because when I called, ye did not answer; when I spake, ye did not hear; but did evil before mine eyes, and did choose that wherein I delighted not. Therefore thus saith the Lord God, Behold, my servants shall eat, but ye shall be hungry: behold, my servants shall drink, but ye shall be thirsty: behold, my servants shall rejoice, but ye shall be ashamed: Behold, my servants shall sing for joy of heart, but ye shall cry for sorrow of heart, and shall howl for vexation of spirit.*

The picture presented is of a rural idyll, a place of peace and prosperity, but this is only for those who have listened to the Lord and carried out their lives according to the way He has shown them whilst patiently waiting for Him. At their end is a place where there is no more remembrance of what has gone before, and this passage can be compared with the [73]*New heavens and new earth* of the book of Revelation, coming after the judgement of the *Great White throne* of Revelation 20:

Isaiah 65:17-25: *For, behold, I create new heavens and a new earth: and the former shall not be remembered, nor come into mind. But be ye glad and rejoice forever in that which I create: for, behold, I create Jerusalem a rejoicing, and her people a joy. And I will rejoice in Jerusalem, and joy in my people: and the voice of weeping shall be no more heard in her, nor the voice of crying. There shall be no more thence an infant of days, nor an old man that hath not filled his days: for the child shall die an hundred years old; but the sinner being an hundred years old shall be accursed. And they shall build houses, and inhabit them; and they shall plant vineyards, and eat the fruit of them. They shall not build, and another inhabit; they shall not plant, and another eat: for as the days of a tree are the days of my people, and mine elect shall long enjoy the work of their hands. They shall not labour in vain, nor bring forth for trouble; for they are the seed of the blessed of the Lord, and their offspring with them. And it shall come to pass, that before they call, I will answer; and while they are yet speaking, I will hear. The wolf and the lamb shall feed together, and the lion shall eat straw like the bullock: and dust shall be the serpent's meat. They shall not hurt nor destroy in all my holy mountain, saith the Lord.*

The last part of this passage may present some difficulties, as we have discussed previously. The wolf and the lamb are not known to be on good terms, and nor as yet is the lion a vegetarian, but even given the descriptive and exaggerated language that we know the Middle Eastern writer to be prone to, these are plain statements which in my view can be taken literally. We must remember though that this is a state of affairs bound up with the *new heavens* and on the *new earth*, and so previous rules do not apply. This is in the kingdom of God, where sin and rebellion against Him do not exist. All the wicked have been judged, the beast and false prophet are long gone, and Satan has now followed them into the lake of fire, so the temptations that were on the earth are gone, allowing men to live without fear of judgement.

Isaiah 66:1-24: *Thus saith the Lord, The heaven is my throne, and the earth is my footstool: where is the house that ye build unto me? and where is the place of my rest? For all those things hath mine hand made, and all those things have been, saith the Lord: but to this man will I look, even to him that is poor and of a contrite spirit, and trembleth at my word. He that killeth an ox is as if he slew a man; he that sacrificeth a lamb, as if he cut off a dog's neck; he that offereth an oblation, as if he offered swine's blood; he that burneth incense, as if he blessed an idol. Yea, they have chosen their own ways, and their soul delighteth in their abominations. I also will choose their delusions, and will bring their fears upon them; because when I called, none did answer; when I spake, they did not hear: but they did evil before mine eyes, and chose that in which I delighted not.*

The theme of judgement being contrasted with that of blessing continues to the very end of Isaiah's vision, where those that have taken God seriously and have suffered as a result are comforted. The promised deliverer is to be sent, and this should have been the signal for national repentance leading to blessing. The required travailing of Israel to be born into the Kingdom of Heaven failed to materialise at that time, and so is deferred to another time, when the faithful will see it.

"BEHOLD, I HAVE FORETOLD YOU ALL THINGS"

Hear the word of the Lord, ye that tremble at his word; Your brethren that hated you, that cast you out for my name's sake, said, Let the Lord be glorified: but he shall appear to your joy, and they shall be ashamed. A voice of noise from the city, a voice from the temple, a voice of the Lord that rendereth recompence to his enemies. Before she travailed, she brought forth; before her pain came, she was delivered of a man child. Who hath heard such a thing? who hath seen such things? Shall the earth be made to bring forth in one day? or shall a nation be born at once? for as soon as Zion travailed, she brought forth her children. Shall I bring to the birth, and not cause to bring forth? saith the Lord : shall I cause to bring forth, and shut the womb? saith thy God. Rejoice ye with Jerusalem, and be glad with her, all ye that love her: rejoice for joy with her, all ye that mourn for her: That ye may suck, and be satisfied with the breasts of her consolations; that ye may milk out, and be delighted with the abundance of her glory. For thus saith the Lord, Behold, I will extend peace to her like a river, and the glory of the Gentiles like a flowing stream: then shall ye suck, ye shall be borne upon her sides, and be dandled upon her knees. As one whom his mother comforteth, so will I comfort you; and ye shall be comforted in Jerusalem. And when ye see this, your heart shall rejoice, and your bones shall flourish like an herb:

In an equal measure there is to be a reckoning up, and the wicked will get their own recompense, as much for their treatment of the righteous, as for anything else. Interestingly, the wicked do not seem content to pursue their own wickedness, but invariably seek to interfere with and oppress the righteous in their cause as well. We should not really be surprised at this for it is Satan's realm after all, at least for a time, and the wicked belong to him and do his bidding!

And the hand of the Lord shall be known toward his servants, and his indignation toward his enemies. For, behold, the Lord will come with fire, and with his chariots like a whirlwind, to render his anger with fury, and his rebuke with flames of fire. For by fire and by his sword will the Lord plead with all flesh: and the slain of the Lord shall be many. They that sanctify themselves, and purify themselves in the gardens behind one tree in the midst, eating swine's flesh, and the abomination, and the mouse, shall be consumed together, saith the Lord. For I know their works and their thoughts:

It shall come, that I will gather all nations and tongues; and they shall come, and see my glory. And I will set a sign among them, and I will send those that escape of them unto the nations, to Tarshish, Pul, and Lud, that draw the bow, to Tubal, and Javan, to the isles afar off, that have not heard my fame, neither have seen my glory; and they shall declare my glory among the Gentiles. And they shall bring all your brethren for an offering unto the Lord out of all nations upon horses, and in chariots, and in litters, and upon mules, and upon swift beasts, to my holy mountain Jerusalem, saith the Lord, as the children of Israel bring an offering in a clean vessel into the house of the Lord. And I will also take of them for priests and for Levites, saith the Lord. For as the new heavens and the new earth, which I will make, shall remain before me, saith the Lord, so shall your seed and your name remain.

The re-establishment of Israel, when it comes, will be accompanied by an evangelistic zeal on a scale never seen before. Those who have escaped, His messengers, will be sent to the nations with a ministry that is seen to have the authority and backing of the Lord. When this takes place is not clear, for in the narrative it follows after His description of the *new heavens and the new earth*. We know that after the *Great tribulation* there is a gathering together of the Jews, and this comes about because of the ministry of the times commenced by the two witnesses. It is therefore difficult to place this exactly in any time period, and these words may not be in chronological order. What is certain is that the faithful are to be rewarded for their patience in tribulation, and will be vindicated eventually in the world's eyes, whilst the wicked can look forward to answering to God for their deeds. Time has no bearing on this prophecy; it can stand on its own, and we can be sure of its fulfilment to the last detail. What is subject to change however, is man's willingness to submit himself to God, and what we have learned from our previous study is that prophecy is able to accommodate delay whilst man, (in particular application to His own people Israel) decides just when they are finally ready to listen, after having realised that their obstinacy towards their creator has got them nowhere. It is in turning to Him that their salvation and eventual restoration will be complete. The rest of the world will follow after them, once they see that the Jewish nation is in its rightful place of blessing.

And it shall come to pass, that from one new moon to another, and from one sabbath to another, shall all flesh come to worship before me, saith the Lord. And they shall go forth, and look upon the carcases of the men that have transgressed against me: for their worm shall not die, neither shall their fire be quenched; and they shall be an abhorring unto all flesh.

CHAPTER SIX

Ezekiel: Four visions, Gog and Magog.

Ezekiel was destined to be a priest, but was taken to Babylon in about the fifth year after the beginning of the captivity. Instead of performing priestly duties, which he could not now do, he was engaged by the Lord to be a prophet to those of the captivity, being contemporary at some points with both Daniel and Jeremiah, who were also active around the same time. Ezekiel's prophecy as a whole is sadly overlooked by some, being overshadowed by the extraordinary vision that is described in the first chapter of the book, which over the years has been subject to a range of interpretations, even being used by some as evidence of the existence of aliens, supposedly travelling in a spaceship when visiting the earth. Fortunately most commentators are more conservative in their views, and can agree that what is described in these first chapters is the manifestation of the Lord's [74]*shekinah* presence, or the inner workings of the cloud that showed the way for the tabernacle in the wilderness, and which later rested on Solomon's temple.

Ezekiel's prophecy covers the judgments of God on His people for their idolatry, and shows that despite His displeasure in them, He will yet reinstate them as His people to their land as He has promised. One of Ezekiel's visions concerns what is known as the Third Temple, which has been the subject of much debate since. Solomon's temple was built after the Jews had established themselves in the land under David, and is known as the First Temple. This was destroyed shortly after Ezekiel began to prophesy, at about 586BC, and when the Jews returned to the land from Babylon they rebuilt Solomon's temple, but only to a measure of its former glory. This is known as the second temple, or *Zerubbabel's* temple, after the leader of the time, and was finished at around 516BC. This same temple was later restored by King Herod, and became what was then known as *Herod's temple,* which was the one in existence when the Lord walked on earth. This was utterly destroyed, as the Lord said it would be, by the Romans when they sacked Jerusalem in AD70. There is no evidence in scripture to suggest that it will ever be rebuilt. The temple that is so meticulously described in Ezekiel's vision has never been built. Its given dimensions bear no resemblance to any of the previous temples that existed, so the question remains for some as to whether it was merely given as a spiritual or idealized vision of what the temple should be, or whether it will become a real and actual future dwelling place of the Lord on the earth, through His *shekinah* presence.

The present situation is that the Jews have no place to sacrifice, so their religion is on hold until such time as they can once again make offerings on the holy site appointed them, which they [75]believe to be the Temple Mount, currently the home of the Dome of the Rock and the Al-Aqsah mosque in Jerusalem. The full dimensions of the Third Temple site make it unlikely that it will be built at this time, as it would engulf most of modern Jerusalem, but it is clear that for the events of the last week, or seventieth week of Daniel, to commence, there must be some form of agreement that will allow the morning and evening sacrifice to take place. This will probably be on that site, and so in my view some form of altar, but not necessarily an actual temple, will have to be erected after having first gained the agreement of the Muslim community. This will not be however the *Third Temple*, which as will be seen later, is to be built on an unprecedented scale, and includes instruction for the reorganization of all Israel, separated horizontally into strips of land for each tribe, and following a boundary line exceeding that of present-day Israel.

The book of Ezekiel is punctuated by his visions, given at various times and covering a range of subjects. These are commonly said to be seven in number, but in addition to specific visions, we are also told on several occasions that the Word of the Lord came to Ezekiel. Whilst interesting in itself, much of what is written in Ezekiel is not directly relevant to our subject, but what becomes clear as we examine the prophecies, is their main subject is the restoration of the people to their own land, after their having being judged in exile (the Book of Ezekiel also covering the judgments of other nations around them) and that when they did return, it would be to a new system, both of temple worship, and of government. I have no doubt that this was the expectation of Ezekiel, and that his understanding was that the third temple would be built soon after the people returned from their captivity. What did actually happen instead was that parts of the old temple were rebuilt under the edict of Cyrus the Persian king. The question for us is whether the third temple remains to be built at some future time.

Commonly it is concluded that there were seven visions, but I have found five visions stated which cover the following subjects, the first four to be considered in this chapter, the fifth in the next:

1   Chapters 1-3:15 The Cherubim and Ezekiel's commission to prophesy.
2   Chapters 3:23- 7:27 In the Plain.
3   Chapters 8:1- 11:23 The Temple in Jerusalem.
4   Chapters 37:1 – 37:28 Valley of dry bones.
5   Chapters 40:1-48:35 The New Temple, New City and divisions of the tribes.

First vision: Ezekiel 1-3:15. The Cherubim, and Ezekiel's commission to prophesy.

Ezekiel 1:1-28 *Now it came to pass in the thirtieth year, in the fourth month, in the fifth day of the month, as I was among the captives by the river of Chebar, that the heavens were opened, and I saw visions of God. In the fifth day of the month, which was the fifth year of king Jehoiachin's captivity, The word of the Lord came expressly unto Ezekiel the priest, the son of Buzi, in the land of the Chaldeans by the river Chebar; and the hand of the Lord was there upon him. And I looked, and, behold, a whirlwind came out of the north, a great cloud, and a fire infolding itself, and a brightness was about it, and out of the midst thereof as the colour of amber, out of the midst of the fire. Also out of the midst thereof came the likeness of four living creatures. And this was their*

CHAPTER SIX

appearance; they had the likeness of a man. And every one had four faces, and every one had four wings. And their feet were straight feet; and the sole of their feet was like the sole of a calf's foot: and they sparkled like the colour of burnished brass. And they had the hands of a man under their wings on their four sides; and they four had their faces and their wings. Their wings were joined one to another; they turned not when they went; they went every one straight-forward. As for the likeness of their faces, they four had the face of a man, and the face of a lion, on the right side: and they four had the face of an ox on the left side; they four also had the face of an eagle. Thus were their faces: and their wings were stretched upward; two wings of every one were joined one to another, and two covered their bodies. And they went every one straight- forward: whither the spirit was to go, they went; and they turned not when they went. As for the likeness of the living creatures, their appearance was like burning coals of fire, and like the appearance of lamps: it went up and down among the living creatures; and the fire was bright, and out of the fire went forth lightning. And the living creatures ran and returned as the appearance of a flash of lightning. Now as I beheld the living creatures, behold one wheel upon the earth by the living creatures, with his four faces. The appearance of the wheels and their work was like unto the colour of a beryl: and they four had one likeness: and their appearance and their work was as it were a wheel in the middle of a wheel. When they went, they went upon their four sides: and they turned not when they went. As for their rings, they were so high that they were dreadful; and their rings were full of eyes round about them four. And when the living creatures went, the wheels went by them: and when the living creatures were lifted up from the earth, the wheels were lifted up. Whithersoever the spirit was to go, they went, thither was their spirit to go; and the wheels were lifted up over against them: for the spirit of the living creature was in the wheels. When those went, these went; and when those stood, these stood; and when those were lifted up from the earth, the wheels were lifted up over against them: for the spirit of the living creature was in the wheels. And the likeness of the firmament upon the heads of the living creature was as the colour of the terrible crystal, stretched forth over their heads above. And under the firmament were their wings straight, the one toward the other: every one had two, which covered on this side, and every one had two, which covered on that side, their bodies. And when they went, I heard the noise of their wings, like the noise of great waters, as the voice of the Almighty, the voice of speech, as the noise of an host: when they stood, they let down their wings. And there was a voice from the firmament that was over their heads, when they stood, and had let down their wings. And above the firmament that was over their heads was the likeness of a throne, as the appearance of a sapphire stone: and upon the likeness of the throne was the likeness as the appearance of a man above upon it. And I saw as the colour of amber, as the appearance of fire round about within it, from the appearance of his loins even upward, and from the appearance of his loins even downward, I saw as it were the appearance of fire, and it had brightness round about. As the appearance of the bow that is in the cloud in the day of rain, so was the appearance of the brightness round about. This was the appearance of the likeness of the glory of the Lord. And when I saw it, I fell upon my face, and I heard a voice of one that spake.

There is no point here trying to elaborate on what Ezekiel saw, except to say that it is consistent with other descriptions in scripture of the means by which the Lord's presence is manifest on the earth. That is not to say that every appearance of the Lord is accompanied by the vision of this chariot, or that it is manifest to everyone. For example, the Lord appeared to Joshua without such a vision, and at various times to the disciples after His resurrection, to Paul, and again to John in his account in Chapter 1 of the book of Revelation. Yet Elisha saw this same chariot appear to take up Elijah, and the cloud was seen to lead the children of Israel in the wilderness, fill the tabernacle, and abide in Solomon's temple. There is no reason to suppose that while its abode was on the temple it was always visible, and it seems that the ability to see it is given at certain times, or to certain people, and not others. However, without trying to examine the description too much, it seems that the carriage has four wheels, each being suspended beneath one of the four cherubim, and above this, the Lord Himself is present. The cherubim act in unison, and the whole thing can move in any direction, in a moment of time.

Ezekiel 2:1-10: *And he said unto me, Son of man, stand upon thy feet, and I will speak unto thee. And the spirit entered into me when he spake unto me, and set me upon my feet, that I heard him that spake unto me. And he said unto me, Son of man, I send thee to the children of Israel, to a rebellious nation that hath rebelled against me: they and their fathers have transgressed against me, even unto this very day. For they are impudent children and stiffhearted. I do send thee unto them; and thou shalt say unto them, Thus saith the Lord God. And they, whether they will hear, or whether they will forbear, (for they are a rebellious house,) yet shall know that there hath been a prophet among them. And thou, son of man, be not afraid of them, neither be afraid of their words, though briers and thorns be with thee, and thou dost dwell among scorpions: be not afraid of their words, nor be dismayed at their looks, though they be a rebellious house. And thou shalt speak my words unto them, whether they will hear, or whether they will forbear: for they are most rebellious. But thou, son of man, hear what I say unto thee; Be not thou rebellious like that rebellious house: open thy mouth, and eat that I give thee. And when I looked, behold, an hand was sent unto me; and, lo, a roll of a book was therein; And he spread it before me; and it was written within and without: and there was written therein lamentations, and mourning, and woe.*

Ezekiel 3:1-27: *Moreover he said unto me, Son of man, eat that thou findest; eat this roll, and go speak unto the house of Israel. So I opened my mouth, and he caused me to eat that roll. And he said unto me, Son of man, cause thy belly to eat, and fill thy bowels with this roll that I give thee. Then did I eat it; and it was in my mouth as honey for sweetness. And he said unto me, Son of man, go, get thee unto the house of Israel, and speak with my words unto them. For thou art not sent to a people of a strange speech and of an hard language, but to the house of Israel; Not to many people of a strange speech and of an hard language, whose words thou canst not understand. Surely, had I sent thee to them, they would have hearkened unto thee. But the house of Israel will not hearken unto thee; for they will not hearken unto me: for all the house of Israel are impudent and hardhearted. Behold, I have made thy face strong against their faces, and thy forehead strong against their foreheads. As an adamant harder than flint have I made thy forehead: fear them not, neither be dismayed at their looks, though they be a rebellious house. Moreover he said unto me, Son of man, all my words that I shall speak unto thee receive in thine heart, and hear with thine ears. And go, get thee to them of the captivity, unto the children of thy people, and speak unto them, and tell them, Thus saith the Lord God; whether they will hear, or whether they will forbear. Then the spirit took me up, and I heard behind me a voice of a great rushing, saying, Blessed be the glory of the Lord from his place. I heard also the noise of the wings of the living creatures that touched one another, and the noise of the wheels over against them, and a noise of a great rushing. So the spirit lifted me up, and took me away, and I went in bitterness, in the heat of my spirit; but the hand of the Lord was strong upon me. Then I came to them of the captivity at Tel-abib, that dwelt by the river of Chebar, and I sat where they sat, and remained there astonished among them seven days.*

The purpose of Ezekiel receiving this vision was not just to show him the chariot, so much as to lend weight to the importance of what he was being commissioned to do. We must consider that this vision was given shortly before the destruction of the first temple took place, a time when the *shekinah* was going to be taken up from the temple, and so Ezekiel's role was to warn the people, both those already in captivity but also more importantly those still in Jerusalem, of the terrible consequences of continuing in their resistance to God's judgment on their idolatry in turning to other gods. The revelation of God to Ezekiel was sweet, but the bitterness for him lay in the message he was to give, and the consequences of their likely refusal to hear it, which was the departing of the presence of God from among them.

End of the first vision

And it came to pass at the end of seven days, that the word of the Lord came unto me, saying, Son of man, I have made thee a watchman unto the house of Israel: therefore hear the word at my mouth, and give them warning from me. When I say unto the wicked, Thou shalt surely die; and thou givest him not warning, nor speakest to warn the wicked from his wicked way, to save his life; the same wicked man shall die in his iniquity; but his blood will I require at thine hand. Yet if thou warn the wicked, and he turn not from his wickedness, nor from his wicked way, he shall die in his iniquity; but thou hast delivered thy soul. Again, When a righteous man doth turn from his righteousness, and commit iniquity, and I lay a stumblingblock before him, he shall die: because thou hast not given him warning, he shall die in his sin, and his righteousness which he hath done shall not be remembered; but his blood will I require at thine hand. Nevertheless if thou warn the righteous man, that the righteous sin not, and he doth not sin, he shall surely live, because he is warned; also thou hast delivered thy soul. And the hand of the Lord was there upon me; and he said unto me, Arise, go forth into the plain, and I will there talk with thee.

Second vision: Ezekiel 3:23- 5:17. In the Plain.
Then I arose, and went forth into the plain: and, behold, the glory of the Lord stood there, as the glory which I saw by the river of Chebar: and I fell on my face. Then the spirit entered into me, and set me upon my feet, and spake with me, and said unto me, Go, shut thyself within thine house. But thou, O son of man, behold, they shall put bands upon thee, and shall bind thee with them, and thou shalt not go out among them: And I will make thy tongue cleave to the roof of thy mouth, that thou shalt be dumb, and shalt not be to them a reprover: for they are a rebellious house. But when I speak with thee, I will open thy mouth, and thou shalt say unto them, Thus saith the Lord God; He that heareth, let him hear; and he that forbeareth, let him forbear: for they are a rebellious house.

Ezekiel again sees the same vision, which he describes as the *glory of the Lord*. Notice that he was not in any way complacent about this, but needed to be set on his feet, as the natural reaction of man in such a presence is to fall on one's face. Anyone who claims to have seen God without having been first lifted up from hiding from Him has a vivid imagination, and has seen nothing. Ezekiel is further shown that he is to be a token to Israel, a sign to them of their disobedience, and is commanded to eat his defiled bread for a representative period where days are substituted for years. In effect, the people are to be shown that they will eat of the fruit of their ways, for initially what was to come out of Ezekiel, his own waste product, was to be used by him to cook with, i.e. dried dung. Ezekiel is shocked by this, and the concession is made that he can use dried cow dung to cook with, but nevertheless, the message is to be that what has come out of them, will be what they are to eat, in effect they gave God bull**** and so now they will receive it back from Him. Ezekiel was a priest and the Lord could see his discomfort in this, but in reality Ezekiel's sensibilities did not take account of the fact that it is the Lord who decides what is clean and acceptable for us in His will, not ourselves. Notice too in these verses that they include both of the houses of Israel, the ten tribes that had long ago been dispersed under the Assyrian captivity, as well as the now disobedient two tribes of Judah, Judah and Benjamin. This shows that the restoration, when it came was to include all of Israel, wherever it was scattered. At that time Israel was only represented by the two tribes of Judah, together with a few of the descendants of the ten tribes that had escaped the first captivity of the Northern kingdom of Israel.

Ezekiel 4:1-17: *Thou also, son of man, take thee a tile, and lay it before thee, and pourtray upon it the city, even Jerusalem: And lay siege against it, and build a fort against it, and cast a mount against it; set the camp also against it, and set battering rams against it round about. Moreover take thou unto thee an iron pan, and set it for a wall of iron between thee and the city: and set thy face against it, and it shall be besieged, and thou shalt lay siege against it. This shall be a sign to the house of Israel. Lie thou also upon thy left side, and lay the iniquity of the house of Israel upon it: according to the number of the days that thou shalt lie upon it thou shalt bear their iniquity. For I have laid upon thee the years of their iniquity, according to the number of the days, three hundred and ninety days: so shalt thou bear the iniquity of the house of Israel. And when thou hast accomplished them, lie again on thy right side, and thou shalt bear the iniquity of the house of Judah forty days: I have appointed thee each day for a year. Therefore thou shalt set thy face toward the siege of Jerusalem, and thine arm shall be uncovered, and thou shalt prophesy against it. And, behold, I will lay bands upon thee, and thou shalt not turn thee from one side to another, till thou hast ended the days of thy siege. Take thou also unto thee wheat, and barley, and beans, and lentiles, and millet, and fitches, and put them in one vessel, and make thee bread thereof, according to the number of the days that thou shalt lie upon thy side, three hundred and ninety days shalt thou eat thereof. And thy meat which thou shalt eat shall be by weight, twenty shekels a day: from time to time shalt thou eat it. Thou shalt drink also water by measure, the sixth part of an hin: from time to time shalt thou drink. And thou shalt eat it as barley cakes, and thou shalt bake it with dung that cometh out of man, in their sight. And the Lord said, Even thus shall the children of Israel eat their defiled bread among the Gentiles, whither I will drive them. Then said I, Ah Lord God! behold, my soul hath not been polluted: for from my youth up even till now have I not eaten of that which dieth of itself, or is torn in pieces; neither came there abominable flesh into my mouth. Then he said unto me, Lo, I have given thee cow's dung for man's dung, and thou shalt prepare thy bread therewith. Moreover he said unto me, Son of man, behold, I will break the staff of bread in Jerusalem: and they shall eat bread by weight, and with care; and they shall drink water by measure, and with astonishment: That they may want bread and water, and be astonied one with another, and consume away for their iniquity.*

Ominously, Ezekiel was also to cut off his beard, and this was to signify the destruction that was to come upon Jerusalem when Nebuchadnezzar returned to deal with it for its rebellion against him. He would utterly destroy the place, and the reason for this was their attitude to God, and *His Sanctuary* the place where His glory rested, the Temple.

Ezekiel 5:1-17: *And thou, son of man, take thee a sharp knife, take thee a barber's razor, and cause it to pass upon thine head and*

CHAPTER SIX

upon thy beard: then take thee balances to weigh, and divide the hair. Thou shalt burn with fire a third part in the midst of the city, when the days of the siege are fulfilled: and thou shalt take a third part, and smite about it with a knife: and a third part thou shalt scatter in the wind; and I will draw out a sword after them. Thou shalt also take thereof a few in number, and bind them in thy skirts. Then take of them again, and cast them into the midst of the fire, and burn them in the fire; for thereof shall a fire come forth into all the house of Israel. Thus saith the Lord God; This is Jerusalem: I have set it in the midst of the nations and countries that are round about her. And she hath changed my judgments into wickedness more than the nations, and my statutes more than the countries that are round about her: for they have refused my judgments and my statutes, they have not walked in them. Therefore thus saith the Lord God; Because ye multiplied more than the nations that are round about you, and have not walked in my statutes, neither have kept my judgments, neither have done according to the judgments of the nations that are round about you; Therefore thus saith the Lord God; Behold, I, even I, am against thee, and will execute judgments in the midst of thee in the sight of the nations. And I will do in thee that which I have not done, and whereunto I will not do any more the like, because of all thine abominations. Therefore the fathers shall eat the sons in the midst of thee, and the sons shall eat their fathers; and I will execute judgments in thee, and the whole remnant of thee will I scatter into all the winds. Wherefore, as I live, saith the Lord God; Surely, because thou hast defiled my sanctuary with all thy detestable things, and with all thine abominations, therefore will I also diminish thee; neither shall mine eye spare, neither will I have any pity. A third part of thee shall die with the pestilence, and with famine shall they be consumed in the midst of thee: and a third part shall fall by the sword round about thee; and I will scatter a third part into all the winds, and I will draw out a sword after them. Thus shall mine anger be accomplished, and I will cause my fury to rest upon them, and I will be comforted: and they shall know that I the Lord have spoken it in my zeal, when I have accomplished my fury in them. Moreover I will make thee waste, and a reproach among the nations that are round about thee, in the sight of all that pass by. So it shall be a reproach and a taunt, an instruction and an astonishment unto the nations that are round about thee, when I shall execute judgments in thee in anger and in fury and in furious rebukes. I the Lord have spoken it. When I shall send upon them the evil arrows of famine, which shall be for their destruction, and which I will send to destroy you: and I will increase the famine upon you, and will break your staff of bread: So will I send upon you famine and evil beasts, and they shall bereave thee; and pestilence and blood shall pass through thee; and I will bring the sword upon thee. I the Lord have spoken it.

End of the second vision

Third vision: Ezekiel 8:1-11:23. The Temple in Jerusalem.

Ezekiel 8:1-18: *And it came to pass in the sixth year, in the sixth month, in the fifth day of the month, as I sat in mine house, and the elders of Judah sat before me, that the hand of the Lord God fell there upon me. Then I beheld, and lo a likeness as the appearance of fire: from the appearance of his loins even downward, fire; and from his loins even upward, as the appearance of brightness, as the colour of amber. And he put forth the form of an hand, and took me by a lock of mine head; and the spirit lifted me up between the earth and the heaven, and brought me in the visions of God to Jerusalem, to the door of the inner gate that looketh toward the north; where was the seat of the image of jealousy, which provoketh to jealousy. And, behold, the glory of the God of Israel was there, according to the vision that I saw in the plain. Then said he unto me, Son of man, lift up thine eyes now the way toward the north. So I lifted up mine eyes the way toward the north, and behold*

CHAPTER SIX

northward at the gate of the altar this image of jealousy in the entry. He said furthermore unto me, Son of man, seest thou what they do? even the great abominations that the house of Israel committeth here, that I should go far off from my sanctuary? but turn thee yet again, and thou shalt see greater abominations. And he brought me to the door of the court; and when I looked, behold a hole in the wall. Then said he unto me, Son of man, dig now in the wall: and when I had digged in the wall, behold a door. And he said unto me, Go in, and behold the wicked abominations that they do here. So I went in and saw; and behold every form of creeping things, and abominable beasts, and all the idols of the house of Israel, pourtrayed upon the wall round about. And there stood before them seventy men of the ancients of the house of Israel, and in the midst of them stood Jaazaniah the son of Shaphan, with every man his censer in his hand; and a thick cloud of incense went up. Then said he unto me, Son of man, hast thou seen what the ancients of the house of Israel do in the dark, every man in the chambers of his imagery? for they say, The Lord seeth us not; the Lord hath forsaken the earth. He said also unto me, Turn thee yet again, and thou shalt see greater abominations that they do. Then he brought me to the door of the gate of the Lord's house which was toward the north; and, behold, there sat women weeping for Tammuz. Then said he unto me, Hast thou seen this, O son of man? turn thee yet again, and thou shalt see greater abominations than these. And he brought me into the inner court of the Lord's house, and, behold, at the door of the temple of the Lord, between the porch and the altar, were about five and twenty men, with their backs toward the temple of the Lord, and their faces toward the east; and they worshipped the sun toward the east. Then he said unto me, Hast thou seen this, O son of man? Is it a light thing to the house of Judah that they commit the abominations which they commit here? for they have filled the land with violence, and have returned to provoke me to anger: and, lo, they put the branch to their nose. Therefore will I also deal in fury: mine eye shall not spare, neither will I have pity: and though they cry in mine ears with a loud voice, yet will I not hear them.

Ezekiel is shown another vision relating to the destruction and desolation of the Temple at Jerusalem. He is shown this whilst sitting with the elders in captivity, yet is transported in spirit to the temple at Jerusalem, to be shown that those still left in the temple had provoked the Lord and brought this destruction, shortly to become a reality, upon themselves. What Ezekiel is shown is the presence of the Lord in the *shekinah* cloud, being removed from the temple because of the idolatry of the people. Notice how the Lord puts it to Ezekiel in Chapter 8:6: *He said furthermore unto me, Son of man, seest thou what they do? even the great abominations that the house of Israel committeth here, that I should go far off from my sanctuary?* And we get the sense in view of this, that the Lord finally has no choice but to leave His own Temple amongst the people because of its defilement. In effect they had driven Him out of it. The real wonder is that it took so long for Him to come to this decision, showing how reluctant He was to follow this line of action. However, even after all of these judgments that are to follow, He says:

Ezekiel 11:16-20: *Therefore say, Thus saith the Lord God; Although I have cast them far off among the heathen, and although I have scattered them among the countries, yet will I be to them as a little sanctuary in the countries where they shall come. Therefore say, Thus saith the Lord God; I will even gather you from the people, and assemble you out of the countries where ye have been scattered, and I will give you the land of Israel. And they shall come thither, and they shall take away all the detestable things thereof and all the abominations thereof from thence. And I will give them one heart, and I will put a new spirit within you; and I will take the stony heart out of their flesh, and will give them an heart of flesh: That they may walk in my statutes, and keep mine ordinances, and do them: and they shall be my people, and I will be their God.*

In spite of their provocation of Him, He was still prepared to be gracious to them, being as a *little sanctuary* to them, in the place of the one that they had lost in Jerusalem. There is no hint in this that they will build another temple in Babylon, or continue their sacrifices, but they were assured of His continued presence in their captivity, and of their eventual restoration in the land once they acknowledge their idolatry. Notice though what happened to the *Shekinah* cloud:

Ezekiel 11:22-23: *Then did the cherubims lift up their wings, and the wheels beside them; and the glory of the God of Israel was over them above. And the glory of the Lord went up from the midst of the city, and stood upon the mountain which is on the east side of the city. Afterwards the spirit took me up, and brought me in a vision by the Spirit of God into Chaldea, to them of the captivity. So the vision that I had seen went up from me. Then I spake unto them of the captivity all the things that the Lord had shewed me.*

When the glory of the Lord departs from the Temple it is seen to stand on the Mount of Olives. The significance of this seems to have been lost through history, but it is from there that the Lord ascended to His Father, as described for us in Acts, and where the angels said in Acts 1:11 *This same Jesus which is taken up from you into heaven, shall so come in like manner as ye have seen Him go into heaven.*

The Lord spent a considerable amount of time in and around the Mount of Olives, which overlooks the Temple site. It was near the place where Bethany was situated, the home of Lazarus, Mary and Martha, and He often resorted there with His disciples. His attachment to the place is more than a coincidence. It is my belief that the *shekinah* cloud indicated the direction from which the Lord would return to the third temple, as we know that the Lord is to return to the mount of Olives, and that He enters into the new Temple by means of the [76]East gate, the one facing the Mount of Olives, which Ezekiel is yet to see and describe. I say this, because there is no further sighting of the *shekinah* cloud stated in scripture on the rebuilt temples that were to follow, until we see it in the yet unbuilt *Third temple* of Ezekiel's later vision:

Ezekiel 43:2-4: *And, behold, the glory of the God of Israel came from the way of the east: and his voice was like a noise of many waters: and the earth shined with his glory. And it was according to the appearance of the vision which I saw, even according to the vision that I saw when I came to destroy the city: and the visions were like the vision that I saw by the river Chebar; and I fell upon my face. And the glory of the Lord came into the house by the way of the gate whose prospect is toward the east. So the spirit took me up, and brought me into the inner court; and, behold, the glory of the Lord filled the house.*

We will come to this shortly, but it remains to say that for the Lord, Herod's Temple, which was the rebuilt second temple, impressive as it seemed to the disciples, was little more than a centre for a dying religion, offering sacrifices that had long since lost their meaning due to the prevailing heart of the people of the Lord's time. In their rejection of Him, the people represented by their leaders, confirmed that their whole attitude to the ordinances of God rendered them meaningless, they were just a going through the motions of religion. It had no future.

End of the third vision

There is a gap of at least [77]6 years between Ezekiel's third and fourth visions, but he is not inactive during this time, and there is a range of information to be found in the intervening chapters concerning the Lord's impending judgments both on Israel and the nations around it, Tyre and Egypt amongst others, through the hand of Nebuchadnezzar and his army. These are beyond the scope of this study, yet there is a relevant chapter here that will have bearing on our later remarks on the Third temple:

Ezekiel 34:1-31: *And the word of the Lord came unto me, saying, Son of man, prophesy against the shepherds of Israel, prophesy, and say unto them, Thus saith the Lord God unto the shepherds; Woe be to the shepherds of Israel that do feed themselves! should not the shepherds feed the flocks? Ye eat the fat, and ye clothe you with the wool, ye kill them that are fed: but ye feed not the flock. The diseased have ye not strengthened, neither have ye healed that which was sick, neither have ye bound up that which was broken, neither have ye brought again that which was driven away, neither have ye sought that which was lost; but with force and with cruelty have ye ruled them. And they were scattered, because there is no shepherd: and they became meat to all the beasts of the field, when they were scattered. My sheep wandered through all the mountains, and upon every high hill: yea, my flock was scattered upon all the face of the earth, and none did search or seek after them. Therefore, ye shepherds, hear the word of the Lord; As I live, saith the Lord God, surely because my flock became a prey, and my flock became meat to every beast of the field, because there was no shepherd, neither did my shepherds search for my flock, but the shepherds fed themselves, and fed not my flock; Therefore, O ye shepherds, hear the word of the Lord; Thus saith the Lord God; Behold, I am against the shepherds; and I will require my flock at their hand, and cause them to cease from feeding the flock; neither shall the shepherds feed themselves any more; for I will deliver my flock from their mouth, that they may not be meat for them.*

Clearly the Lord held the leaders of the people, the priesthood, responsible in large measure both for what had happened and what was about to happen to His people. Their power and influence is to be curtailed in the time when the Lord restores the land, and notice that there is to be once again a leader raised up who will rule the people justly, under God's direction.

For thus saith the Lord God; Behold, I, even I, will both search my sheep, and seek them out. As a shepherd seeketh out his flock in the day that he is among his sheep that are scattered; so will I seek out my sheep, and will deliver them out of all places where they have been scattered in the cloudy and dark day. And I will bring them out from the people, and gather them from the countries, and will bring them to their own land, and feed them upon the mountains of Israel by the rivers, and in all the inhabited places of the country. I will feed them in a good pasture, and upon the high mountains of Israel shall their fold be: there shall they lie in a good fold, and in a fat pasture shall they feed upon the mountains of Israel. I will feed my flock, and I will cause them to lie down, saith the Lord God. I will seek that which was lost, and bring again that which was driven away, and will bind up that which was broken, and will strengthen that which was sick: but I will destroy the fat and the strong; I will feed them with judgment. And as for you, O my flock, thus saith the Lord God; Behold, I judge between cattle and cattle, between the rams and the he goats. Seemeth it a small thing unto you to have eaten up the good pasture, but ye must tread down with your feet the residue of your pastures? and to have drunk of the deep waters, but ye must foul the residue with your feet? And as for my flock, they eat that which ye have trodden with your feet; and they drink that which ye have fouled with your feet. Therefore thus saith the Lord God unto them; Behold, I, even I, will judge between the fat cattle and between the lean cattle. Because ye have thrust with side and with shoulder, and pushed all the diseased with your horns, till ye have scattered them abroad; Therefore will I save my flock, and they shall no

CHAPTER SIX

more be a prey; and I will judge between cattle and cattle. And I will set up one shepherd over them, and he shall feed them, even my servant David; he shall feed them, and he shall be their shepherd. And I the Lord will be their God, and my servant David a prince among them; I the Lord have spoken it. And I will make with them a covenant of peace, and will cause the evil beasts to cease out of the land: and they shall dwell safely in the wilderness, and sleep in the woods. And I will make them and the places round about my hill a blessing; and I will cause the shower to come down in his season; there shall be showers of blessing. And the tree of the field shall yield her fruit, and the earth shall yield her increase, and they shall be safe in their land, and shall know that I am the Lord, when I have broken the bands of their yoke, and delivered them out of the hand of those that served themselves of them. And they shall no more be a prey to the heathen, neither shall the beast of the land devour them; but they shall dwell safely, and none shall make them afraid. And I will raise up for them a plant of renown, and they shall be no more consumed with hunger in the land, neither bear the shame of the heathen any more. Thus shall they know that I the Lord their God am with them, and that they, even the house of Israel, are my people, saith the Lord God. And ye my flock, the flock of my pasture, are men, and I am your God, saith the Lord God.

The *one shepherd, my servant David* is raised up to guide the people in this time of restoration, and as Ezekiel had written some 400 years after the death of the original David, we can safely conclude that this character, whilst being of a similar nature, is not the same man. Similar, perhaps in the sense of his being of the same spirit as David, and of necessity from Judah, as David was, but therefore not a priest of the Levitical line. It is tempting to assume that this is a description of the Lord Himself come to restore Israel, and then to apply these words to His coming for Israel, but in the context of Ezekiel's writings this is to occur when the Jews return to their land and commence their period of blessing, and this David is a servant of the Lord, acting under Him as an earthly ruler. He appears again later, and is identified with the description given of the third Temple, as the prince, having a [78]strip of land for his exclusive use on either side of the Temple precinct.

Ezekiel 36:21-38: *But I had pity for mine holy name, which the house of Israel had profaned among the heathen whither they went. Therefore say unto the house of Israel, Thus saith the Lord God; I do not this for your sakes, O house of Israel, but for mine holy name's sake, which ye have profaned among the heathen, whither ye went. And I will sanctify my great name, which was profaned among the heathen, which ye have profaned in the midst of them; and the heathen shall know that I am the Lord, saith the Lord God, when I shall be sanctified in you before their eyes. For I will take you from among the heathen, and gather you out of all countries, and will bring you into your own land. Then will I sprinkle clean water upon you, and ye shall be clean: from all your filthiness, and from all your idols, will I cleanse you. A new heart also will I give you, and a new spirit will I put within you: and I will take away the stony heart out of your flesh, and I will give you an heart of flesh. And I will put my spirit within you, and cause you to walk in my statutes, and ye shall keep my judgments, and do them. And ye shall dwell in the land that I gave to your fathers; and ye shall be my people, and I will be your God. I will also save you from all your uncleannesses: and I will call for the corn, and will increase it, and lay no famine upon you. And I will multiply the fruit of the tree, and the increase of the field, that ye shall receive no more reproach of famine among the heathen. Then shall ye remember your own evil ways, and your doings that were not good, and shall lothe yourselves in your own sight for your iniquities and for your abominations. Not for your sakes do I this, saith the Lord God, be it known unto you: be ashamed and confounded for your own ways, O house of Israel. Thus saith the Lord God; In the day that I shall have cleansed you from all your iniquities I will also cause you to dwell in the cities, and the wastes shall be builded. And the desolate land shall be tilled, whereas it lay desolate in the sight of all that passed by. And they shall say, This land that was desolate is become like the garden of Eden; and the waste and desolate and ruined cities are become fenced, and are inhabited. Then the heathen that are left round about you shall know that I the Lord build the ruined places, and plant that that was desolate: I the Lord have spoken it, and I will do it. Thus saith the Lord God; I will yet for this be enquired of by the house of Israel, to do it for them; I will increase them with men like a flock. As the holy flock, as the flock of Jerusalem in her solemn feasts; so shall the waste cities be filled with flocks of men: and they shall know that I am the Lord.*

Again we find some verses that may give a context to words later found in the New Testament where Paul is addressing the Hebrews. In these verses it is clear that when the Lord says:

A new heart also will I give you, and a new spirit will I put within you: and I will take away the stony heart out of your flesh, and I will give you an heart of flesh. And I will put my spirit within you, and cause you to walk in my statutes, and ye shall keep my judgments, and do them. And ye shall dwell in the land that I gave to your fathers; and ye shall be my people, and I will be your God. I will also save you from all your uncleannesses: and I will call for the corn, and will increase it, and lay no famine upon you.

…He is talking about their restoration in the land, and that the new heart and spirit is towards His statutes and judgments, or the Law that they already had. In [79]Hebrews Paul also quotes from similar verses in Jeremiah 31:31, written at around the same time and referring to the same event, which is the restoration of Israel in the land. But note that these words apply to the new covenant with the *house of Israel, and the house of Judah* and it is the *Law,* albeit a revised one, that is to be written into their hearts and minds. Paul recognized that this was yet future to him, and that although the first covenant was still *ready to vanish away* it had not yet completely gone when Paul ministered, as the conditions for it had not been met by Israel. What we are looking at in both Ezekiel's, and Jeremiah's words is a situation that when the people return to the land it would be under a new covenant where the Law was written into their hearts and minds, yet we see that Paul recognized even in his day, that this had not yet become a reality for Israel, and remained to be fulfilled.

Fourth vision: Ezekiel 37:1 – 37:28 The valley of dry bones.
Ezekiel 37:1-28 *The hand of the Lord was upon me, and carried me out in the spirit of the Lord, and set me down in the midst of the valley which was full of bones, And caused me to pass by them round about: and, behold, there were very many in the open valley; and, lo, they were very dry. And he said unto me, Son of man, can these bones live? And I answered, O Lord God, thou knowest. Again he said unto me, Prophesy upon these bones, and say unto them, O ye dry bones, hear the word of the Lord. Thus saith the Lord God unto these bones; Behold, I will cause breath to enter into you, and ye shall live: And I will lay sinews upon you, and will bring up flesh upon you, and cover you with skin, and put breath in you, and ye shall live; and ye shall know that I am the Lord. So I prophesied as I was commanded: and as I prophesied, there was a noise, and behold a shaking, and the bones came together, bone to his bone. And when I beheld, lo, the sinews and the flesh came up upon them, and the skin covered them above: but there was no breath in them. Then said he unto me, Prophesy unto the wind,*

CHAPTER SIX

prophesy, son of man, and say to the wind, Thus saith the Lord God; Come from the four winds, O breath, and breathe upon these slain, that they may live. So I prophesied as he commanded me, and the breath came into them, and they lived, and stood up upon their feet, an exceeding great army. Then he said unto me, Son of man, these bones are the whole house of Israel: behold, they say, Our bones are dried, and our hope is lost: we are cut off for our parts. Therefore prophesy and say unto them, Thus saith the Lord God; Behold, O my people, I will open your graves, and cause you to come up out of your graves, and bring you into the land of Israel. And ye shall know that I am the Lord, when I have opened your graves, O my people, and brought you up out of your graves, And shall put my spirit in you, and ye shall live, and I shall place you in your own land: then shall ye know that I the Lord have spoken it, and performed it, saith the Lord. The word of the Lord came again unto me, saying, Moreover, thou son of man, take thee one stick, and write upon it, For Judah, and for the children of Israel his companions: then take another stick, and write upon it, For Joseph, the stick of Ephraim, and for all the house of Israel his companions: And join them one to another into one stick; and they shall become one in thine hand. And when the children of thy people shall speak unto thee, saying, Wilt thou not shew us what thou meanest by these? Say unto them, Thus saith the Lord God; Behold, I will take the stick of Joseph, which is in the hand of Ephraim, and the tribes of Israel his fellows, and will put them with him, even with the stick of Judah, and make them one stick, and they shall be one in mine hand. And the sticks whereon thou writest shall be in thine hand before their eyes. And say unto them, Thus saith the Lord God; Behold, I will take the children of Israel from among the heathen, whither they be gone, and will gather them on every side, and bring them into their own land: And I will make them one nation in the land upon the mountains of Israel; and one king shall be king to them all: and they shall be no more two nations, neither shall they be divided into two kingdoms any more at all: Neither shall they defile themselves any more with their idols, nor with their detestable things, nor with any of their transgressions: but I will save them out of all their dwellingplaces, wherein they have sinned, and will cleanse them: so shall they be my people, and I will be their God. And David my servant shall be king over them; and they all shall have one shepherd: they shall also walk in my judgments, and observe my statutes, and do them. And they shall dwell in the land that I have given unto Jacob my servant, wherein your fathers have dwelt; and they shall dwell therein, even they, and their children, and their children's children for ever: and my servant David shall be their prince for ever. Moreover I will make a covenant of peace with them; it shall be an everlasting covenant with them: and I will place them, and multiply them, and will set my sanctuary in the midst of them for evermore. My tabernacle also shall be with them: yea, I will be their God, and they shall be my people. And the heathen shall know that I the Lord do sanctify Israel, when my sanctuary shall be in the midst of them for evermore.

End of the fourth vision

This fourth vision of Ezekiel where he is taken either bodily or by spirit to this valley of bones, whether [80]real or representative we are not told, concerns the *whole house of Israel*. We do not know when exactly this took place, but it is clear from the dates given that Judah had been in captivity for at least six years and the hope of the people at this time is likened to these dry bones, whose attitude now was that they were cut off as scattered bones, both from their own land and their promises. Israel's ten tribes of course had long since been scattered throughout the Assyrian Empire, with only remnants of the tribes represented in Judah, but this vision concerns the whole house including both Judah and Benjamin, with the other so-called ten *lost tribes*, and the prophecy indicates not only a physical restoration of this renewed Israel to the land, but also a restoration of their spiritual state under God's law. This prophecy, the Word of God, was to be the glue, the spirit of God in them through which the unity would take place, and in which they would be joined together. Notice again that this now-cleansed people would serve God under *my servant David, their prince for ever.* Also notice that He said:

I will make a covenant of peace with them; it shall be an everlasting covenant with them: and I will place them, and multiply them, and will set my sanctuary in the midst of them for evermore. My tabernacle also shall be with them: yea, I will be their God, and they shall be my people. And the heathen shall know that I the Lord do sanctify Israel, when my sanctuary shall be in the midst of them for evermore.

Quite apart from their being returned to the land as one people unified under the Law, albeit a modified Law that was to be written in their hearts, there was also to be a new covenant of peace, and a new sanctuary or Temple, which was to be *in the midst of them for evermore.*

These promises were not only given to Ezekiel for the people but were also the subject of the prophecies of [81]Jeremiah, and were later to be clarified through the visions given to [82]Daniel. From the start of the captivities, there was a limit set on their duration, and although it was later extended because of the refusal of the people to submit to Nebuchadnezzar as they were told to, yet the set timings remained. Such was the devastation of the nation that even within this short time of captivity they had already given up all hope of restoration. However, returning to Ezekiel's account we notice that the sanctuary that was yet to be built was to be in the midst of them for *evermore* which could not be said of the temple that was rebuilt and modified under Herod, and which the Lord condemned to obscurity.

We have to conclude from these words that not only were there to be changes in the Law when the people returned, there would also need to be a change of heart, of governors, and of the temple that was to be built. What actually took place on their return appears to be a compromise of the people on all points, for these conditions remain unfulfilled to this day, and it has become increasingly obvious that the eventual return to Israel did not fulfil the conditions for blessing that God intended for the nation. In fact the land fell to the Greeks, the Romans, and eventually the Ottomans, then briefly after the First World War to the British, before it finally became a Jewish homeland in 1947. But even now we see neither a Jewish revival of unity under their God, nor a rebuilt temple for their worship to recommence. The reason is shown in Ezekiel's fifth vision, but let us first consider Gog and Magog, drawing from Ezekiel Chapters 38-39.

With one [83]exception the names of Gog the prince and of Magog his realm are only mentioned by Ezekiel here, and by John in the Book of Revelation. Clearly in Ezekiel's account Gog is brought by the Lord to try Israel, after they have been restored to the land. The description given shows that not only must the Jews have returned from captivity for this to happen, but they would have done so long enough to be at ease, hence disregarding the need for protection of their borders and considering themselves safe from invasion. Ezekiel was looking forward to the *latter years* but not I believe in his own mind, to

CHAPTER SIX

the much later time that John describes, which was to be the subject of further revelation. However the wording here allows scope for an alternative timescale, whilst at the same time describing what would be expected to take place some time after, when the Jews returned to their homeland from captivity. Talking of Gog:

Ezekiel 38:8-12: *in the latter years thou shalt come into the land that is brought back from the sword, and is gathered out of many people, against the mountains of Israel, which have been always waste: but it is brought forth out of the nations, and they shall dwell safely all of them. Thou shalt ascend and come like a storm, thou shalt be like a cloud to cover the land, thou, and all thy bands, and many people with thee. Thus saith the Lord God; It shall also come to pass, that at the same time shall things come into thy mind, and thou shalt think an evil thought: And thou shalt say, I will go up to the land of unwalled villages; I will go to them that are at rest, that dwell safely, all of them dwelling without walls, and having neither bars nor gates, To take a spoil, and to take a prey; to turn thine hand upon the desolate places that are now inhabited.*

The essence of both Ezekiel's and John's message is that at some time in the future, Israel would be subject to trial by the threat of invasion by a great army, loosely described as coming from the North, but more likely an alliance drawn from many nations who eventually are made to come to fight against Israel. This is not altogether a voluntary act on their part, as they are under Gods control, being brought back from their own intentions, as a fish when it is hooked, trying to pull away but inevitably drawn in, for it is God's will to use this army to try His own nation:

And I will turn thee back, and put hooks into thy jaws, and I will bring thee forth, and all thine army, horses and horsemen, all of them clothed with all sorts of armour, even a great company with bucklers and shields, all of them handling swords: Persia, Ethiopia, and Libya with them; all of them with shield and helmet: Gomer, and all his bands; the house of Togarmah of the north quarters, and all his bands: and many people with thee.

This alliance consists of many nations, not easily identified, but includes some African nations. The downfall of this army is a foregone conclusion, and eventually God's purpose in allowing this attempted invasion is seen: to make *my holy name known in the midst of my people Israel.*

Ezekiel 39:4-9: *Thou shalt fall upon the open field: for I have spoken it, saith the Lord God. And I will send a fire on Magog, and among them that dwell carelessly in the isles: and they shall know that I am the Lord. So will I make my holy name known in the midst of my people Israel; and I will not let them pollute my holy name any more: and the heathen shall know that I am the Lord, the Holy One in Israel. Behold, it is come, and it is done, saith the Lord God; this is the day whereof I have spoken. And they that dwell in the cities of Israel shall go forth, and shall set on fire and burn the weapons, both the shields and the bucklers, the bows and the arrows, and the handstaves, and the spears, and they shall burn them with fire seven years:*

John has less to say about Gog and Magog, but there are some interesting comparisons to be made:

Revelation 20:1-15: *And I saw an angel come down from heaven, having the key of the bottomless pit and a great chain in his hand. And he laid hold on the dragon, that old serpent, which is the Devil, and Satan, and bound him a thousand years, And cast him into the bottomless pit, and shut him up, and set a seal upon him, that he should deceive the nations no more, till the thousand years should be fulfilled: and after that he must be loosed a little season. And I saw thrones, and they sat upon them, and judgment was given unto them: and I saw the souls of them that were beheaded for the witness of Jesus, and for the word of God, and which had not worshipped the beast, neither his image, neither had received his mark upon their foreheads, or in their hands; and they lived and reigned with Christ a thousand years. But the rest of the dead lived not again until the thousand years were finished. This is the first resurrection. Blessed and holy is he that hath part in the first resurrection: on such the second death hath no power, but they shall be priests of God and of Christ, and shall reign with him a thousand years. And when the thousand years are expired, Satan shall be loosed out of his prison, And shall go out to deceive the nations which are in the four quarters of the earth, Gog and Magog, to gather them together to battle: the number of whom is as the sand of the sea. And they went up on the breadth of the earth, and compassed the camp of the saints about, and the beloved city: and fire came down from God out of heaven, and devoured them. And the devil that deceived them was cast into the lake of fire and brimstone, where the beast and the false prophet are, and shall be tormented day and night for ever and ever. And I saw a great white throne, and him that sat on it, from whose face the earth and the heaven fled away; and there was found no place for them. And I saw the dead, small and great, stand before God; and the books were opened: and another book was opened, which is the book of life: and the dead were judged out of those things which were written in the books, according to their works. And the sea gave up the dead which were in it; and death and hell delivered up the dead which were in them: and they were judged every man according to their works. And death and hell were cast into the lake of fire. This is the second death. And whosoever was not found written in the book of life was cast into the lake of fire.*

The fundamental truth that we need to understand about these events is that they take place at the end of the millennium reign, long after the beast and his false prophet have been cast into the lake of fire, from which there is no return. When we understand this, we will not confuse the events that have to do with Gog and Magog with those that have taken place around a thousand years previously at Armageddon where the armies of the beast and the false prophet were destroyed. They are separate events, as can be easily seen provided we read the text properly. Here we have Israel blessed in the land, no longer under threat from Satan, as he has been bound in the bottomless pit (not the same as the lake of fire). We see that there is a period of relative peace until he is later released for a short time, when he once again tries to deceive the nations, stirring them up against Israel. Gog, and his realm of Magog, are the instruments that he now uses, and these are drawn from the *four quarters of the earth* to form this massive alliance. These finally encircle Jerusalem, but are then destroyed by fire from God. After this, the devil is cast permanently into the lake of fire, and the Great white throne is revealed, where eventually all will stand to face God. Notice that the Beast, the false Prophet and Satan are not presented here, as their judgment has already been set, there is no justification for what they have done, and no one to speak for them in their defence. Eventually death, hell, and *whosoever was not found written in the book of life* are sent to the same place. After this, the old earth is destroyed and a new one set up.

John's Book of Revelation as a whole was the final unveiling of how God would pull together the various prophecies of scripture, and make sense of them all. It becomes more apparent as we progress, that during the ages God has tried to reason with man, and His own nation in particular, but has met with refusal and failure, at every turn. Where He would have intervened with blessing, and averted the worst of the judgments, He has been unable to do so except in the case of those few individuals in

CHAPTER SIX

His will who have listened.

There is no doubt in my mind that the Lord's coming to earth should have been the time of universal blessing for mankind, had the Jews in the first instance, accepted Him and the sacrifice He made. If that had happened then the timescale for these events might have been dramatically reduced, and in all likelihood the severity of His judgments on this earth muted. It is also clear to me that Ezekiel was given the blueprint for the Jews blessing when they returned to the land, the ordinances and building of the Third Temple, which we will consider in the next chapter.

CHAPTER SEVEN

Fifth vision, the Third Temple and its Ordinances

This final vision given to Ezekiel comes about eighteen or so years after the previous one, according to the dates we are given, and concerns the setting up of the Third Temple with its ordinances, including instructions for the division of the land amongst the twelve tribes, the priests and the prince, with the new city at its centre.

The book of Ezekiel deserves a more in-depth study, but it is not the intention here to examine in too much detail what is written, more to give an outline with particular reference to any points that may be relevant to our study of the Millennium period. I gladly refer you to the many and varied illustrations of the Third Temple that are available on the internet, some of which are based on the dimensions given in scripture. These are of course, however well-presented they might be, at best only artists' impressions, but often they are the result of many years of study, and will give an idea at least, of what we are considering here.

Even a brief glance at Ezekiel's description should convince us that this is a blueprint for real walls and real buildings, with precise and correct dimensions which will enable the builders to complete it in due course using modern methods and materials. It is sufficient to note here that the Lord intended the rebuilding of the temple, the city, the divisions of the tribes, and the new borders of Israel to be new and according to this detailed plan, shortly after they returned from captivity. Ezekiel was to show the people the vision, but its acceptance, and subsequent reality was to depend on how they received his prophecy:

Ezekiel 43:10-11: *Thou son of man, shew the house to the house of Israel, that they may be ashamed of their iniquities: and let them measure the pattern. And if they be ashamed of all that they have done, shew them the form of the house, and the fashion thereof, and the goings out thereof, and the comings in thereof, and all the forms thereof, and all the ordinances thereof, and all the forms thereof, and all the laws thereof: and write it in their sight, that they may keep the whole form thereof, and all the ordinances thereof, and do them.*

The condition given is seen as their being *ashamed of their iniquities*, which was obviously not to be the case, as both history and scripture inform us that the return to the land involved a rebuilding of Jerusalem according to its former boundary walls, and with a partial reconstruction of Solomon's temple, as described for us by Ezra and Nehemiah. The only two possible conclusions to be drawn from this are that either the remainder of the plan was not shown to the Jews because they did not show proper regard to Ezekiel's message, or that the vision was shown to them in full but they disregarded it. On return to the land the Jews wanted to rebuild the city and temple as it was before, which turned out to be a compromise far short of what the Lord intended. They had a blank canvas on which to rebuild, as Jerusalem was in ruins anyway, but we cannot tell if the plan was actually in their possession, although we know it was written down somewhere because we have it recorded here in Ezekiel. Either way, they were obviously not *ashamed* enough to take this vision seriously and so it remains for them to build it as God intended at a later time when they actually are ready.

It might be as well to remember that Israel on the Earth, with its priesthood and ordinances, was the only true religion there ever was, having been set up by the Lord Himself, and [84]representing things in heaven not always openly revealed or understood. Where the plans for the tabernacle, and Solomon's temple were followed for example, they were of precise dimensions, materials and method of construction, given by God to glorify Himself in His own perfect way. It is in the same detailed manner that this temple is shown to Ezekiel, and he wrote it down as it was shown him. We can only wonder why they failed to build it and opted for something inferior instead. There is no evidence that the glory of God in the form of the *shekinah* cloud ever descended into the rebuilt Temple of Zerubbabel, as it did in Solomon's, but Ezekiel did see this happen in his own vision of the third Temple, and so it must be that this whole experience is still in abeyance, awaiting a later fulfilment. Remember that God still wishes to abide with His people in this place, and whilst He reluctantly, and temporarily, removed His presence from them, Ezekiel records that He intends to return to them in the form of the *shekinah,* but only on His own terms, and when conditions are right.

For the sake of simplicity let us consider Ezekiel's final vision in scripture, by its natural divisions:

(a) Measuring the Temple Ezekiel 40:1-42:20. Layout of the gates and courts (40:1-47), Layout of the three divisions of the temple (40:48-41:26), Layout of the chambers (42:1-14), Outside measurements (42:15-20)

Ezekiel is once again taken by the Lord's hand to Israel, to a mountain, to the south of which was laid out the *frame* of a city. We remember that by this time the city, and temple of Jerusalem had been destroyed, and so what Ezekiel is being shown is the pattern for it to be rebuilt. The city is not named here as Jerusalem, but is later referred to as the same that he saw in his other [85]visions:

Ezekiel 40:1-49: *In the five and twentieth year of our captivity, in the beginning of the year, in the tenth day of the month, in the fourteenth year after that the city was smitten, in the selfsame day the hand of the Lord was upon me, and brought me thither. In the visions of God brought he me into the land of Israel, and set me upon a very high mountain, by which was as the frame of a city on the south. And he brought me thither, and, behold, there was a man, whose appearance was like the appearance of brass, with a line of flax in his hand, and a measuring reed; and he stood in the gate. And the man said unto me, Son of man, behold with thine eyes, and hear with thine ears, and set thine heart upon all that I shall shew thee; for to the intent that I might shew them unto thee art thou brought hither: declare all that thou seest to the house of Israel.*

There follows a detailed description of the measurements of the new temple, its three gates, north, south and east, their porch areas, with the outer walls, and chambers. The east gate is distinguished from the other two, in that there are seven steps leading up to it, rather than the eight of the north and south gates. After this we are shown the dimensions of the inner court and buildings, and note that near to the inner north gate are the eight tables for sacrifice:

And behold a wall on the outside of the house round about, and in the man's hand a measuring reed of six cubits long by the cubit and an hand breadth: so he measured the breadth of the building, one reed; and the height, one reed. Then came he unto the gate which looketh toward the east, and went up the stairs thereof, and measured the threshold of the gate, which was one reed broad; and the other threshold of the gate, which was one reed broad. And every little chamber was one reed long, and one reed broad; and between the little chambers were five cubits; and the threshold of the gate by the porch of the gate within was one reed. He measured also the porch of the gate within, one reed. Then measured he the porch of the gate, eight cubits; and the posts thereof, two cubits; and the porch of the gate was inward. And the little chambers of the gate eastward were three on this side, and three on that side; they three were of one measure: and the posts had one measure on this side and on that side. And he measured the breadth of the entry of the gate, ten cubits; and the length of the gate, thirteen cubits. The space also before the little chambers was one cubit on this side, and the space was one cubit on that side: and the little chambers were six cubits on this side, and six cubits on that side. He measured then the gate from the roof of one little chamber to the roof of another: the breadth was five and twenty cubits, door against door. He made also posts of threescore cubits, even unto the post of the court round about the gate. And from the face of the gate of the entrance unto the face of the porch of the inner gate were fifty cubits. And there were narrow windows to the little chambers, and to their posts within the gate round about, and likewise to the arches: and windows were round about inward: and upon each post were palm trees. Then brought he me into the outward court, and, lo, there were chambers, and a pavement made for the court round about: thirty chambers were upon the pavement. And the pavement by the side of the gates over against the length of the gates was the lower pavement. Then he measured the breadth from the forefront of the lower gate unto the forefront of the inner court without, an hundred cubits eastward and northward. And the gate of the outward court that looked toward the north, he measured the length thereof, and the breadth thereof. And the little chambers thereof were three on this side and three on that side; and the posts thereof and the arches thereof were after the measure of the first gate: the length thereof was fifty cubits, and the breadth five and twenty cubits. And their windows, and their arches, and their palm trees, were after the measure of the gate that looketh toward the east; and they went up unto it by seven steps; and the arches thereof were before them. And the gate of the inner court was over against the gate toward the north, and toward the east; and he measured from gate to gate an hundred cubits.

After that he brought me toward the south, and behold a gate toward the south: and he measured the posts thereof and the arches thereof according to these measures. And there were windows in it and in the arches thereof round about, like those windows: the length was fifty cubits, and the breadth five and twenty cubits. And there were seven steps to go up to it, and the arches thereof were before them: and it had palm trees, one on this side, and another on that side, upon the posts thereof. And there was a gate in the inner court toward the south: and he measured from gate to gate toward the south an hundred cubits. And he brought me to the inner court by the south gate: and he measured the south gate according to these measures; And the little chambers thereof, and the posts thereof, and the arches thereof, according to these measures: and there were windows in it and in the arches thereof round about: it was fifty cubits long, and five and twenty cubits broad. And the arches round about were five and twenty cubits long, and five cubits broad. And the arches thereof were toward the utter court; and palm trees were upon the posts thereof: and the going up to it had eight steps.

And he brought me into the inner court toward the east: and he measured the gate according to these measures. And the little chambers thereof, and the posts thereof, and the arches thereof, were according to these measures: and there were windows therein and in the arches thereof round about: it was fifty cubits long, and five and twenty cubits broad. And the arches thereof were toward the outward court; and palm trees were upon the posts thereof, on this side, and on that side: and the going up to it had eight steps. And he brought me to the north gate, and measured it according to these measures; The little chambers thereof, the posts thereof, and the arches thereof, and the windows to it round about: the length was fifty cubits, and the breadth five and twenty cubits. And the posts thereof were toward the utter court; and palm trees were upon the posts thereof, on this side, and on that side: and the going up to it had eight steps.

And the chambers and the entries thereof were by the posts of the gates, where they washed the burnt offering. And in the porch of the gate were two tables on this side, and two tables on that side, to slay thereon the burnt offering and the sin offering and the trespass offering. And at the side without, as one goeth up to the entry of the north gate, were two tables; and on the other side, which was at the porch of the gate, were two tables. Four tables were on this side, and four tables on that side, by the side of the gate; eight tables, whereupon they slew their sacrifices. And the four tables were of hewn stone for the burnt offering, of a cubit and an half long, and a cubit and an half broad, and one cubit high: whereupon also they laid the instruments wherewith they slew the burnt offering and the sacrifice. And within were hooks, an hand broad, fastened round about: and upon the tables was the flesh of the offering.

Notice that these offerings are to continue in this temple: *to slay thereon the burnt offering and the sin offering and the trespass offering,* so if we accept that this temple is to be built in the future to the same pattern, this necessarily includes the fact that sacrifices are to be made there. This may be a cause of difficulty for some of us as believers, for we know that the Lord made the one necessary sacrifice for all time[86], but when we consider that the restoration of the Jewish nation in prophecy commences at the last week of Daniel with an agreement concerning the morning and evening sacrifices[87], then the concept of sacrifices becomes more meaningful, for this not only heralds the recommencement of the Jewish *religion,* but also the conclusion of the gospel of the grace of God that we now enjoy.

This may be hard for us to accept, but accept it we must, for the truth is that under the Jewish law sacrifices were offered continually, and although they were never intended to be an alternative to Christ's sacrifice, they were still required as a reminder to the nation of their need of Christ to redeem them from sin. In that respect nothing has changed, for as in the days before Christ they could look forward to the sacrifice He was about to make, in the last days of this Temple and reinstituted worship under the Law, they will look back to what He achieved for them in a sense of remembrance. The sacrifices themselves only ever served as a pattern for heavenly things, and were never intended to be effective in removing sin. This will remain their purpose in times to come.

Returning to Ezekiel's account we see the inner house, and most holy place described:

Ezekiel 41:1-26: *Afterward he brought me to the temple, and measured the posts, six cubits broad on the one side, and six cubits broad on the other side, which was the breadth of the tabernacle. And the breadth of the door was ten cubits; and the sides of the door were five cubits on the one side, and five cubits on the other side: and he measured the length thereof, forty cubits: and the breadth, twenty cubits. Then went he inward, and measured the post of the door, two cubits; and the door, six cubits; and the breadth of the door, seven cubits. So he measured the length thereof, twenty cubits; and the breadth, twenty cubits, before the temple: and he said unto me, This is the most holy place. After he measured the wall of the house, six cubits; and the breadth of every side chamber, four cubits, round about the house on every side. And the side chambers were three, one over another, and thirty in order; and they entered into the wall which was of the house for the side chambers round about, that they might have hold, but they had not hold in the wall of the house. And there was an enlarging, and a winding about still upward to the side chambers: for the winding about of the house went still upward round about the house: therefore the breadth of the house was still upward, and so increased from the lowest chamber to the highest by the midst.*

Again this description owes nothing to any previous sanctuary or tabernacle, as we see the building itself is on three storeys, each extending outwards from the one below it, with the point made that there are no pillars supporting the extended storeys. Inside, the building is decorated with alternating cherubim and palm trees, with the face of a young lion and a man facing inward.

Of course from Ezekiel's previous description of *cherubim* we know there are two other faces on the left side, not seen here, the eagle and the ox, so we might presume these are represented as facing outward from Ezekiel's previous description of them, Ezekiel 1:10: *As for the likeness of their faces, they four had the face of a man, and the face of a lion on the right side; and they four had the face of an ox on the left side, they four also had the face of an eagle.*

This is pure conjecture on my part, but I like to think that the man and the lion represent Israel and the Lord, and the palms represent His coming to His temple, as when the people praised Him and laid [88]palm branches before Him. This holy place is where the Lord meets with His people, who are represented here by the priests, the sons of Zadok. If we are to continue this analogy, the eagle facing outward could represent the fowls of the air, the ox as man working the earth. The [89]opposition of the fowls of the air and the [90]labour of man imposed at his removal from Eden could then be seen as outside, and removed from, the Lord's fellowship with man in this place. Such a simple explanation may not please everyone, I suppose, but we will never really know the truth of this until we reach heaven and see the real thing, and not the just pattern of it.

And it was made with cherubims and palm trees, so that a palm tree was between a cherub and a cherub; and every cherub had two faces; So that the face of a man was toward the palm tree on the one side, and the face of a young lion toward the palm tree on the other side: it was made through all the house round about. From the ground unto above the door were cherubims and palm trees made, and on the wall of the temple. The posts of the temple were squared, and the face of the sanctuary; the appearance of the one as the appearance of the other. The altar of wood was three cubits high, and the length thereof two cubits; and the corners thereof, and the length thereof, and the walls thereof, were of wood: and he said unto me, This is the table that is before the Lord. And the temple and the sanctuary had two doors. And the doors had two leaves apiece, two turning leaves; two leaves for the one door, and two leaves for the other door. And there were made on them, on the doors of the temple, cherubims and palm trees, like as were made upon the walls; and there were thick planks upon the face of the porch without. And there were narrow windows and palm trees on the one side and on the other side, on the sides of the porch, and upon the side chambers of the house, and thick planks.

Ezekiel 42:1-20: *Then he brought me forth into the utter court, the way toward the north: and he brought me into the chamber that was over against the separate place, and which was before the building toward the north. Before the length of an hundred cubits was the north door, and the breadth was fifty cubits. Over against the twenty cubits which were for the inner court, and over against the pavement which was for the utter court, was gallery against gallery in three stories. And before the chambers was a walk of ten cubits breadth inward, a way of one cubit; and their doors toward the north. Now the upper chambers were shorter: for the galleries were higher than these, than the lower, and than the middlemost of the building. For they were in three stories, but had not pillars as the pillars of the courts: therefore the building was straitened more than the lowest and the middlemost from the ground. And the wall that was without over against the chambers, toward the utter court on the forepart of the chambers, the length thereof was fifty cubits. For the length of the chambers that were in the utter court was fifty cubits: and, lo, before the temple were an hundred cubits. And from under these chambers was the entry on the east side, as one goeth into them from the utter court. The chambers were in the thickness of the wall of the court toward the east, over against the separate place, and over against the building. And the way before them was like the appearance of the chambers which were toward the north, as long as they, and as broad as they: and all their goings out were both according to their fashions, and according to their doors. And according to the doors of the chambers that were toward the south was a door in the head of the way, even the way directly before the wall toward the east, as one entereth into them.*

Then said he unto me, The north chambers and the south chambers, which are before the separate place, they be holy chambers, where the priests that approach unto the Lord shall eat the most holy things: there shall they lay the most holy things, and the meat offering, and the sin offering, and the trespass offering; for the place is holy. When the priests enter therein, then shall they not go out of the holy place into the utter court, but there they shall lay their garments wherein they minister; for they are holy; and shall put on other garments, and shall approach to those things which are for the people. Now when he had made an end of measuring the inner house, he brought me forth toward the gate whose prospect is toward the east, and measured it round about. He measured the east side with the measuring reed, five hundred reeds, with the measuring reed round about. He measured the north side, five hundred reeds, with the measuring reed round about. He measured the south side, five hundred reeds, with the measuring reed. He turned about to the west side, and measured five hundred reeds with the measuring reed. He measured it by the four sides: it had a wall round about, five hundred reeds long, and five hundred broad, to make a separation between the sanctuary and the profane place.

(b) The return of the *shekinah* to the Temple, and the conditions applying to its return (43:1-11)

Ezekiel 43:1-11: *Afterward he brought me to the gate, even the gate that looketh toward the east: And, behold, the glory of the God of Israel came from the way of the east: and his voice was like a noise of many waters: and the earth shined with his glory. And it was according to the appearance of the vision which I saw, even according to the vision that I saw when I came to destroy the city: and the visions were like the vision that I saw by the river Chebar; and I fell upon my face. And the glory of the Lord came into the house by the way of the gate whose prospect is toward the east. So the spirit took me up, and brought me into the inner court; and, behold, the glory of the Lord filled the house. And I heard him speaking unto me out of the house; and the man stood by me. And he said unto me, Son of man, the place of my throne, and the place of the soles of my feet, where I will dwell in the midst of the children of Israel for ever, and my holy name, shall the house of Israel no more defile, neither they, nor their kings, by their whoredom, nor by the carcases of their kings in their high places. In their setting of their threshold by my thresholds, and their post by my posts, and the wall between me and them, they have even defiled my holy name by their abominations that they have committed: wherefore I have consumed them in mine anger. Now let them put away their whoredom, and the carcases of their kings, far from me, and I will dwell in the midst of them for ever.*

Here Ezekiel is shown the return of the glory of God, the *shekinah* presence to the temple. We remember that he was previously shown its [91]departure, and its return follows the same route, coming from the east, then through the outer east gate. Ezekiel establishes that this is the same vision that he has previously seen of the glory of God, so there is no mistaking what is meant here. Also notice that this place is *forever* or at least while the earth is standing, and so it is inconceivable that this temple is in existence when the beast desecrates the place with his own *abomination of desolation*. I cannot see how this temple can be in place before this event, to be desecrated by the beast, so it must be built after the tribulation period for the Jews, and therefore after the beast and false prophet have been destroyed. I know this is not the belief of some present Jews, who at this very time are preparing to build a Temple, but all that really needs to be in place here to start with is an altar of burnt offering, so that the daily sacrifice can be made, and this is probably where the false prophet sets up the *abomination of desolation*. Once the *shekinah* presence returns to the Temple, it does not leave again, and here in Ezekiel's account is the only place where this phenomenon is described, where God, in this form, once again dwells on the earth. The condition for this return is seen: *Now let them put away their whoredom, and the carcases of their kings, far from me, and I will dwell in the midst of them for ever.*

Back now in real time, Ezekiel is commissioned to go to the elders of the house of Israel, and present this vision to them. Notice however, the condition for all of this is *if they be ashamed of all that they have done* and assuming they were, then he was to show them the whole vision so they could consequently measure it from the description, and build it. As previously noted, this never happened, nor do we know whether or not Ezekiel felt comfortable enough with their response to show them the whole vision. We are not told what their reaction was, so we have to draw our own conclusions about it. Certainly, when they finally did return from captivity, this was not the temple that was built.

Thou son of man, shew the house to the house of Israel, that they may be ashamed of their iniquities: and let them measure the pattern. And if they be ashamed of all that they have done, shew them the form of the house, and the fashion thereof, and the goings out thereof, and the comings in thereof, and all the forms thereof, and all the ordinances thereof, and all the forms thereof, and all the laws thereof: and write it in their sight, that they may keep the whole form thereof, and all the ordinances thereof, and do them.

(c) The Law of the house, the altar of burnt offering and its consecration (43:12-27)

Returning to the vision, the law of the house, a new law was to be added in that the whole area was to be considered holy, or separated to the Lord. In addition, the altar of burnt offering was to be constructed to these exact specifications, and there were to be steps leading up to it. This of course is man-made, in contrast with the previous altars that were not to be made of [92]*hewn stone.* Its consecration is described, and we are reminded that it is the *sons of Zadok* who have the privilege of serving in the temple proper, although other branches of the Levites were to perform some external duties.

This is the law of the house; Upon the top of the mountain the whole limit thereof round about shall be most holy. Behold, this is the law of the house. And these are the measures of the altar after the cubits: The cubit is a cubit and an hand breadth; even the bottom shall be a cubit, and the breadth a cubit, and the border thereof by the edge thereof round about shall be a span: and this shall be the higher place of the altar. And from the bottom upon the ground even to the lower settle shall be two cubits, and the breadth one cubit; and from the lesser settle even to the greater settle shall be four cubits, and the breadth one cubit. So the altar shall be four cubits; and from the altar and upward shall be four horns. And the altar shall be twelve cubits long, twelve broad, square in the four squares thereof. And the settle shall be fourteen cubits long and fourteen broad in the four squares thereof; and the border about it shall be half a cubit; and the bottom thereof shall be a cubit about; and his stairs shall look toward the east. And he said unto me, Son of man, thus saith the Lord God; These are the ordinances of the altar in the day when they shall make it, to offer burnt offerings thereon, and to sprinkle blood thereon

And thou shalt give to the priests the Levites that be of the seed of Zadok, which approach unto me, to minister unto me, saith the Lord God, a young bullock for a sin offering. And thou shalt take of the blood thereof, and put it on the four horns of it, and on the four corners of the settle, and upon the border round about: thus shalt thou cleanse and purge it. Thou shalt take the bullock also of the sin offering, and he shall burn it in the appointed place of the house, without the sanctuary. And on the second day thou shalt offer a kid of the goats without blemish for a sin offering; and they shall cleanse the altar, as they did cleanse it with the bullock. When thou hast made an end of cleansing it, thou shalt offer a young bullock without blemish, and a ram out of the flock without blemish. And thou shalt offer them before the Lord, and the priests shall cast salt upon them, and they shall offer them up for a burnt offering unto the Lord. Seven days shalt thou prepare every day a goat for a sin offering: they shall also prepare a young bullock, and a ram out of the flock, without blemish. Seven days shall they purge the altar and purify it; and they shall consecrate themselves. And when these days are expired, it shall be, that upon the eighth day, and so forward, the priests shall make your burnt offerings upon the altar, and your peace offerings; and I will accept you, saith the Lord God.

(d) Ordinances of the Temple (44:1-31) Restricted access to the Temple (44:1-9), Status of Levites (44:10-14), the priesthood of Zadok (44:15-31)

Ezekiel 44:1-31: *Then he brought me back the way of the gate of the outward sanctuary which looketh toward the east; and it was shut. Then said the Lord unto me; This gate shall be shut, it shall not be opened, and no man shall enter in by it; because the Lord, the God of Israel, hath entered in by it, therefore it shall be shut. It is for the prince; the prince, he shall sit in it to eat bread before the Lord; he shall enter by the way of the porch of that gate, and shall go out by the way of the same.*

The outwards east gate is described here, and this is to be kept shut, as this is where the glory of the Lord had entered in. The description of the prince here, sitting in the porch accessed from inside the temple suggests to me that he is symbolically waiting, on behalf of the people, for the Lord Himself to return through this gate. This would reflect the spirit of what the Lord said in His parables, where the people were to wait for His final return, and would also suggest that the prince in these days also represents the high priest's office (there is no description of a high priest given anywhere in Ezekiel's vision of the temple) thus the royal line and earthly priesthood are combined in this man, until such time as the Lord returns to the Mount of Olives, and onwards into His temple. Although the priesthood itself remains Levitical, the representative of the high priest is now from [93]Judah, the Lord's own tribe, about which Moses [94]*spake nothing concerning the priesthood*. This in my view opens the way for the priesthood to be changed when the Lord returns to His temple, for He is the high priest in the order of Melchizedec, the everlasting priesthood, going beyond that of the sons of Aaron. All of the offerings of the people were to be for the maintenance of the priests that served in the temple, as they were not given any other means of support. The Levites were given certain duties around the temple, but it was to be the role of the sons of Zadok to offer the sacrifices, both for the prince, themselves and the people, and to enter into the sanctuary to eat before the Lord, having first changed their clothes, and then changing them back on exit. They were also more importantly, to:

Teach my people the difference between the holy and profane, and cause them to discern between the unclean and the clean. And in controversy they shall stand in judgment; and they shall judge it according to my judgments: and they shall keep my laws and my statutes in all mine assemblies; and they shall hallow my sabbaths.

(e) The land divided: Sacred Things (45:1-46:24) The Holy District (45:1-9) Weights and measures, standards for offerings (45:10-17) Passover regulations (45:18-25), The Prince (46:1-18), Temple accommodations (46:19-24)

Ezekiel 45:1-25: *Moreover, when ye shall divide by lot the land for inheritance, ye shall offer an oblation unto the Lord, an holy portion of the land: the length shall be the length of five and twenty thousand reeds, and the breadth shall be ten thousand. This shall be holy in all the borders thereof round about. Of this there shall be for the sanctuary five hundred in length, with five hundred in breadth, square round about; and fifty cubits round about for the suburbs thereof. And of this measure shalt thou measure the length of five and twenty thousand, and the breadth of ten thousand: and in it shall be the sanctuary and the most holy place. The holy portion of the land shall be for the priests the ministers of the sanctuary, which shall come near to minister unto the Lord: and it shall be a place for their houses, and an holy place for the sanctuary. And the five and twenty thousand of length, and the ten thousand of breadth, shall also the Levites, the ministers of the house, have for themselves, for a possession for twenty chambers. And ye shall appoint the possession of the city five thousand broad, and five and twenty thousand long, over against the oblation of the holy portion: it shall be for the whole house of Israel. And a portion shall be for the prince on the one side and on the other side of the oblation of the holy portion, and of the possession of the city, before the oblation of the holy portion, and before the possession of the city, from the west side westward, and from the east side eastward: and the length shall be over against one of the portions, from the west border unto the east border. In the land shall be his possession in Israel: and my princes shall no more oppress my people; and the rest of the land shall they give to the house of Israel according to their tribes.*

Thus saith the Lord God; Let it suffice you, O princes of Israel: remove violence and spoil, and execute judgment and justice, take away your exactions from my people, saith the Lord God. Ye shall have just balances, and a just ephah, and a just bath. The ephah and the bath shall be of one measure, that the bath may contain the tenth part of an homer, and the ephah the tenth part of an homer: the measure thereof shall be after the homer. And the shekel shall be twenty gerahs: twenty shekels, five and twenty shekels, fifteen shekels, shall be your maneh.

This is the oblation that ye shall offer; the sixth part of an ephah of an homer of wheat, and ye shall give the sixth part of an ephah of an homer of barley: Concerning the ordinance of oil, the bath of oil, ye shall offer the tenth part of a bath out of the cor, which is an homer of ten baths; for ten baths are an homer: And one lamb out of the flock, out of two hundred, out of the fat pastures of Israel; for a meat offering, and for a burnt offering, and for peace offerings, to make reconciliation for them, saith the Lord God. All the people of the land shall give this oblation for the prince in Israel.

And it shall be the prince's part to give burnt offerings, and meat offerings, and drink offerings, in the feasts, and in the new moons, and in the sabbaths, in all solemnities of the house of Israel: he shall prepare the sin offering, and the meat offering, and the burnt offering, and the peace offerings, to make reconciliation for the house of Israel. Thus saith the Lord God; In the first month, in the first day of the month, thou shalt take a young bullock without blemish, and cleanse the sanctuary: And the priest shall take of the blood of the sin offering, and put it upon the posts of the house, and upon the four corners of the settle of the altar, and upon the posts of the gate of the inner court. And so thou shalt do the seventh day of the month for every one that erreth, and for him that is simple: so shall ye reconcile the house. In the first month, in the fourteenth day of the month, ye shall have the passover, a feast of seven days; unleavened bread shall be eaten. And upon that day shall the prince prepare for himself and for all the people of the land a bullock for a sin offering. And seven days of the feast he shall prepare a burnt offering to the Lord, seven bullocks and seven rams without blemish daily the seven days; and a kid of the goats daily for a sin offering. And he shall prepare a meat offering of an ephah for a bullock, and an ephah for a ram, and an hin of oil for an ephah. In the seventh month, in the fifteenth day of the month, shall he do the like in the feast of the seven days, according to the sin offering, according to the burnt offering, and according to the meat offering, and according to the oil.

Above we have the *Holy portion* of the division of the land specified. This is to be in the form of a strip of land running from North to South [95]25000 reeds by 10000 reeds in width. It is to be in the seventh section down, from Judah in the overall division of the land, and the whole area is considered an oblation, or an offering to the Lord. In the centre is the sanctuary itself, 500 reeds square, and surrounding this the city, in which the Levites have their houses. The whole area is considered holy, and on either side of the city will be two sections, given to the prince and his family. From this area he is to get his income, and is also to provide the general offerings for the feasts for himself and the people. So there is to be no taxing of the people to support either the Prince or the priesthood, as everyone is provided for. The narrative also provides for fair, tamper-proof weights and balances:

Ezekiel 46:1-24: *Thus saith the Lord God; The gate of the inner court that looketh toward the east shall be shut the six working days; but on the sabbath it shall be opened, and in the day of the new moon it shall be opened. And the prince shall enter by the way of the porch of that gate without, and shall stand by the post of the gate, and the priests shall prepare his burnt offering and his peace offerings, and he shall worship at the threshold of the gate: then he shall go forth; but the gate shall not be shut until the evening. Likewise the people of the land shall worship at the door of this gate before the Lord in the sabbaths and in the new moons. And the burnt offering that the prince shall offer unto the Lord in the sabbath day shall be six lambs without blemish, and a ram without blemish. And the meat offering shall be an ephah for a ram, and the meat offering for the lambs as he shall be able to give, and an hin of oil to an ephah. And in the day of the new moon it shall be a young bullock without blemish, and six lambs, and a ram: they shall be without blemish. And he shall prepare a meat offering, an ephah for a bullock, and an ephah for a ram, and for the lambs according as his hand shall attain unto, and an hin of oil to an ephah. And when the prince shall enter, he shall go in by the way of the porch of that gate, and he shall go forth by the way thereof. But when the people of the land shall come before the Lord in the solemn feasts, he that entereth in by the way of the north gate to worship shall go out by the way of the south gate; and he that entereth by the way of the south gate shall go forth by the way of the north gate: he shall not return by the way of the gate whereby he came in, but shall go forth over against it. And the prince in the midst of them, when they go in, shall go in; and when they go forth, shall go forth. And in the feasts and in the solemnities the meat offering shall be an ephah to a bullock, and an ephah to a ram, and to the lambs as he is able to give, and an hin of oil to an ephah. Now when the prince shall prepare a voluntary burnt offering or peace offerings voluntarily unto the Lord, one shall then open him the gate that looketh toward the east, and he shall prepare his burnt offering and his peace offerings, as he did on the sabbath day: then he shall go forth; and after his going forth one shall shut the gate. Thou shalt daily prepare a burnt offering unto the Lord of a lamb of the first year without blemish: thou shalt prepare it every morning. And thou shalt prepare a meat offering for it every morning, the sixth part of an ephah, and the third part of an hin of oil, to temper with the fine flour; a meat offering continually by a perpetual ordinance unto the Lord. Thus shall they prepare the lamb, and the meat offering, and the oil, every morning for a continual burnt offering.*

Above we have the instruction for worship, and we see that the east gate of the inner sanctuary is for the sole use of the Prince, while the people themselves are to worship outside the gate. They are directed to come in either at the north or the south gates, with the proviso that they exit by a different gate from the one they entered by. The prince makes his offering every sabbath and new moon, but can also make freewill offerings, when the gate will be opened for him. In addition there is a daily burnt offering, but this is for the priesthood to make, although probably also provided by the prince.

Thus saith the Lord God; If the prince give a gift unto any of his sons, the inheritance thereof shall be his sons'; it shall be their possession by inheritance. But if he give a gift of his inheritance to one of his servants, then it shall be his to the year of liberty; after it shall return to the prince: but his inheritance shall be his sons' for them. Moreover the prince shall not take of the people's inheritance by oppression, to thrust them out of their possession; but he shall give his sons inheritance out of his own possession: that my people be not scattered every man from his possession.

Interestingly the Jubilee years, every seven years, still seem to apply, for in giving gifts from the Prince's own inheritance, they can only be enjoyed by his servants till the jubilee year, then returned. This ensures that the inheritance is not eroded, so any gift to them is effectively a loan. The prince's sons however, can keep their gifts.

After he brought me through the entry, which was at the side of the gate, into the holy chambers of the priests, which looked toward the north: and, behold, there was a place on the two sides westward. Then said he unto me, This is the place where the priests shall boil the trespass offering and the sin offering, where they shall bake the meat offering; that they bear them not out into the utter court, to sanctify the people. Then he brought me forth into the utter court, and caused me to pass by the four corners of the court; and, behold, in every corner of the court there was a court. In the four corners of the court there were courts joined of forty cubits long and thirty broad: these four corners were of one measure. And there was a row of building round about in them, round about them four, and it was made with boiling places under the rows round about. Then said he unto me, These are the places of them that boil, where the ministers of the house shall boil the sacrifice of the people.

(f) The Restored Community: The Land (47:1-48:3), The River (47:1-12), Allotment of the land (47:13-48:29) (boundaries of the land (47:13-20) equal distribution (47:21-23) allotment by tribes (48:1-7) land reserved for the Temple and priestly use (48:8-14) land for the city and the Prince (48:15-22) the tribes' allotment (48:23-29)

Ezekiel 47:1-23: *Afterward he brought me again unto the door of the house; and, behold, waters issued out from under the threshold of the house eastward: for the forefront of the house stood toward the east, and the waters came down from under from the right side of the house, at the south side of the altar. Then brought he me out of the way of the gate northward, and led me about the way without unto the utter gate by the way that looketh eastward; and, behold, there ran out waters on the right side. And when the man that had the line in his hand went forth eastward, he measured a thousand cubits, and he brought me through the waters; the waters were to the ancles. Again he measured a thousand, and brought me through the waters; the waters were to the knees. Again he measured a thousand, and brought me through; the waters were to the loins. Afterward he measured a thousand; and it was a river that I could not pass over: for the waters were risen, waters to swim in, a river that could not be passed over. And he said unto me, Son of man, hast thou seen this? Then he brought me, and caused me to return to the brink of the river. Now when I had returned, behold, at the bank of the river were very many trees on the one side and on the other. Then said he unto me, These waters issue out toward the east country, and go down into the desert, and go into the sea: which being brought forth into the sea, the waters shall be healed. And it shall come to pass, that every thing that liveth, which moveth, whithersoever the rivers shall come, shall live: and there shall be a very great multitude of fish, because these waters shall come thither: for they shall be healed; and every thing shall live whither the river cometh. And it shall come to pass, that the fishers shall stand upon it from Engedi even unto Eneglaim; they shall be a place to spread forth nets; their fish shall be according to their kinds, as the fish of the great sea, exceeding many. But the miry places thereof and the marshes thereof shall not be healed; they shall be given to salt. And by the river upon the bank thereof, on this side and on that side, shall grow all trees for meat, whose leaf shall not fade, neither shall the fruit thereof be consumed: it shall bring forth new fruit according to his months, because their waters they issued out of the sanctuary: and the fruit thereof shall be for meat, and the leaf thereof for medicine.*

Ezekiel is brought to the inner east gate to observe water coming out from the right side of the house, passing the south side of the altar, therefore as we look towards the gate it comes from the left, and exits the temple itself on the left side of the outer east gate. The really interesting thing is that what starts as a relative trickle as it exits becomes within the space of four thousand cubits a river that cannot be crossed other than by swimming. Where all this water comes from we are not told, but this cannot be a [96]normal spring by any means, although the water is fresh, not salt, for it heals wherever it touches, except for the salt pans of the Dead Sea into which it finally enters. Clearly the topography of the land has changed for this river to be able to course through to the Dead Sea on the east, but we know that the mountains have been divided at some point, and the land no longer looks the same. We are reminded in this of the description in John's Book of Revelation:

Revelation 22:1-3: *And he shewed me a pure river of water of life, clear as crystal, proceeding out of the throne of God and of the Lamb.*

In the midst of the street of it, and on either side of the river, was there the tree of life, which bare twelve manner of fruits, and yielded her fruit every month: and the leaves of the tree were for the healing of the nations. And there shall be no more curse: but the throne of God and of the Lamb shall be in it; and his servants shall serve him:

And while this Temple of Ezekiel is not the same place as we have described for us in Revelation, we can see that it is the earthly representative, the shadow of the New Heavens and new earth, which are yet to come.

Thus saith the Lord God; This shall be the border, whereby ye shall inherit the land according to the twelve tribes of Israel: Joseph shall have two portions. And ye shall inherit it, one as well as another: concerning the which I lifted up mine hand to give it unto your fathers: and this land shall fall unto you for inheritance. And this shall be the border of the land toward the north side, from the great sea, the way of Hethlon, as men go to Zedad; Hamath, Berothah, Sibraim, which is between the border of Damascus and the border of Hamath; Hazar-hatticon, which is by the coast of Hauran. And the border from the sea shall be Hazarenan, the border of Damascus, and the north northward, and the border of Hamath. And this is the north side. And the east side ye shall measure from Hauran, and from Damascus, and from Gilead, and from the land of Israel by Jordan, from the border unto the east sea. And this is the east side. And the south side southward, from Tamar even to the waters of strife in Kadesh, the river to the great sea. And this is the south side southward. The west side also shall be the great sea from the border, till a man come over against Hamath. This is the west side. So shall ye divide this land unto you according to the tribes of Israel. And it shall come to pass, that ye shall divide it by lot for an inheritance unto you, and to the strangers that sojourn among you, which shall beget children among you: and they shall be unto you as born in the country among the children of Israel; they shall have inheritance with you among the tribes of Israel. And it shall come to pass, that in what tribe the stranger sojourneth, there shall ye give him his inheritance, saith the Lord God.

Ezekiel 48:1-35 *Now these are the names of the tribes. From the north end to the coast of the way of Hethlon, as one goeth to Hamath, Hazar-enan, the border of Damascus northward, to the coast of Hamath; for these are his sides east and west; a portion for Dan.*

And by the border of Dan, from the east side unto the west side, a portion for Asher.

And by the border of Asher, from the east side even unto the west side, a portion for Naphtali.

And by the border of Naphtali, from the east side unto the west side, a portion for Manasseh.

And by the border of Manasseh, from the east side unto the west side, a portion for Ephraim.

And by the border of Ephraim, from the east side even unto the west side, a portion for Reuben.

And by the border of Reuben, from the east side unto the west side, a portion for Judah.

And by the border of Judah, from the east side unto the west side, shall be the offering which ye shall offer of five and twenty thousand reeds in breadth, and in length as one of the other parts, from the east side unto the west side: and the sanctuary shall be in the midst of it. The oblation that ye shall offer unto the Lord shall be of five and twenty thousand in length, and of ten thousand in breadth. And for them, even for the priests, shall be this holy oblation; toward the north five and twenty thousand in length, and toward the west ten thousand in breadth, and toward the east ten thousand in breadth, and toward the south five and twenty thousand in length: and the sanctuary of the Lord shall be in the midst thereof. It shall be for the priests that are sanctified of the sons of Zadok; which have kept my charge, which went not astray when the children of Israel went astray, as the Levites went astray. And this oblation of the land that is offered shall be unto them a thing most holy by the border of the Levites. And over against the border of the priests the Levites shall have five and twenty thousand in length, and ten thousand in breadth: all the length shall be five and twenty thousand, and the breadth ten thousand. And they shall not sell of it, neither exchange, nor alienate the firstfruits of the land: for it is holy unto the Lord. And the five thousand, that are left in the breadth over against the five and twenty thousand, shall be a profane place for the city, for dwelling, and for suburbs: and the city shall be in the midst thereof. And these shall be the measures thereof; the north side four thousand and five hundred, and the south side four thousand and five hundred, and on the east side four thousand and five hundred, and the west side four thousand and five hundred. And the suburbs of the city shall be toward the north two hundred and fifty, and toward the south two hundred and fifty, and toward the east two hundred and fifty, and toward the west two hundred and fifty. And the residue in length over against the oblation of the holy portion shall be ten thousand eastward, and ten thousand westward: and it shall be over against the oblation of the holy portion; and the increase thereof shall be for food unto them that serve the city. And they that serve the city shall serve it out of all the tribes of Israel. All the oblation shall be five and twenty thousand by five and twenty thousand: ye shall offer the holy oblation foursquare, with the possession of the city. And the residue shall be for the prince, on the one side and on the other of the holy oblation, and of the possession of the city, over against the five and twenty thousand of the oblation toward the east border, and westward over against the five and twenty thousand toward the west border, over against the portions for the prince: and it shall be the holy oblation; and the sanctuary of the house shall be in the midst thereof. Moreover from the possession of the Levites, and from the possession of the city, being in the midst of that which is the prince's, between the border of Judah and the border of Benjamin, shall be for the prince.

As for the rest of the tribes, from the east side unto the west side, Benjamin shall have a portion.

And by the border of Benjamin, from the east side unto the west side, Simeon shall have a portion.

And by the border of Simeon, from the east side unto the west side, Issachar a portion.

And by the border of Issachar, from the east side unto the west side, Zebulun a portion.

And by the border of Zebulun, from the east side unto the west side, Gad a portion. And by the border of Gad, at the south side southward, the border shall be even from Tamar unto the waters of strife in Kadesh, and to the river toward the great sea. This is the land which ye shall divide by lot unto the tribes of Israel for inheritance, and these are their portions, saith the Lord God.

This is fairly self-explanatory, but the point should be emphasized that at no point in Israel's history has the land ever been divided up between the tribes as horizontal strips, much less have the twelve tribes been reunited or identified since their dispersal. Our overall conclusion from Ezekiel's vision of the Temple must either be that this plan has been superseded, and God has given up altogether on Israel as His nation, or that it is a future event, delayed until such time as His people begin to seek Him again as their God. For myself I have no doubts as Paul, the apostle to the Gentiles and therefore of our present church, taught us:

Romans 11:25-33: *For I would not, brethren, that ye should be ignorant of this mystery, lest ye should be wise in your own conceits; that blindness in part is happened to Israel, until the fulness of the Gentiles be come in. And so all Israel shall be saved: as it is written, There shall come out of Sion the Deliverer, and shall turn away ungodliness from Jacob: For this is my covenant unto them, when I shall take away their sins. As concerning the gospel, they are enemies for your sakes: but as touching the election, they are beloved for the fathers' sakes. For the gifts and calling of God are without repentance. For as ye in times past have not believed God, yet have now obtained mercy through their unbelief: Even so have these also now not believed, that through your mercy they also may obtain mercy. For God hath concluded them all in unbelief, that he might have mercy upon all. O the depth of the riches both of the wisdom and knowledge of God! how unsearchable are his judgments, and his ways past finding out!*

(g) The New Jerusalem (48:30-35)
And these are the goings out of the city on the north side, four thousand and five hundred measures. And the gates of the city shall be after the names of the tribes of Israel: three gates northward; one gate of Reuben, one gate of Judah, one gate of Levi. And at the east side four thousand and five hundred: and three gates; and one gate of Joseph, one gate of Benjamin, one gate of Dan. And at the south side four thousand and five hundred measures: and three gates; one gate of Simeon, one gate of Issachar, one gate of Zebulun. At the west side four thousand and five hundred, with their three gates; one gate of Gad, one gate of Asher, one gate of Naphtali. It was round about eighteen thousand measures: and the name of the city from that day shall be, The Lord is there.

The Lord clearly identifies Himself with the new city through His *shekinah* presence, and the people of Israel are identified by tribe in the gates, so there is no mistake who is meant. They await His coming as the Judge of all the earth to finally vindicate His trust in them as His people, His representatives on this earth.

End of fifth vision, and of the Book of Ezekiel.

CHAPTER EIGHT

Zechariah: *And many nations shall be joined to the Lord in that day*

As can be seen from its content, the book of [97]Zechariah contains prophecies regarding the reinstatement of the Jews to their homeland after their return from captivity in Babylon. Zechariah is often paired with Haggai, whose prophesies began at around the same time, and were intended to be an encouragement to both Zerubbabel (as the governor of Judah) and Joshua (the high priest) as well as being an exhortation to the people to show that the Lord was with them in their return and rebuilding of Jerusalem and its Temple. Unlike Haggai whose prophecy mainly concerned his own times, the prophecies of Zechariah are more far reaching, extending to the

Day of the Lord, and showing that while the Lord's initial intention was to bless the people in the land, their failure would not alter His determination to fulfil all of His promises to them in due time. These writings show that even in their subsequent falling away, the promises to Israel would still be in effect and that ultimately the Lord would have His way, despite the fact that Israel would have to learn to respect His Laws before this could become a reality. At the time that Zechariah wrote this however, the message was a positive one, and looked forward to their success, now that they had returned from captivity in Babylon.

Zechariah 1:7-21:` *Upon the four and twentieth day of the eleventh month, which is the month Sebat, in the second year of Darius, came the word of the Lord unto Zechariah, the son of Berechiah, the son of Iddo the prophet, saying, I saw by night, and behold a man riding upon a red horse, and he stood among the myrtle trees that were in the bottom; and behind him were there red horses, speckled, and white. Then said I, O my Lord, what are these? And the angel that talked with me said unto me, I will shew thee what these be. And the man that stood among the myrtle trees answered and said, These are they whom the Lord hath sent to walk to and fro through the earth. And they answered the angel of the Lord that stood among the myrtle trees, and said, We have walked to and fro through the earth, and, behold, all the earth sitteth still, and is at rest. Then the angel of the Lord answered and said, O Lord of hosts, how long wilt thou not have mercy on Jerusalem and on the cities of Judah, against which thou hast had indignation these threescore and ten years? And the Lord answered the angel that talked with me with good words and comfortable words. So the angel that communed with me said unto me, Cry thou, saying, Thus saith the Lord of hosts; I am jealous for Jerusalem and for Zion with a great jealousy. And I am very sore displeased with the heathen that are at ease: for I was but a little displeased, and they helped forward the affliction. Therefore thus saith the Lord; I am returned to Jerusalem with mercies: my house shall be built in it, saith the Lord of hosts, and a line shall be stretched forth upon Jerusalem. Cry yet, saying, Thus saith the Lord of hosts; My cities through prosperity shall yet be spread abroad; and the Lord shall yet comfort Zion, and shall yet choose Jerusalem. Then lifted I up mine eyes, and saw, and behold four horns. And I said unto the angel that talked with me, What be these? And he answered me, These are the horns which have scattered Judah, Israel, and Jerusalem. And the Lord shewed me four carpenters. Then said I, What come these to do? And he spake, saying, These are the horns which have scattered Judah, so that no man did lift up his head: but these are come to fray them, to cast out the horns of the Gentiles, which lifted up their horn over the land of Judah to scatter it.*

We are again given an insight into the workings of heavenly beings regarding events on earth, being shown either the work of the *cherubim*, or of the *seven spirits* that are associated with the throne. I would suggest that the later appearances of the four chariots are more likely to be the *cherubim*, and that the spirits described here are the *watchers*, the seven spirits before the throne with a special commission regarding the affairs of the Earth, and the Jewish nation in particular. The angel questions the fact that the Jews have been in captivity for seventy years now, and the Lord responds with the answer that He will now have mercy on them, and *return to His house with mercies*, as promised. He will also judge those nations who have been instrumental in keeping Israel subject for their own misdeeds, but note that there are four carpenters or tradesmen, to 'fray' the four horns that dominate them, but up to this time the Jews had been subject to only two of the four great empires that were to dominate them according to Daniel, Babylon and Persia, so these horns

CHAPTER EIGHT

may well refer to previous nations. The Greek and Roman parts of Nebuchadnezzar's vision have not yet appeared, but Israel had previously been subject to Egypt and Assyria, before Babylon and Persia came, so perhaps these are the nations meant here. In any event the vision seems to be retrospective, looking back on the heavenly process that has already taken place in order to restore the nation Israel to its own land. Thus Zechariah is brought up to date.

Zechariah 2:1-13: *I lifted up mine eyes again, and looked, and behold a man with a measuring line in his hand. Then said I, Whither goest thou? And he said unto me, To measure Jerusalem, to see what is the breadth thereof, and what is the length thereof. And, behold, the angel that talked with me went forth, and another angel went out to meet him, And said unto him, Run, speak to this young man, saying, Jerusalem shall be inhabited as towns without walls for the multitude of men and cattle therein: For I, saith the Lord, will be unto her a wall of fire round about, and will be the glory in the midst of her. Ho, ho, come forth, and flee from the land of the north, saith the Lord: for I have spread you abroad as the four winds of the heaven, saith the Lord. Deliver thyself, O Zion, that dwellest with the daughter of Babylon. For thus saith the Lord of hosts; After the glory hath he sent me unto the nations which spoiled you: for he that toucheth you toucheth the apple of his eye. For, behold, I will shake mine hand upon them, and they shall be a spoil to their servants: and ye shall know that the Lord of hosts hath sent me. Sing and rejoice, O daughter of Zion: for, lo, I come, and I will dwell in the midst of thee, saith the Lord. And many nations shall be joined to the Lord in that day, and shall be my people: and I will dwell in the midst of thee, and thou shalt know that the Lord of hosts hath sent me unto thee. And the Lord shall inherit Judah his portion in the holy land, and shall choose Jerusalem again. Be silent, O all flesh, before the Lord: for he is raised up out of his holy habitation.*

Here we have described the figure of a man with a measuring line, as if laying out the footings of the rebuilt city of Jerusalem. This figure is employed several times in scripture to denote something being built that is yet future, and as the setting up of any building involves laying out the ground beforehand, this is what is meant by the 'spiritual surveyors' that we [98]sometimes come across. As we have seen before, once God's will is revealed, the opposition immediately takes steps to try and prevent it happening, and here is no different, for we are now shown in heavenly places how Satan is resisting the man on earth whose job it is to make this work a reality:

Zechariah 3:1-10 *And he shewed me Joshua the high priest standing before the angel of the Lord, and Satan standing at his right hand to resist him. And the Lord said unto Satan, The Lord rebuke thee, O Satan; even the Lord that hath chosen Jerusalem rebuke thee: is not this a brand plucked out of the fire? Now Joshua was clothed with filthy garments, and stood before the angel. And he answered and spake unto those that stood before him, saying, Take away the filthy garments from him. And unto him he said, Behold, I have caused thine iniquity to pass from thee, and I will clothe thee with change of raiment. And I said, Let them set a fair mitre upon his head. So they set a fair mitre upon his head, and clothed him with garments. And the angel of the Lord stood by. And the angel of the Lord protested unto Joshua, saying, Thus saith the Lord of hosts; If thou wilt walk in my ways, and if thou wilt keep my charge, then thou shalt also judge my house, and shalt also keep my courts, and I will give thee places to walk among these that stand by. Hear now, O Joshua the high priest, thou, and thy fellows that sit before thee: for they are men wondered at: for, behold, I will bring forth my servant the Branch. For behold the stone that I have laid before Joshua; upon one stone shall be seven eyes: behold, I will engrave the graving thereof, saith the Lord of hosts, and I will remove*

CHAPTER EIGHT

the iniquity of that land in one day. In that day, saith the Lord of hosts, shall ye call every man his neighbour under the vine and under the fig tree.

It is unlikely that Joshua was aware of the heavenly nature of the spiritual opposition he faced, but this small glimpse into heaven illustrates that difficulties do not always originate from earthly sources, as men seek to find God's will. Interestingly too, we are shown that Joshua is promised a place to walk in heaven amongst the angels, and again, his own status is probably not apparent to him in his daily struggles, until of course he is shown it. The importance of what Joshua is tasked with is seen in the bringing forth of *my servant the Branch,* for this is nothing less than the promise of the Lord's appearing to rule on Earth, should the pre-conditions be met by the people. He is also described as the 'stone with seven eyes', the same stone that will eventually smash the image Nebuchadnezzar had dreamt of in its toes, prior to the everlasting kingdom appearing. This is quite a promise to Joshua, and clearly he is intended to be both the appointed and anointed one who is to lay the foundation with this people, leading to the Lord's appearance as Israel's king. All this shows that shortly after the return to Israel it should have been possible for events to move forward quickly, allowing Israel to be established as God's kingdom on Earth a lot sooner. As it stands, they still await this promise, despite the Lord's appearing as it was foretold He would.

Zechariah 4:1-14: *And the angel that talked with me came again, and waked me, as a man that is wakened out of his sleep, And said unto me, What seest thou? And I said, I have looked, and behold a candlestick all of gold, with a bowl upon the top of it, and his seven lamps thereon, and seven pipes to the seven lamps, which are upon the top thereof: And two olive trees by it, one upon the right side of the bowl, and the other upon the left side thereof. So I answered and spake to the angel that talked with me, saying, What are these, my Lord? Then the angel that talked with me answered and said unto me, Knowest thou not what these be? And I said, No, my Lord. Then he answered and spake unto me, saying, This is the word of the Lord unto Zerubbabel, saying, Not by might, nor by power, but by my spirit, saith the Lord of hosts. Who art thou, O great mountain? before Zerubbabel thou shalt become a plain: and he shall bring forth the headstone thereof with shoutings, crying, Grace, grace unto it. Moreover the word of the Lord came unto me, saying, The hands of Zerubbabel have laid the foundation of this house; his hands shall also finish it; and thou shalt know that the Lord of hosts hath sent me unto you. For who hath despised the day of small things? for they shall rejoice, and shall see the plummet in the hand of Zerubbabel with those seven; they are the eyes of the Lord, which run to and fro through the whole earth. Then answered I, and said unto him, What are these two olive trees upon the right side of the candlestick and upon the left side thereof? And I answered again, and said unto him, What be these two olive branches which through the two golden pipes empty the golden oil out of themselves? And he answered me and said, Knowest thou not what these be? And I said, No, my Lord. Then said he, These are the two anointed ones, that stand by the Lord of the whole earth.*

Next Zechariah is woken from sleep and asked by the angel to describe his dream. The words are now for Zerubbabel, who was governor in Judah at the time and also responsible for the rebuilding of Jerusalem and the Temple. He is not on his own in this, for further described here are the candlestick with seven lamps, the bowl, and the two olive trees. The seven spirits being also associated with this work, and the Holy Spirit Himself represented by the *golden oil* is involved too. Zechariah's attention and question is regarding the two olive trees, as the vessels used for distributing the golden oil, and he is told that they are the *two anointed ones, that stand by the Lord of the whole earth.*

These are not, of course, the only two *olive trees* noted in scripture, for in Revelation 11:4 we see that the two later witnesses to Israel are described in a similar way. We should be careful to understand that these two are not the same people, although their roles are similar as heralds of the Lord's coming, sent to prepare the hearts of the people for His imminent return, in much the same way as John the Baptist was also used to prepare the people for His appearance as a man. All of these men are inspired by the Holy Spirit, and are used to enable an outpouring of the Spirit to the people in their respective times. The two in question here are in my view Zerubbabel the Governor and Joshua the High Priest, who were both commissioned to prepare Israel and Jerusalem in anticipation of the Lord's coming. Who the two are in Revelation remains to be seen, but there is no necessity to jump to conclusions, falling into the trap of assuming that they are same two as here, or that they have to be reincarnations of Moses and Elijah, as is commonly supposed because of the type of miracles they produce. After all it is the same Holy Spirit producing these miracles, so can He not use whom He wishes as vessels for His own purpose? We remember that from the Lord's own words, John the Baptist fulfilled the promise of the sending of Elijah through his own ministry, so there is a precedent in scripture set for naming someone in prophecy as someone else, if they fulfil the same prophetic role. As the Lord said, it was up to them to believe this… [99]*if you will receive it!*

Zechariah 5:1-11: *Then I turned, and lifted up mine eyes, and looked, and behold a flying roll. And he said unto me, What seest thou? And I answered, I see a flying roll; the length thereof is twenty cubits,*

"BEHOLD, I HAVE FORETOLD YOU ALL THINGS"

and the breadth thereof ten cubits. Then said he unto me, This is the curse that goeth forth over the face of the whole earth: for every one that stealeth shall be cut off as on this side according to it; and every one that sweareth shall be cut off as on that side according to it. I will bring it forth, saith the Lord of hosts, and it shall enter into the house of the thief, and into the house of him that sweareth falsely by my name: and it shall remain in the midst of his house, and shall consume it with the timber thereof and the stones thereof. Then the angel that talked with me went forth, and said unto me, Lift up now thine eyes, and see what is this that goeth forth. And I said, What is it? And he said, This is an ephah that goeth forth. He said moreover, This is their resemblance through all the earth. And, behold, there was lifted up a talent of lead: and this is a woman that sitteth in the midst of the ephah. And he said, This is wickedness. And he cast it into the midst of the ephah; and he cast the weight of lead upon the mouth thereof. Then lifted I up mine eyes, and looked, and, behold, there came out two women, and the wind was in their wings; for they had wings like the wings of a stork: and they lifted up the ephah between the earth and the heaven. Then said I to the angel that talked with me, Whither do these bear the ephah? And he said unto me, To build it an house in the land of Shinar: and it shall be established, and set there upon her own base.

We are now faced again with the problem of deciding whether this vision relates to the future for the nation, or whether it is a retrospective look at what had happened to Israel in the past for both Zechariah's and our own understanding. If we accept that the *flying roll* is representative of the Law, God's Word to Israel, which included the curse proclaimed to those who did not obey it at [100]Mt Ebal, then it is a short step to accept that the woman that was revealed to Zechariah when the weight was lifted, was Israel, burdened by its sin, a nation which had now become recognised worldwide (its *resemblance*) as being just as wicked, and therefore no different to other nations. When the measure of this wickedness (the *ephah*) was complete, the whole thing was sealed and taken to Babylon, where the *wickedness* would remain, so when the Jews returned it was without the idolatry they left with. This would explain what had taken place prior to Zechariah's prophecy, but if we look forward to [101]Revelation, then we see that there is further involvement of Israel and the wickedness emanating from Babylon, to which this passage could also refer. It's probably best to keep an open mind on both applications here, as it is not altogether clear what is meant, and it could refer to either or both possibilities. There was no subsequent carrying away to Babylon on any significant scale after the Jews returned, so it is unlikely that that's what was meant, but Babylon certainly figures prominently in the judgments of God in the last days, so it is possible that some Jews are again taken to Babylon in the final conclusion of the judgement for both nations.

Zechariah 6:1-15: *And I turned, and lifted up mine eyes, and looked, and, behold, there came four chariots out from between two mountains; and the mountains were mountains of brass. In the first chariot were red horses; and in the second chariot black horses; And in the third chariot white horses; and in the fourth chariot grisled and bay horses. Then I answered and said unto the angel that talked with me, What are these, my Lord? And the angel answered and said unto me, These are the four spirits of the heavens, which go forth from standing before the Lord of all the earth. The black horses which are therein go forth into the north country; and the white go forth after them; and the grisled go forth toward the south country. And the bay went forth, and sought to go that they might walk to and fro through the earth: and he said, Get you hence, walk to and fro through the earth. So they walked to and fro through the earth. Then cried he upon me, and spake unto me, saying, Behold, these that go toward the north country have quieted my spirit in the north country. And the word of the Lord came unto me, saying, Take of them of the captivity, even of Heldai, of Tobijah, and of Jedaiah, which are come from Babylon, and come thou the same day, and go into the house of Josiah the son of Zephaniah;Then take silver and gold, and make crowns, and set them upon the head of Joshua the son of Josedech, the high priest; And speak unto him, saying, Thus speaketh the Lord of hosts, saying, Behold the man whose name is The Branch; and he shall grow up out of his place, and he shall build the temple of the Lord: Even he shall build the temple of the Lord; and he shall bear the glory, and shall sit and rule upon his throne; and he shall be a priest upon his throne: and the counsel of peace shall be between them both. And the crowns shall be to Helem, and to Tobijah, and to Jedaiah, and to Hen the son of Zephaniah, for a memorial in the temple of the Lord. And they that are far off shall come and build in the temple of the Lord, and ye shall know that the Lord of hosts hath sent me unto you. And this shall come to pass, if ye will diligently obey the voice of the Lord your God.*

The description here is not the same as in the earlier vision of the horses of the first chapter, as the horses described above are also accompanied by chariots, but clearly these are spirits that are not only *before the throne,* but who are also directly concerned with the affairs of Earth, so this description more likely depicts the *cherubim*, who are four in number. In any event, the two chariots that set off towards the north, with both black and white horses, are said to have *quieted my spirit,* which suggests in the original Hebrew 'rest and anger', so that God's anger rested or remained upon, or is confirmed upon, the North or Persian Empire, at the reporting back of these two spirits. This area also included the old Babylonian and Assyrian empires from which the Israelites had now returned from exile. The manifestation of this anger could signal the passing of the Persian Empire to the Greek, but historically this was not to take place for a further 90 years, so it is more likely that His anger towards the north will be manifest in the very end days when the four [102]empires are destroyed together. In any event we now see that God's rekindled favour towards His people is contrasted with His anger towards the nations they had been subject to previously. From reading the narrative we see that it leads directly to the anointing of Joshua, who is crowned in anticipation of the coming Branch. He, the Branch, is the one who is to incorporate the role of both High Priest and King in His own person, and this can only be the Lord Himself. We are reminded that in the eleventh chapter of Isaiah there is another [103]mention of the Branch, who is clearly associated there with the final restoration of Israel, in what we now call the Millennium reign, or Kingdom of Heaven. There are also crowns given to the four others named, who were to wear them in their temple duties, as a memorial, or token that the *Branch* was on His way. There is no suggestion here that the kingdom and priesthood were united in Joshua the High Priest, but certainly the Lord is showing that this is the eventual intention when He comes both as the promised king in the line of David, and also as high priest in the [104]Melchizedec order. Again, the promises are conditional upon whether Israel would *diligently obey the voice of the Lord.*

Zechariah 7:1-14 *And it came to pass in the fourth year of king Darius, that the word of the Lord came unto Zechariah in the fourth day of the ninth month, even in Chisleu; When they had sent unto the house of God Sherezer and Regem-melech, and their men, to pray before the Lord, And to speak unto the priests which were in the house of the Lord of hosts, and to the prophets, saying, Should I weep in the fifth month, separating myself, as I have done these so many years? Then came the word of the Lord of hosts unto me, saying, Speak unto all the people of the land, and to the priests, saying, When ye fasted and mourned in the fifth and seventh month, even those seventy years, did ye at all fast unto me, even to me? And when ye did eat, and when ye did drink, did not ye eat for yourselves, and drink for yourselves? Should ye not hear the words which the Lord hath cried by the former prophets, when Jerusalem was inhabited and in prosperity, and the cities thereof round about her, when men inhabited the south and the plain? And the word of the Lord came unto Zechariah, saying, Thus speaketh the Lord of hosts, saying, Execute true judgment, and shew mercy and compassions every man to his brother: And oppress not the widow, nor the fatherless, the stranger, nor the poor; and let none of you imagine evil against his brother in your heart. But they refused to hearken, and pulled away the shoulder, and stopped their ears, that they should not hear. Yea, they made their hearts as an adamant stone, lest they should hear the law, and the words which the Lord of hosts hath sent in his spirit by the former prophets: therefore came a great wrath from the Lord of hosts. Therefore it is come to pass, that as he cried, and they would not hear; so they cried, and I would not hear, saith the Lord of hosts: But I scattered them with a whirlwind among all the nations whom they knew not. Thus the land was desolate after them, that no man passed through nor returned: for they laid the pleasant land desolate.*

After about two years, Zechariah is given these words in response to the inquiry concerning fasting, notably in the *fifth and seventh month*. The Lord's answer is that these fasts meant very little to Him, as they were more of a performance by the people who, feeling sorry for themselves in captivity, performed them as an outward show, as many of their actions were. We should not be surprised at the Lord's reaction here as after all, it was He who had placed them in captivity in Babylon in the first place, as a result of their own error, and He was not going to be impressed with mere gesturing on their part. We only have to read Ezekiel again to see how reluctantly the Lord left them to it, but once His decision was made, He had no further regrets. Again He shows, anticipating the Lord's later words in the Sermon of the Mount, what He really required of them from their adherence to the Law. It was for them to *execute true judgement,* and not a pretence or outward show in observing formalities. This was the cause of their exile in the first place, the breakdown of their real relationship with God, whilst they continued in the outward formality but not in the spirit of real observance of the law. Sadly, despite this and other prophecies, this state of affairs was to continue until the Lord's time and beyond it, even to the present day.

Zechariah 8:1-23: *Again the word of the Lord of hosts came to me, saying, Thus saith the Lord of hosts; I was jealous for Zion with great jealousy, and I was jealous for her with great fury. Thus saith the Lord; I am returned unto Zion, and will dwell in the midst of Jerusalem: and Jerusalem shall be called a city of truth; and the mountain of the Lord of hosts the holy mountain. Thus saith the Lord of hosts; There shall yet old men and old women dwell in the streets of Jerusalem, and every man with his staff in his hand for very age. And the streets of the city shall be full of boys and girls playing in the streets thereof. Thus saith the Lord of hosts; If it be marvellous in the eyes of the remnant of this people in these days, should it also be marvellous in mine eyes? saith the Lord of hosts. Thus saith the Lord of hosts; Behold, I will save my people from the east country, and from the west country; And I will bring them, and they shall dwell in the midst of Jerusalem: and they shall be my people, and I will be their God, in truth and in righteousness. Thus saith the Lord of hosts; Let your hands be strong, ye that hear in these days these words by the mouth of the prophets, which were in the day that the foundation of the house of the Lord of hosts was laid, that the temple might be built. For before these days there was no hire for man, nor any hire for beast; neither was there any peace to him that went out or came in because of the affliction: for I set all men every one against his neighbour. But now I will not be unto the residue of this people as in the former days, saith the Lord of hosts. For the seed shall be prosperous; the vine shall give her fruit, and the ground shall give her increase, and the heavens shall give their dew; and I will cause the remnant of this people to possess all these things. And it shall come to pass, that as ye were a curse among the heathen, O house of Judah, and house of Israel; so will I save you, and ye shall be a blessing: fear not, but let your hands be strong.*

For thus saith the Lord of hosts; As I thought to punish you, when your fathers provoked me to wrath, saith the Lord of hosts, and I repented not: So again have I thought in these days to do well unto Jerusalem and to the house of Judah: fear ye not. These are the things that ye shall do; Speak ye every man the truth to his neighbour; execute the judgment of truth and peace in your gates: And let none of you imagine evil in your hearts against his neighbour; and love no false oath: for all these are things that I hate, saith the Lord. And the word of the Lord of hosts came unto me, saying, Thus saith the Lord of hosts; The fast of the fourth month, and the fast of the fifth, and the fast of the seventh, and the fast of the tenth, shall be to the house of Judah joy and gladness, and cheerful feasts; therefore love the truth and peace. Thus saith the Lord of hosts; It shall yet come to pass, that there shall come people, and the inhabitants of many cities: And the inhabitants of one city shall go to another, saying, Let us go speedily to pray before the Lord, and to seek the Lord of hosts: I will go also. Yea, many people and strong nations shall come to seek the Lord of hosts in Jerusalem, and to pray before the Lord. Thus saith the Lord of hosts; In those days it shall come to pass, that ten men shall

CHAPTER EIGHT

take hold out of all languages of the nations, even shall take hold of the skirt of him that is a Jew, saying, We will go with you: for we have heard that God is with you.

The past however was to be forgotten, and the new dawn was to be accomplished through their reacquaintance with the Lord, in His presence among them. Although it is not said here, this would probably be understood as being accomplished through His *shekinah* presence in the temple, but there is no record that this ever materialised. Eventually the Lord Himself did come as the Branch, but when He did, He was rejected and crucified at the hand of the leaders. Despite all of the Lord's efforts to prepare them, the people were not ready for Him when He came. However, in answer to their enquiry, they were to have [105]four *cheerful feasts*, as opposed to fasts, a new approach that was in its turn intended to inspire those around them, other cities and nations, to seek the Lord at Jerusalem. Being a Jew would no more be a reproachful or shameful title, but would mean being sought out by others because of the manifest blessing of having Gods presence amongst them.

Zechariah 9:1-17: *The burden of the word of the Lord in the land of Hadrach, and Damascus shall be the rest thereof: when the eyes of man, as of all the tribes of Israel, shall be toward the Lord. And Hamath also shall border thereby; Tyrus, and Zidon, though it be very wise. And Tyrus did build herself a strong hold, and heaped up silver as the dust, and fine gold as the mire of the streets. Behold, the Lord will cast her out, and he will smite her power in the sea; and she shall be devoured with fire. Ashkelon shall see it, and fear; Gaza also shall see it, and be very sorrowful, and Ekron; for her expectation shall be ashamed; and the king shall perish from Gaza, and Ashkelon shall not be inhabited. And a bastard shall dwell in Ashdod, and I will cut off the pride of the Philistines. And I will take away his blood out of his mouth, and his abominations from between his teeth: but he that remaineth, even he, shall be for our God, and he shall be as a governor in Judah, and Ekron as a Jebusite. And I will encamp about mine house because of the army, because of him that passeth by, and because of him that returneth: and no oppressor shall pass through them any more: for now have I seen with mine eyes.*

Rejoice greatly, O daughter of Zion; shout, O daughter of Jerusalem: behold, thy King cometh unto thee: he is just, and having salvation; lowly, and riding upon an ass, and upon a colt the foal of an ass. And I will cut off the chariot from Ephraim, and the horse from Jerusalem, and the battle bow shall be cut off: and he shall speak peace unto the heathen: and his dominion shall be from sea even to sea, and from the river even to the ends of the earth. As for thee also, by the blood of thy covenant I have sent forth thy prisoners out of the pit wherein is no water. Turn you to the strong hold, ye prisoners of hope: even to day do I declare that I will render double unto thee; When I have bent Judah for me, filled the bow with Ephraim, and raised up thy sons, O Zion, against thy sons, O Greece, and made thee as the sword of a mighty man. And the Lord shall be seen over them, and his arrow shall go forth as the lightning: and the Lord GOD shall blow the trumpet, and shall go with whirlwinds of the south. The Lord of hosts shall defend them; and they shall devour, and subdue with sling stones; and they shall drink, and make a noise as through wine; and they shall be filled like bowls, and as the corners of the altar. And the Lord their God shall save them in that day as the flock of his people: for they shall be as the stones of a crown, lifted up as an ensign upon his land. For how great is his goodness, and how great is his beauty! corn shall make the young men cheerful, and new wine the maids.

The above verses suggest that in the coming times, although there will be another attempt to occupy Israel by an invading army from the North, probably of Syrian/Greek origins, it would be contested by the Lord through his army of Israel. The reference to Tyre of course, is something that had happened under the reign of Nebuchadnezzar, where it had been destroyed utterly, and this seems to be a reminder to others who might have the same intent of pursuing greatness in the area, that God is in charge, and can make or break nations regardless of how powerful they seem to be. The sons of Zion, in effect, would take on the sons of Greece and win.

The difficulty with this is that history records that actually the reverse happened, and that Antiochus Epiphanes of Syria, did in fact sack and subdue Jerusalem on his return from his Egyptian campaign, and although there was a rebellion after this, named the Maccabean revolt, it did not conclude with the end of oppression for Israel, as the Romans then came as conquerors, to subject Israel to their own rule. Israel's brief spell of independence under the Maccabees could hardly be said to be the period of blessing that God had promised.

It is just a guess on my part, but the above passage may refer to a possible scenario that would have been in place had the Jews been ready for the Lord's return earlier. Then the final confrontation may have been with the Greeks, under Antiochus the Syrian, who could have fulfilled the role of the beast. Certainly he had some of those characteristics, and was to defile the Temple with the slaughter of pigs on the altar. If the last week of Daniel was brought forward, this may have meant that their conflict could have been with the Greeks (or Seleucid tribes of Syria) rather than with Rome later. Providing Israel had remained faithful, the Lord may have come to them sooner and fulfilled Daniel's prophecies under slightly different circumstances. In this case, when the Lord came it would have been to a people that had already been proved faithful, and were ready for His return. As I said before, prophecy has a built-in flexibility that allows for men to either accept or reject the truth. In any event, there is a passage here with which we are all probably familiar:

Rejoice greatly, O daughter of Zion; shout, O daughter of Jerusalem: behold, thy King cometh unto thee: he is just, and having salvation; lowly, and riding upon an ass, and upon a colt the foal of an ass.

We know that when the Lord did come to the [106]temple in Jerusalem, and when He should have come in victory, it was in this manner, and in full knowledge of what was written. He fulfilled His own part, but sadly Israel had not fulfilled theirs. The deliverance of Israel was never going to be straightforward or trouble free, for prophecies both here and elsewhere always include the fact that there was to be a final purging of the nation, a completion of the judgements of the seventy years, which was going to see a period of tribulation preceding the eventual time of prosperity and blessing under the Lord's rule.

Zechariah 12:1-14: *The burden of the word of the Lord for Israel, saith the Lord, which stretcheth forth the heavens, and layeth the foundation of the earth, and formeth the spirit of man within him. Behold, I will make Jerusalem a cup of trembling unto all the people round about, when they shall be in the siege both against Judah and against Jerusalem. And in that day will I make Jerusalem a burdensome stone for all people: all that burden themselves with it shall be cut in pieces, though all the people of the earth be gathered together against it. In that day, saith the Lord, I will smite every horse with astonishment, and his rider with madness: and I will open mine eyes upon the house of Judah, and will smite every horse of the people with blindness. And the governors of Judah shall say in their heart, The inhabitants of Jerusalem shall be my strength in the Lord of hosts their God. In that day will I make the governors of Judah like an hearth of fire among the wood, and like a torch of fire in a sheaf; and they shall devour all the people round about, on the right hand and on the left: and Jerusalem shall be inhabited again in her own place, even in Jerusalem. The Lord also shall save the tents of Judah first, that the glory of the house of David and the glory of the inhabitants of Jerusalem do not magnify themselves against Judah. In that day shall the Lord defend the inhabitants of Jerusalem; and he that is feeble among them at that day shall be as David; and the house of David shall be as God, as the angel of the Lord before them. And it shall come to pass in that day, that I will seek to destroy all the nations that come against Jerusalem. And I will pour upon the house of David, and upon the inhabitants of Jerusalem, the spirit of grace and of supplications: and they shall look upon me whom they have pierced, and they shall mourn for him, as one mourneth for his only son, and shall be in bitterness for him, as one that is in bitterness for his firstborn.*

Nor was there going to be any reprieve for the Lord when He came, for even in the best-case scenario, He was going to have to die as the cleansing sacrifice for His people, the nations, the world and the heavens themselves in order to reconcile all things which had been defiled by Satan's fall to God. If things had been different His death might have been at the hands of the Greek or Roman authorities of the time, but in the event, because of the Jewish leaders' fear of losing their position with the Romans, it was they who caused His death, claiming He was a threat to the peace. *In that day shall there be a great mourning in Jerusalem, as the mourning of Hadadrimmon in the valley of Megiddon. And the land shall mourn, every family apart; the family of the house of David apart, and their wives apart; the family of the house of Nathan apart, and their wives apart; The family of the house of Levi apart, and their wives apart; the family of Shimei apart, and their wives apart; All the families that remain, every family apart, and their wives apart.*

Israel would eventually *mourn for him, as one mourning for his only son,* when they realised what had happened and what He had done on their behalf. This mourning marks their reinstatement in favour, and the real healing for the other nations through Israel:

Zechariah 13:1-9: *In that day there shall be a fountain opened to the house of David and to the inhabitants of Jerusalem for sin and for uncleanness. And it shall come to pass in that day, saith the Lord of hosts, that I will cut off the names of the idols out of the land, and they shall no more be remembered: and also I will cause the prophets and the unclean spirit to pass out of the land. And it shall come to pass, that when any shall yet prophesy, then his father and his mother that begat him shall say unto him, Thou shalt not live; for thou speakest lies in the name of the Lord: and his father and his mother that begat him shall thrust him through when he prophesieth. And it shall come to pass in that day, that the prophets shall be ashamed every one of his vision, when he hath prophesied; neither shall they wear a rough garment to deceive: But he shall say, I am no prophet, I am an husbandman; for man taught me to keep cattle from my youth. And one shall say unto him, What are these wounds in thine hands? Then he shall answer, Those with which I was wounded in the house of my friends. Awake, O sword, against my shepherd, and against the man that is my fellow, saith the Lord of hosts: smite the shepherd, and the sheep shall be scattered: and I will turn mine hand upon the little ones. And it shall come to pass, that in all the land, saith the Lord, two parts therein shall be cut off and die; but the third shall be left therein. And I will bring the third part through the fire, and will refine them as silver is refined, and will try them as gold is tried: they shall call on my name, and I will hear them: I will say, It is my people: and they shall say, The Lord is my God.*

These figures, of two-thirds of the population perishing in

this final tribulation, are also reflected in the Book of Revelation, showing the terrible cost of a nation once so favoured, flagrantly turning against its own God, and despising His laws.

Zechariah 14:1-21: *Behold, the day of the Lord cometh, and thy spoil shall be divided in the midst of thee. For I will gather all nations against Jerusalem to battle; and the city shall be taken, and the houses rifled, and the women ravished; and half of the city shall go forth into captivity, and the residue of the people shall not be cut off from the city.*

The deliverance from these armies comes in the form of an earthquake, which divides the Mount of Olives in two, creating a valley through which the people can escape to Jordan beyond, which in all likelihood has not joined itself with the other nations in persecuting Israel. This is not the return prophesied by the angel in Acts, but the Lord's intervention for the faithful in providing an escape from certain destruction at the hands of the encircling armies

Then shall the Lord go forth, and fight against those nations, as when he fought in the day of battle. And his feet shall stand in that day upon the mount of Olives, which is before Jerusalem on the east, and the mount of Olives shall cleave in the midst thereof toward the east and toward the west, and there shall be a very great valley; and half of the mountain shall remove toward the north, and half of it toward the south. And ye shall flee to the valley of the mountains; for the valley of the mountains shall reach unto Azal: yea, ye shall flee, like as ye fled from before the earthquake in the days of Uzziah king of Judah: and the Lord my God shall come, and all the saints with thee. And it shall come to pass in that day, that the light shall not be clear, nor dark: But it shall be one day which shall be known to the Lord, not day, nor night: but it shall come to pass, that at evening time it shall be light.

It is later on that the following description becomes a reality, for the events described here are mirrored in Ezekiel's description of the new temple, along with the added information that the waters that proceed from under the temple go towards both the Dead Sea and the Mediterranean Sea, and are not affected by Earth's seasons or drought. Jerusalem, probably as a result of the earthquake, is to be lifted above all else around, which is another reason why it is unlikely that any temple on the scale of Ezekiel's will be built before the end of this tribulation period, as it could not remain unaffected by such traumatic changes in the landscape, and being so close to the Mount of Olives, it simply would not survive such an upheaval.

And it shall be in that day, that living waters shall go out from Jerusalem; half of them toward the former sea, and half of them toward the hinder sea: in summer and in winter shall it be. And the Lord shall be king over all the earth: in that day shall there be one Lord, and his name one. All the land shall be turned as a plain from Geba to Rimmon south of Jerusalem: and it shall be lifted up, and inhabited in her place, from Benjamin's gate unto the place of the first gate, unto the corner gate, and from the tower of Hananeel unto the king's winepresses. And men shall dwell in it, and there shall be no more utter destruction; but Jerusalem shall be safely inhabited.

We are now shown that the armies that surround Jerusalem, the forces of the *beast,* combined with those of other nations, are destroyed by a similarly miraculous event, which at first glance seems to mirror the effects of a nuclear strike. This cannot be the case however, for the fallout from anything nuclear would last for many years, and make Israel uninhabitable. The other more likely possibility is an airburst, which is the explosion caused by the disintegration of a small comet or meteor as it approaches Earth and breaks up. Such phenomena are evidenced, there being a known site in Russia, and there is current conjecture about the site of [107]Sodom, which is strongly suspected of having suffered the same fate. Airbursts cause immense blast pressure and heat in a moment of time, but otherwise leave little trace on the landscape, apart from the destruction of trees or buildings. This seems more appropriate to what is described here and the panic and suspicion caused, perhaps some accusing the others of having used a secret weapon, causes the meltdown of any previous alliances, so that the survivors turn on themselves, as is noted in the Book of Revelation.[108]

And this shall be the plague wherewith the Lord will smite all the people that have fought against Jerusalem; Their flesh shall consume away while they stand upon their feet, and their eyes shall consume away in their holes, and their tongue shall consume away in their mouth. And it shall come to pass in that day, that a great tumult from the Lord shall be among them; and they shall lay hold every one on the hand of his neighbour, and his hand shall rise up against the hand of his neighbour. And Judah also shall fight at Jerusalem; and the wealth of all the heathen round about shall be gathered together, gold, and silver, and apparel, in great abundance. And so shall be the plague of the horse, of the mule, of the camel, and of the ass, and of all the beasts that shall be in these tents, as this plague.

This debacle of the armies of the *beast*, along with the destruction of Babylon, is effectively the end of any opposition to Israel, and what we see next is its restoration as God's nation, which includes Judaism as its religion, and therefore a return to the law. This will now be in a new context, as the Lord taught in Matthew, and elsewhere.

And it shall come to pass, that every one that is left of all the nations which came against Jerusalem shall even go up from year to year to worship the King, the Lord of hosts, and to keep the feast of tabernacles. And it shall be, that whoso will not come up of all the families of the earth unto Jerusalem to worship the King, the Lord of hosts, even upon them shall be no rain. And if the family of Egypt go not up, and come not, that have no rain; there shall be the plague, wherewith the Lord will smite the heathen that come not up to keep the feast of tabernacles. This shall be the punishment of Egypt, and the punishment of all nations that come not up to keep the feast of tabernacles. In that day shall there be upon the bells of the horses, Holiness unto the Lord; and the pots in the Lord's house shall be like the bowls before the altar. Yea, every pot in Jerusalem and in Judah shall be holiness unto the Lord of hosts: and all they that sacrifice shall come and take of them, and seethe therein: and in that day there shall be no more the Canaanite in the house of the Lord of hosts.

Notice that acceptance of this state of affairs is more or less compulsory, and any refusal to comply, or to be represented here, has repercussions in terms of prosperity, or even the survival of that nation, ie, there being no rain for the dissidents. The time of idolatry and rebellion is finished, and any left alive are now subject to God's rule on earth through His chosen people. This does not yet necessarily imply that He dwells on the earth, except in the sense that His *shekinah* presence is upon the new temple, but it does mean that in His rule the Kingdom of Heaven has become a reality, awaiting its conclusion, and further transformation into the Kingdom of God.

CHAPTER NINE

Malachi. *Behold, I will send my messenger*

We are not given the date of Malachi's prophecy, but from the content we know that it must have been given some years after the restoration of the temple and its worship, with the best scholars giving us a date of around 374BC, roughly 30 years after the restoration of the Temple worship. It is known by the Jews as the 'seal of the prophets', and links together the Old and the New Testament by its reference to John the Baptist, whose appearance essentially broke the silence of God some 400 years later, when he began to prophesy of the coming of the long-awaited Messiah. Sadly the tone of Malachi's prophesy is far less optimistic than that of Zechariah's, and shows that the Temple worship had deteriorated to the point where God no longer recognised or responded to the sacrifices made by the priesthood, who are themselves accused of being unwilling to do anything without reward, offering the *torn, and the lame and the sick to God* whilst keeping the best back for themselves.

Malachi 1:1-14: *The burden of the word of the Lord to Israel by Malachi. I have loved you, saith the Lord. Yet ye say, Wherein hast thou loved us? Was not Esau Jacob's brother? saith the Lord: yet I loved Jacob, And I hated Esau, and laid his mountains and his heritage waste for the dragons of the wilderness. Whereas Edom saith, We are impoverished, but we will return and build the desolate places; thus saith the Lord of hosts, They shall build, but I will throw down; and they shall call them, The border of wickedness, and, The people against whom the Lord hath indignation for ever. And your eyes shall see, and ye shall say, The Lord will be magnified from the border of Israel. A son honoureth his father, and a servant his master: if then I be a father, where is mine honour? and if I be a master, where is my fear? saith the Lord of hosts unto you, O priests, that despise my name. And ye say, Wherein have we despised thy name. Ye offer polluted bread upon mine altar; and ye say, Wherein have we polluted thee? In that ye say, The table of the Lord is contemptible. And if ye offer the blind for sacrifice, is it not evil? and if ye offer the lame and sick, is it not evil? offer it now unto thy governor; will he be pleased with thee, or accept thy person? saith the Lord of hosts. And now, I pray you, beseech God that he will be gracious unto us: this hath been by your means: will he regard your persons? saith the Lord of hosts. Who is there even among you that would shut the doors for nought? neither do ye kindle fire on mine altar for nought. I have no pleasure in you, saith the Lord of hosts, neither will I accept an offering at your hand. For from the rising of the sun even unto the going down of the same my name shall be great among the Gentiles; and in every place incense shall be offered unto my name, and a pure offering: for my name shall be great among the heathen, saith the Lord of hosts. But ye have profaned it, in that ye say, The table of the Lord is polluted; and the fruit thereof, even his meat, is contemptible. Ye said also, Behold,*

CHAPTER NINE

what a weariness is it! and ye have snuffed at it, saith the Lord of hosts; and ye brought that which was torn, and the lame, and the sick; thus ye brought an offering: should I accept this of your hand? saith the Lord. But cursed be the deceiver, which hath in his flock a male, and voweth, and sacrificeth unto the Lord a corrupt thing: for I am a great King, saith the Lord of hosts, and my name is dreadful among the heathen.

Clearly the Lord is unhappy with this state of affairs, and threatens them with dire consequences if they do not change their attitude towards Him and their office.

Malachi 2:1-17: *And now, O ye priests, this commandment is for you. If ye will not hear, and if ye will not lay it to heart, to give glory unto my name, saith the Lord of hosts, I will even send a curse upon you, and I will curse your blessings: yea, I have cursed them already, because ye do not lay it to heart. Behold, I will corrupt your seed, and spread dung upon your faces, even the dung of your solemn feasts; and one shall take you away with it. And ye shall know that I have sent this commandment unto you, that my covenant might be with Levi, saith the Lord of hosts. My covenant was with him of life and peace; and I gave them to him for the fear wherewith he feared me, and was afraid before my name. The law of truth was in his mouth, and iniquity was not found in his lips: he walked with me in peace and equity, and did turn many away from iniquity.*

The real spirit of what the priesthood was about is seen in the following, and their failure to uphold God's laws was the cause of many of their flock falling short. The Lord lays the blame for this squarely on their shoulders. Although the Jews never returned to idolatry after their captivity in Babylon, they are here accused of a similar desertion of the Lord in their attitudes, yet their response is that they have done nothing wrong. In the light of history, we know that things never really improved from this time, which was the period when the sects of the Pharisees and Sadducees were founded, and as a consequence Israel became in essence a self-righteous but altogether godless nation, with the notable exception of the small remnant who mourned for their former state under God's laws.

For the priest's lips should keep knowledge, and they should seek the law at his mouth: for he is the messenger of the Lord of hosts. But ye are departed out of the way; ye have caused many to stumble at the law; ye have corrupted the covenant of Levi, saith the Lord of hosts. Therefore have I also made you contemptible and base before all the people, according as ye have not kept my ways, but have been partial in the law. Have we not all one father? hath not one God created us? why do we deal treacherously every man against his brother, by profaning the covenant of our fathers? Judah hath dealt treacherously, and an abomination is committed in Israel and in Jerusalem; for Judah hath profaned the holiness of the Lord which he loved, and hath married the daughter of a strange god. The Lord will cut off the man that doeth this, the master and the scholar, out of the tabernacles of Jacob, and him that offereth an offering unto the Lord of hosts. And this have ye done again, covering the altar of the Lord with tears, with weeping, and with crying out, insomuch that he regardeth not the offering any more, or receiveth it with good will at your hand.

The priests had begun to take ownership of the law for themselves, and this continued until the Lord's time, where there was one set of rules for the priesthood and the rich and quite another for the people themselves; under this regime they had no voice at all, and were made to bear the [109]heavy burdens of the Law that the Pharisees and Sadducees had fabricated, their 'oral law' or 'traditions'. By the time the Lord came, Israel had become like any other nation, and any fairness and equity inbuilt into God's Law had been replaced by a man's government, going under the guise of being divinely appointed although in reality it had been corrupted by the leaders, who were far more worried about not upsetting their Roman masters than they were about serving their own God.

Yet ye say, Wherefore? Because the Lord hath been witness between thee and the wife of thy youth, against whom thou hast dealt treacherously: yet is she thy companion, and the wife of thy covenant. And did not he make one? Yet had he the residue of the spirit. And wherefore one? That he might seek a godly seed. Therefore take heed to your spirit, and let none deal treacherously against the wife of his youth. For the Lord, the God of Israel, saith that he hateth putting away: for one covereth violence with his garment, saith the Lord of hosts: therefore take heed to your spirit, that ye deal not treacherously. Ye have wearied the Lord with your words. Yet ye say, Wherein have we wearied him? When ye say, Every one that doeth evil is good in the sight of the Lord, and he delighteth in them; or, Where is the God of judgment?

Remarkably, this does not affect the faithfulness of God in sending His Son to redeem the Earth, but what could have been a time of blessing, while the people, having returned from captivity and enjoying God's favour in walking in His judgements, should have been waiting quietly for their Messiah to come as was intended for them, is now to turn into a time of silence from God, and one of general oppression for the nation. When the Lord did come, because the nation for the most part had not listened to this last opportunity to change, it was to a nation that had been spoiled and corrupted. Only a few of the faithful now looked forward to His appearance. The sign of His coming was to be John the Baptist, who would herald His appearance, and did his best to shake the nation from their lethargy in anticipation of their Messiah:

Malachi 3:1-18: *Behold, I will send my messenger, and he shall prepare the way before me: and the Lord, whom ye seek, shall suddenly come to his temple, even the messenger of the covenant, whom ye delight in: behold, he shall come, saith the Lord of hosts. But who may abide the day of his coming? and who shall stand when he appeareth? for he is like a refiner's fire, and like fullers' soap: And he shall sit as a refiner and purifier of silver: and he shall purify the sons of Levi, and purge them as gold and silver, that they may offer unto the Lord an offering in righteousness.*

The chance for them to be purged and refined was to be offered to them again at the Lord's appearing, and their acceptance of Him should have commenced the events of the last seven years of the seventieth week of the desolations of Jeremiah's prophecy, as explained in Daniel's visions. There would have undoubtedly been a time of judgement, but after this would have come the Kingdom of Heaven, a short time of probation, soon to be followed by the Kingdom of God. What could have been the time of probation for Israel, after the return from Babylon, the restoration of the its true religion and the building of Ezekiel's third Temple, is yet to materialize, and although it should have occurred before the Lord came in the flesh, it was offered again afterwards through the apostles' ministry. The truth is that the nation failed to recognise these opportunities, both rejecting and crucifying the Lord when He came, and also refusing the apostolic ministry, the preaching of the Kingdom gospel that followed after His resurrection. Eventually Paul, speaking at the end of the book of Acts, conceded that the main thrust of his ministry was now going to be to the Gentile nations, those despised by the Jews, who considered themselves the people of God, and looked down on everyone else.

This change of dispensation, the preaching of the gospel of

the grace of God to all nations, was to lead to the formation of a predominantly gentile church, of which we are now members. This church embraces both Jew and gentile, as it is inclusive for all believers, but it has a limited time frame and we understand, because Paul explained it clearly, that when the [110]fullness of the gentiles is come in, the ministry concerning the Kingdom Gospel will once more be preached to the world, and then events will return to the original intention, where Israel will be seen to represent God on this earth through the Jewish religion and law. It is then that the [111]new covenant will be made with the Jew, and the Israel that will appear then will be a very different nation from the one we see now.

After seeing these truths in their biblical perspective we can only marvel at God's patience towards Israel, for it seems that there is no end to His mercy and grace towards them. Although we may consider His Judgements on His own people to have been severe in the past, and yet more severe in the future, He has never forsaken them as His people, despite the countless times they have forsaken Him as their God.

He will finally glorify Himself in them, justifying Himself to all concerned, both in heaven and earth, for as He says below in 3:6 *For I am the Lord, I change not; therefore ye sons of Jacob are not consumed.*

The period he has set for this new and final probation period is what we call the millennium, the thousand years of His rule on earth through Israel, but we must not forget that this set length of time is a comparatively recent revelation, only mentioned in vision to John after sufficient time for the nation to repent was given, at the end of the apostolic period. John of course, being the last one left of the apostles who walked with Him on earth.

"BEHOLD, I HAVE FORETOLD YOU ALL THINGS"

After this time, we see in heaven the [112]Great throne of Judgement, and following after this the appearance of the [113]New Heavens and New earth, where finally all of the righteous are to be gathered into God's kingdom.

Then shall the offering of Judah and Jerusalem be pleasant unto the Lord, as in the days of old, and as in former years. And I will come near to you to judgment; and I will be a swift witness against the sorcerers, and against the adulterers, and against false swearers, and against those that oppress the hireling in his wages, the widow, and the fatherless, and that turn aside the stranger from his right, and fear not me, saith the Lord of hosts. For I am the Lord, I change not; therefore ye sons of Jacob are not consumed. Even from the days of your fathers ye are gone away from mine ordinances, and have not kept them. Return unto me, and I will return unto you, saith the Lord of hosts. But ye said, Wherein shall we return? Will a man rob God? Yet ye have robbed me. But ye say, Wherein have we robbed thee? In tithes and offerings. Ye are cursed with a curse: for ye have robbed me, even this whole nation. Bring ye all the tithes into the storehouse, that there may be meat in mine house, and prove me now herewith, saith the Lord of hosts, if I will not open you the windows of heaven, and pour you out a blessing, that there shall not be room enough to receive it. And I will rebuke the devourer for your sakes, and he shall not destroy the fruits of your ground; neither shall your vine cast her fruit before the time in the field, saith the Lord of hosts. And all nations shall call you blessed: for ye shall be a delightsome land, saith the Lord of hosts. Your words have been stout against me, saith the Lord. Yet ye say, What have we spoken so much against thee? Ye have said, It is vain to serve God: and what profit is it that we have kept his ordinance, and that we have walked mournfully before the Lord of hosts? And now we call the proud happy; yea, they that work wickedness are set up; yea, they that tempt God are even delivered. Then

CHAPTER NINE

they that feared the Lord spake often one to another: and the Lord hearkened, and heard it, and a book of remembrance was written before him for them that feared the Lord, and that thought upon his name. And they shall be mine, saith the Lord of hosts, in that day when I make up my jewels; and I will spare them, as a man spareth his own son that serveth him. Then shall ye return, and discern between the righteous and the wicked, between him that serveth God and him that serveth him not.

Malachi 4:1-6: *For, behold, the day cometh, that shall burn as an oven; and all the proud, yea, and all that do wickedly, shall be stubble: and the day that cometh shall burn them up, saith the Lord of hosts, that it shall leave them neither root nor branch. But unto you that fear my name shall the Sun of righteousness arise with healing in his wings; and ye shall go forth, and grow up as calves of the stall. And ye shall tread down the wicked; for they shall be ashes under the soles of your feet in the day that I shall do this, saith the Lord of hosts. Remember ye the law of Moses my servant, which I commanded unto him in Horeb for all Israel, with the statutes and judgments.*

This book closes the Old Testament with the promise of another witness to herald the Lord's appearance, another attempt to turn this people round, so that they are prepared to meet their God:

Behold, I will send you Elijah the prophet before the coming of the great and dreadful day of the Lord: And he shall turn the heart of the fathers to the children, and the heart of the children to their fathers, lest I come and smite the earth with a curse.

In its rejection of the Lord, Israel and the world can look forward to the curse that is to come, the inevitable consequence of refusing His righteousness and sacrifice, in favour of its own. His church meanwhile looks forward to His appearance in the clouds, when at some point He will take us to be with Him. However, He has not forsaken His people Israel, and He will remain their God throughout, eventually cleansing them and proving once and for all that He at least is faithful, and remains true to His word.

Amen.

Endnotes

1   Mark 13:23 *But take ye heed: behold, I have foretold you all things.*

2   The Catholic Church may hold a different view, of course! See also Jeremiah Chapter 3:14-20 *Turn, O backsliding children, saith the Lord; for I am married unto you: and I will take you one of a city, and two of a family, and I will bring you to Zion: And I will give you pastors according to mine heart, which shall feed you with knowledge and understanding. And it shall come to pass, when ye be multiplied and increased in the land, in those days, saith the Lord, they shall say no more, The ark of the covenant of the Lord: neither shall it come to mind: neither shall they remember it; neither shall they visit it; neither shall that be done any more. At that time they shall call Jerusalem the throne of the Lord; and all the nations shall be gathered unto it, to the name of the Lord, to Jerusalem: neither shall they walk any more after the imagination of their evil heart. In those days the house of Judah shall walk with the house of Israel, and they shall come together out of the land of the north to the land that I have given for an inheritance unto your fathers. But I said, How shall I put thee among the children, and give thee a pleasant land, a goodly heritage of the hosts of nations? and I said, Thou shalt call me, My father; and shalt not turn away from me. Surely as a wife treacherously departeth from her husband, so have ye dealt treacherously with me, O house of Israel, saith the Lord.*

3   Ephesians 3:1-10 *For this cause I Paul, the prisoner of Jesus Christ for you Gentiles, If ye have heard of the dispensation of the grace of God which is given me to you-ward: How that by revelation he made known unto me the mystery; (as I wrote afore in few words, Whereby, when ye read, ye may understand my*

> *knowledge in the mystery of Christ)* **Which in other ages was not made known unto the sons of men, as it is now revealed unto his holy apostles and prophets by the Spirit; That the Gentiles should be fellowheirs, and of the same body, and partakers of his promise in Christ by the gospel:** *Whereof I was made a minister, according to the gift of the grace of God given unto me by the effectual working of his power. Unto me, who am less than the least of all saints, is this grace given, that I should preach among the Gentiles the unsearchable riches of Christ; And to make all men see what is the fellowship of* **the mystery, which from the beginning of the world hath been hid in God, who created all things by Jesus Christ: To the intent that now unto the principalities and powers in heavenly places might be known by the church the manifold wisdom of God.**

4   Galatians 3:28-29 *There is neither Jew nor Greek, there is neither bond nor free, there is neither male nor female: for ye are all one in Christ Jesus. And if ye be Christ's, then are ye Abraham's seed, and heirs according to the promise.*

5   Of course Jews and Gentiles, or non-Jews, are still present in a demographic sense.

6   It is a fact that there are occasional errors of translation in the King James Bible and these are well documented, but this is not what is being discussed here.

7   For example Mark 1:15 *And saying, The time is fulfilled, and the kingdom of God is at hand: repent ye, and believe the gospel.*

8   But only for those that would receive it. Malachi 4:5 *Behold, I will send you Elijah the prophet before the coming of the great and dreadful day of the Lord.*

9   Mark 6:17 *For Herod himself had sent forth and laid hold upon John, and bound him in prison for Herodias' sake, his brother Philip's wife: for he had married her. For John had said unto Herod, It is not lawful for thee to have thy brother's wife. Therefore Herodias had a quarrel against him, and would have killed him; but she could not: For Herod feared John, knowing that he was a just man and an holy, and observed him; and when he heard him, he did many things, and heard him gladly. And when a convenient day was come, that Herod on his birthday made a supper to his Lord's, high captains, and chief estates of Galilee; And when the daughter of the said Herodias came in, and danced, and pleased Herod and them that sat with him, the king said unto the damsel, Ask of me*

whatsoever thou wilt, and I will give it thee. And he sware unto her, Whatsoever thou shalt ask of me, I will give it thee, unto the half of my kingdom. And she went forth, and said unto her mother, What shall I ask? And she said, The head of John the Baptist.

10   Luke 1:17 *And he shall go before him in the spirit and power of Elias, to turn the hearts of the fathers to the children, and the disobedient to the wisdom of the just; to make ready a people prepared for the Lord.*

11   John 4:1-2 *When therefore the Lord knew how the Pharisees had heard that Jesus made and baptised more disciples than John (Though Jesus Himself baptized not, but His disciples)*

12   Matthew 3:13-15 *Then cometh Jesus from Galilee to Jordan unto John, to be baptized of him. But John forbad him, saying, I have need to be baptized of thee, and comest thou to me? And Jesus answering said unto him, Suffer it to be so now: for thus it becometh us to fulfil all righteousness. Then he suffered him.*

13   John 15:1-5 *I am the true vine, and my Father is the husbandman. Every branch in me that beareth not fruit he taketh away: and every branch that beareth fruit, he purgeth it, that it may bring forth more fruit.* **Now ye are clean through the word which I have spoken unto you.** *Abide in me, and I in you. As the branch cannot bear fruit of itself, except it abide in the vine; no more can ye, except ye abide in me. I am the vine, ye are the branches: He that abideth in me, and I in him, the same bringeth forth much fruit: for without me ye can do nothing.*

Paul too, in his later ministry did not insist on baptism in water for believers, saying: 1 Corinthians 1:14-18 *I thank God that I baptized none of you, but Crispus and Gaius; Lest any should say that I had baptized in mine own name. And I baptized also the household of Stephanas: besides, I know not whether I baptized any other. For Christ sent me not to baptize, but to preach the gospel: not with wisdom of words, lest the cross of Christ should be made of none effect. For the preaching of the cross is to them that perish foolishness; but unto us which are saved it is the power of God.*

This may seem controversial or hard to accept for some, but if like me you have already been baptized in water, or perhaps still want to be, it will do you no harm!

14   Isaiah 42:21 *The Lord is well pleased for his righteousness sake, he will magnify the Law and make it honourable.*

15 Luke 6:17 *And He came down with them, and stood in the plain, and the company of His disciples, and a great multitude of people out of all Judea, and Jerusalem, and from the sea coast of Tyre and Sidon which came to hear Him, and be healed of their diseases.*

16 John 19:15 *But they cried out, away with him, crucify him. Pilate saith unto them, shall I crucify your king. The chief priests answered, we have no king but Caesar.*

17 Matthew 11:29 *Take my yoke upon you and learn of me, for I am meek and lowly in heart, and ye shall find rest unto your souls.* And: 21:5 *Tell ye the daughter of Zion Behold thy king cometh unto thee, meek and sitting upon an ass, and a colt, the foal of an ass.*

18 1 Peter 3:4 *But let it be the hidden man of the heart, in that which is not corruptible, even the ornament of a meek and quiet spirit, which is in the sight of God of great price.*

19 Acts 12:2 *And he killed James the brother of John with the sword.*

20 Romans 10:12 *For there is no difference between the Jew and the Greek, for the same Lord is rich unto all that call upon Him.* Also: Galatians 3:28 *There is neither Jew nor Greek, there is neither bond nor free there is neither male nor female, for ye are all one in Jesus Christ.* And: Colossians 3:11 *Where there is neither Greek nor Jew, circumcision nor un-circumcision, Barbarian, Scythian, bond nor free, but Christ is all, and in all.*

21 Romans 11:25-26 *For I would not brethren that you be ignorant of this mystery, lest ye should be wise in your own conceits, that blindness in part is happened to Israel, until the fullness of the Gentiles be come in, and so all Israel shall be saved, as it is written, There shall come out of Sion the deliverer, and shall turn away ungodliness from Jacob.*

22 The Pharisees held that that the 'oral law' (the Talmud, comprising Mishnah and Gemarah) had been given to Moses at the same time as the 'written law', and was communicated to Aaron and his sons, and then on to the seventy elders. It was claimed by the Pharisees to be as binding as the written law, or Torah.

23 Luke 10:27 *And he answering said, thou shalt love the Lord thy God with all*

thy heart, and with all thy soul and with all thy strength, and with all thy mind, and thy neighbour as thyself. Compare with 1 John 4:20-21 *If a man say I love God, and hateth his brother, he is a liar, for he that loveth not his brother whom he hath seen, how can he love God whom he hath not seen?*

24 Hebrews 4:15 *For we have not an high priest that cannot be touched with the feeling of our infirmities, but was in all points tempted like as we are, yet without sin.*

25 Now known as a *get*.

26 Matthew 1:19 *Then Joseph her husband, being a just man, and not willing to make her a publick example was minded to put her away privily.*

27 Matthew 19:3 *Is it lawful for a man to put away his wife for every cause?*

28 We have the right in UK courts to give an *affirmation*, an alternatively worded script.

29 Matthew 22:21 *They say unto Him Caesar's, then saith He unto them, Render unto Caesar the things which are Caesars, and unto God the things that are Gods.*

30 1 Corinthians 6:7 *Now therefore there is utterly a fault among you, because ye go to law one with another. Why do ye not rather take wrong? why do ye not rather suffer yourselves to be defrauded?*

31 Matthew 4:2 *And when he had fasted forty days and forty nights, he was afterward an hungered.*

32 1 Corinthians 7:5 *Defraud ye not one the other, except it be with consent for a time, that ye may give yourselves to fasting and prayer; and come together again, that Satan tempt you not for your incontinency which includes sexual acts within marriage.*

33 Daniel 9:3 for example *And I set my face unto the Lord God, to seek by prayer and supplications, with fasting, and sackcloth, and ashes.*

34 1 John 3:20 *For if our heart condemn us, God is greater than our heart, and knoweth all things.*

35   35 Luke 10:40 for example: *But Martha was cumbered about much serving, and came to him, and said, Lord, dost thou not care that my sister hath left me to serve alone? bid her therefore that she help me.*

36   36 Jeremiah 17:9: *The heart is deceitful above all things, and desperately wicked, who can know it?*

37   These same examples are used when the Lord goes on to talk about the giving of the Holy Spirit in Luke 11:13 *If ye then, being evil, know how to give good gifts unto your children: how much more shall your heavenly Father give the Holy Spirit to them that ask him?*

38   Mark 4:31 *It is like a grain of mustard seed, which, when it is sown in the earth, is less than all the seeds that be in the earth.*

Also Luke 13:19 *It is like a grain of mustard seed, which a man took, and cast into his garden; and it grew, and waxed a great tree; and the fowls of the air lodged in the branches of it.*

39   Matthew 17:20 *And Jesus said unto them, Because of your unbelief: for verily I say unto you, If ye have faith as a grain of mustard seed, ye shall say unto this mountain, Remove hence to yonder place; and it shall remove; and nothing shall be impossible unto you.*

Also: Luke 17:6 *And the Lord said, If ye had faith as a grain of mustard seed, ye might say unto this sycamine tree, Be thou plucked up by the root, and be thou planted in the sea; and it should obey you.*

40   Matthew 13:47-49 *Again, the Kingdom of Heaven is like unto a net, that was cast into the sea, and gathered of every kind: Which, when it was full, they drew to shore, and sat down, and gathered the good into vessels, but cast the bad away. So shall it be at the end of the world: the angels shall come forth, and sever the wicked from among the just.*

41   Greek: Zizanion, darnel, or false wheat, understood to be bearded darnel, Latin: *Lolium temulentum*, a form of rye grass that appears as wheat until its full development, whose seeds are smaller than wheat and coloured dark brown/purple. When darnel is fully mature it maintains an upright appearance, whereas wheat tends to droop, which is one way it can be distinguished and dealt with. It is particularly competitive, and is a threat

to wheat crops to this day. The plant itself is not proved to be poisonous, but it is host to a fungus that develops within it, which in extreme cases can kill when taken. The Greeks used a form of it as a medicine.

42 See Paul's wonderful discourse in his letter to the Romans on the place of the Jew, for a more perfect appreciation, of what being a descendant of Abraham should mean.

43 In the light of the Lord's words that there would not remain one stone upon another, this seems unlikely.

44 I have attempted to cover this more comprehensively in my book 'Alpha and Omega'.

45 Revelation 11:6-10 *These have power to shut heaven, that it rain not in the days of their prophecy: and have power over waters to turn them to blood, and to smite the earth with all plagues, as often as they will. And when they shall have finished their testimony, the beast that ascendeth out of the bottomless pit shall make war against them, and shall overcome them, and kill them. And their dead bodies shall lie in the street of the great city, which spiritually is called Sodom and Egypt, where also our Lord was crucified. And they of the people and kindreds and tongues and nations shall see their dead bodies three days and an half, and shall not suffer their dead bodies to be put in graves. And they that dwell upon the earth shall rejoice over them, and make merry, and shall send gifts one to another; because these two prophets tormented them that dwelt on the earth.*

46 There are of course many schools of thought concerning the End Days, and it can be quite a divisive issue for some churches. The *Historicist* for example, would say that these events are over, and were fulfilled by events of the past. We shall see! Better, I believe, not to call ourselves anything, but rather to read what the scriptures clearly state, whilst praying for more understanding, and then as Paul says *rightly dividing the word of truth* so that we are not blindly following the opinions of scholars, or church leaders, or anything else but that which is revealed to us through the Word of God. If you do not agree with anything written in this book, then please check it through, and see whether or not it can be either justified or negated by other scriptures. The truth will always stand this test, and I welcome your comments, criticisms or questions. It may be that you can show me something that I had not considered, in which case we will both be the richer for it?

47 Daniel 12:11 *And from the time that the daily sacrifice shall be taken away, and the abomination that maketh desolate set up, there shall be a thousand two hundred and ninety days.* And: Revelation Chapter 13:13-15 *And he doeth great wonders, so that he maketh fire come down from heaven on the earth in the sight of men, and deceiveth them that dwell on the earth by the means of those miracles which he had power to do in the sight of the beast; saying to them that dwell on the earth, that they should make an image to the beast, which had the wound by a sword, and did live. And he had power to give life unto the image of the beast, that the image of the beast should both speak, and cause that as many as would not worship the image of the beast should be killed.*

48 A fuller explanation can be found in *Alpha and Omega*, by the same author.

49 This creates difficulties for some as the Temple no longer exists, and the site is generally believed to be occupied by the Dome of the Rock, a sacred Muslim building, as well as the Al-Aqsa Mosque, currently regulated by the Jordanian Government. Some argue that the Temple must be rebuilt on this site for the Lord's words to be fulfilled, but nowhere does the Lord say that this particular Temple will be rebuilt, although He does talk about its destruction. The important criterion is that the daily sacrifice morning and evening is reinstated, and this is part of the very agreement that is broken by the beast in the middle of the prophetic week (Daniel 12:11). It remains to be seen what the final conditions of this agreement are between Jew and Muslim, but undoubtedly it will be a triumph of statesmanship accredited to the *Beast,* when a compromise is reached between Jews and Muslims allowing the daily sacrifice to recommence, in a place acceptable to both parties. To complicate matters further, there is a *Third Temple* not yet built, as described by Ezekiel, which we shall consider in due course. A further complication is the likelihood that the original temple was not even located on the Temple mount, as widely accepted, but slightly further south, at a place called Ophel.

50 Jeremiah 25:8-14 *Therefore thus saith the Lord of hosts; Because ye have not heard my words, Behold, I will send and take all the families of the north, saith the Lord, and Nebuchadnezzar the king of Babylon, my servant, and will bring them against this land, and against the inhabitants thereof, and against all these nations round about, and will utterly destroy them, and make them an*

astonishment, and an hissing, and perpetual desolations. Moreover I will take from them the voice of mirth, and the voice of gladness, the voice of the bridegroom, and the voice of the bride, the sound of the millstones, and the light of the candle. And this whole land shall be a desolation, and an astonishment; and these nations shall serve the king of Babylon seventy years. And it shall come to pass, when seventy years are accomplished, that I will punish the king of Babylon, and that nation, saith the Lord, for their iniquity, and the land of the Chaldeans, and will make it perpetual desolations. And I will bring upon that land all my words which I have pronounced against it, even all that is written in this book, which Jeremiah hath prophesied against all the nations. For many nations and great kings shall serve themselves of them also: and I will recompense them according to their deeds, and according to the works of their own hands. And Jeremiah 29:10-14: *For thus saith the LORD, That after seventy years be accomplished at Babylon I will visit you, and perform my good word toward you, in causing you to return to this place. For I know the thoughts that I think toward you, saith the LORD, thoughts of peace, and not of evil, to give you an expected end. Then shall ye call upon me, and ye shall go and pray unto me, and I will hearken unto you. And ye shall seek me, and find me, when ye shall search for me with all your heart. And I will be found of you, saith the Lord: and I will turn away your captivity, and I will gather you from all the nations, and from all the places whither I have driven you, saith the Lord; and I will bring you again into the place whence I caused you to be carried away captive.* For a fuller explanation of this please refer to Chapter 3 of Alpha and Omega.

51   Revelation 20:2-5 *And he laid hold on the dragon, that old serpent, which is the Devil, and Satan, and bound him a thousand years, And cast him into the bottomless pit, and shut him up, and set a seal upon him, that he should deceive the nations no more, till the thousand years should be fulfilled: and after that he must be loosed a little season. And I saw thrones, and they sat upon them, and judgment was given unto them: and I saw the souls of them that were beheaded for the witness of Jesus, and for the word of God, and which had not worshipped the beast, neither his image, neither had received his mark upon their foreheads, or in their hands; and they lived and reigned with Christ a thousand years. But the rest of the dead lived not again until the thousand years were finished. This is the first resurrection.*

52   Revelation 20:1-3 *And I saw an angel come down from heaven, having the key of the bottomless pit and a great chain in his hand. And he laid hold on the*

dragon, that old serpent, which is the Devil, and Satan, and bound him a thousand years, And cast him into the bottomless pit, and shut him up, and set a seal upon him, that he should deceive the nations no more, till the thousand years should be fulfilled: and after that he must be loosed a little season.

53   1 Thessalonians 2:8-9 *And then shall that Wicked be revealed, whom the Lord shall consume with the spirit of his mouth, and shall destroy with the brightness of his coming: Even him, whose coming is after the working of Satan with all power and signs and lying wonders.*

54   This is confusing, but in 2 Thessalonians 2:2 the *Day of Christ* is wrongly translated, and should read the *Day of the Lord*.

55   Acts 1:6-7 *When they therefore were come together, they asked of him, saying, Lord, wilt thou at this time restore again the kingdom to Israel? And he said unto them, It is not for you to know the times or the seasons, which the Father hath put in his own power.*

56   Galatians 4:4-7 *But when the fulness of the time was come, God sent forth his Son, made of a woman, made under the law, To redeem them that were under the law, that we might receive the adoption of sons. And because ye are sons, God hath sent forth the Spirit of his Son into your hearts, crying, Abba, Father. Wherefore thou art no more a servant, but a son; and if a son, then an heir of God through Christ.*

57   Revelation 19:9 *And he saith unto me, Write, Blessed are they which are called unto the marriage supper of the Lamb. And he saith unto me, These are the true sayings of God.*

58   For further details of this please refer to items 79-80 in the appendix section of the 'Companion Bible' by E.W. Bullinger.

59   Jonah 4:1-2 Jonah's anger was that if Nineveh was spared, it might later be used to judge Israel. He was not afraid to minister to them, but was afraid that his ministry would be effective. He is overruled by God, see Jonah 4:11.

60   Romans 9:27-29 *Esaias also crieth concerning Israel, Though the number of the children of Israel be as the sand of the sea, a remnant shall be saved: For he will finish the work, and cut it short in righteousness: because a short work will*

ENDNOTES

the Lord make upon the earth. And as Esaias said before, Except the Lord of Sabaoth had left us a seed, we had been as Sodoma, and been made like unto Gomorrha. Paul the Apostle must have found encouragement from these verses that Israel would never be totally destroyed.

61 The perversions that Sodom has become famous for are only one aspect of the Lord's anger with them, as Ezekiel 16:49-50 *Behold, this was the iniquity of thy sister Sodom, pride, fulness of bread, and abundance of idleness was in her and in her daughters, neither did she strengthen the hand of the poor and needy. And they were haughty, and committed abomination before me: therefore I took them away as I saw good.*

62 The *Branch* is also referred to in a similar context in Zechariah's prophecy.

63 Malachi 4:4-5 *5 Behold, I will send you Elijah the prophet before the coming of the great and dreadful day of the Lord: And he shall turn the heart of the fathers to the children, and the heart of the children to their fathers, lest I come and smite the earth with a curse.*

See also:

Revelation 11:3-6 *And I will give power unto my two witnesses, and they shall prophesy a thousand two hundred and threescore days, clothed in sackcloth. These are the two olive trees, and the two candlesticks standing before the God of the earth. And if any man will hurt them, fire proceedeth out of their mouth, and devoureth their enemies: and if any man will hurt them, he must in this manner be killed. These have power to shut heaven that it rain not in the days of their prophecy: and have power over waters to turn them to blood, and to smite the earth with all plagues, as often as they will.*

64 Romans 15:12 *And again, Esaias saith, There shall be a root of Jesse, and he that shall rise to reign over the Gentiles; in him shall the Gentiles trust.*

65 Revelation 19:19 *And I saw the beast, and the kings of the earth, and their armies, gathered together to make war against him that sat on the horse, and against his army. And the beast was taken, and with him the false prophet that wrought miracles before him, with which he deceived them that had received the mark of the beast, and them that worshipped his image. These both were cast alive into a lake of fire burning with brimstone.*

And see also:

Revelation 20:1-3 *And I saw an angel come down from heaven, having the key of the bottomless pit and a great chain in his hand. And he laid hold on the dragon, that old serpent, which is the Devil, and Satan, and bound him a thousand years, And cast him into the bottomless pit, and shut him up, and set a seal upon him, that he should deceive the nations no more, till the thousand years should be fulfilled: and after that he must be loosed a little season.*

66 Ephesians 2:6-7 *And hath raised us up together, and made us sit together in heavenly places in Christ Jesus: that in the ages to come He might show the exceeding riches of His grace in His kindness toward us through Christ Jesus.*

67 Ezekiel 38: 8-23 *After many days thou shalt be visited: in the latter years thou shalt come into the land that is brought back from the sword, and is gathered out of many people, against the mountains of Israel, which have been always waste: but it is brought forth out of the nations, and they shall dwell safely all of them. Thou shalt ascend and come like a storm, thou shalt be like a cloud to cover the land, thou, and all thy bands, and many people with thee. Thus saith the Lord God; It shall also come to pass, that at the same time shall things come into thy mind, and thou shalt think an evil thought: And thou shalt say, I will go up to the land of unwalled villages; I will go to them that are at rest, that dwell safely, all of them dwelling without walls, and having neither bars nor gates, To take a spoil, and to take a prey; to turn thine hand upon the desolate places that are now inhabited, and upon the people that are gathered out of the nations, which have gotten cattle and goods, that dwell in the midst of the land. Sheba, and Dedan, and the merchants of Tarshish, with all the young lions thereof, shall say unto thee, Art thou come to take a spoil? hast thou gathered thy company to take a prey? to carry away silver and gold, to take away cattle and goods, to take a great spoil? Therefore, son of man, prophesy and say unto Gog, Thus saith the Lord God; In that day when my people of Israel dwelleth safely, shalt thou not know it? And thou shalt come from thy place out of the north parts, thou, and many people with thee, all of them riding upon horses, a great company, and a mighty army: And thou shalt come up against my people of Israel, as a cloud to cover the land; it shall be in the latter days, and I will bring thee against my land, that the heathen may know me, when I shall be sanctified in thee, O Gog, before their eyes. Thus saith the Lord God; Art thou he of whom I have spoken in old time by my servants the prophets of Israel, which prophesied in those days many years that I would bring thee against them? And it shall come to pass at the same*

ENDNOTES

time when Gog shall come against the land of Israel, saith the Lord God, that my fury shall come up in my face. For in my jealousy and in the fire of my wrath have I spoken, Surely in that day there shall be a great shaking in the land of Israel; So that the fishes of the sea, and the fowls of the heaven, and the beasts of the field, and all creeping things that creep upon the earth, and all the men that are upon the face of the earth, shall shake at my presence, and the mountains shall be thrown down, and the steep places shall fall, and every wall shall fall to the ground. And I will call for a sword against him throughout all my mountains, saith the Lord God: every man's sword shall be against his brother. And I will plead against him with pestilence and with blood; and I will rain upon him, and upon his bands, and upon the many people that are with him, an overflowing rain, and great hailstones, fire, and brimstone. Thus will I magnify myself, and sanctify myself; and I will be known in the eyes of many nations, and they shall know that I am the Lord.

68   I fully accept that the term *Millennium reign* cannot be found in scripture, but it simply means a thousand years, which is referred to in the book of Revelation.

69   Galatians 2:11-14 *But when Peter was come to Antioch, I withstood him to the face, because he was to be blamed. For before that certain came from James, he did eat with the Gentiles: but when they were come, he withdrew and separated himself, fearing them which were of the circumcision. And the other Jews dissembled likewise with him; insomuch that Barnabas also was carried away with their dissimulation. But when I saw that they walked not uprightly according to the truth of the gospel, I said unto Peter before them all, If thou, being a Jew, livest after the manner of Gentiles, and not as do the Jews, why compellest thou the Gentiles to live as do the Jews?*

70   Please refer to *Alpha and Omega* by the same author for a more detailed description of how this takes place.

71   Or perhaps it isn't! Luke 4:18-20 *The Spirit of the Lord is upon me, because he hath anointed me to preach the gospel to the poor; he hath sent me to heal the broken hearted, to preach deliverance to the captives, and recovering of sight to the blind, to set at liberty them that are bruised, To preach the acceptable year of the Lord. And he closed the book, and he gave it again to the minister, and sat down. And the eyes of all them that were in the synagogue were fastened on him.*

72 Deuteronomy 30:1-19 *And it shall come to pass, when all these things are come upon thee, the blessing and the curse, which I have set before thee, and thou shalt call them to mind among all the nations, whither the Lord thy God hath driven thee, And shalt return unto the Lord thy God, and shalt obey his voice according to all that I command thee this day, thou and thy children, with all thine heart, and with all thy soul; That then the Lord thy God will turn thy captivity, and have compassion upon thee, and will return and gather thee from all the nations, whither the Lord thy God hath scattered thee. If any of thine be driven out unto the outmost parts of heaven, from thence will the Lord thy God gather thee, and from thence will he fetch thee: And the Lord thy God will bring thee into the land which thy fathers possessed, and thou shalt possess it; and he will do thee good, and multiply thee above thy fathers. And the Lord thy God will circumcise thine heart, and the heart of thy seed, to love the Lord thy God with all thine heart, and with all thy soul, that thou mayest live. And the Lord thy God will put all these curses upon thine enemies, and on them that hate thee, which persecuted thee. And thou shalt return and obey the voice of the Lord, and do all his commandments which I command thee this day. And the Lord thy God will make thee plenteous in every work of thine hand, in the fruit of thy body, and in the fruit of thy cattle, and in the fruit of thy land, for good: for the Lord will again rejoice over thee for good, as he rejoiced over thy fathers: If thou shalt hearken unto the voice of the Lord thy God, to keep his commandments and his statutes which are written in this book of the law, and if thou turn unto the Lord thy God with all thine heart, and with all thy soul. For this commandment which I command thee this day, it is not hidden from thee, neither is it far off. It is not in heaven, that thou shouldest say, Who shall go up for us to heaven, and bring it unto us, that we may hear it, and do it? Neither is it beyond the sea, that thou shouldest say, Who shall go over the sea for us, and bring it unto us, that we may hear it, and do it? But the word is very nigh unto thee, in thy mouth, and in thy heart, that thou mayest do it. See, I have set before thee this day life and good, and death and evil; In that I command thee this day to love the Lord thy God, to walk in his ways, and to keep his commandments and his statutes and his judgments, that thou mayest live and multiply: and the Lord thy God shall bless thee in the land whither thou goest to possess it. But if thine heart turn away, so that thou wilt not hear, but shalt be drawn away, and worship other gods, and serve them; I denounce unto you this day, that ye shall surely perish, and that ye shall not prolong your days upon the land, whither thou passest over Jordan to go to possess it I call heaven and earth to record this day against you, that I have set before you life and death, blessing and cursing: therefore choose life, that both thou and thy seed may live:*

ENDNOTES

73 Revelation 21:1-5 *And I saw a new heaven and a new earth: for the first heaven and the first earth were passed away; and there was no more sea. And I John saw the holy city, new Jerusalem, coming down from God out of heaven, prepared as a bride adorned for her husband. And I heard a great voice out of heaven saying, Behold, the tabernacle of God is with men, and he will dwell with them, and they shall be his people, and God himself shall be with them, and be their God. And God shall wipe away all tears from their eyes; and there shall be no more death, neither sorrow, nor crying, neither shall there be any more pain: for the former things are passed away. And he that sat upon the throne said, Behold, I make all things new.*

74 This word *shekinah* is not found in scripture, but is the word that the Jews later took to describe the phenomenon of the Lord's presence manifested in the cloud. It means dwelling or settling, and is used to describe Gods dwelling place on earth, ie the tabernacle, and later Solomon's temple, where it was seen to descend. Some, because of its feminine origins in Hebrew take it to refer to Gods feminine side. You are welcome to form your own opinion on this, but as the word is not found in scripture, I personally doubt that it has any bearing on Gods gender!

75 Whether it is or not is yet to be proved, for there is good evidence that the old Temple site was located about 300 metres further south within the old city walls, called Ophel.

76 Ezekiel 43:4 *And the glory of the Lord came into the house by the way of the gate whose prospect is towards the East*

77 Ezekiel 8:1 *And it came to pass in the sixth year, in the sixth month, in the fifth day of the month, as I sat in my house and the elders of Judah sat before me, that the hand of God there fell upon me.*

See also: Ezekiel 32:1 *And it came to pass in the twelfth year, in the twelfth month, in the first day of the month, that the word of the Lord came to me, saying…*

78 Ezekiel 48:21-22 *And the residue shall be for the prince, on the one side and on the other of the holy oblation, and of the possession of the city, over and against the five and twenty thousand of the oblation towards the east border, and westward over and against the five and twenty thousand of the west border, over against the*

portions for the prince, and it shall be the holy oblation, and the sanctuary of the house shall be in the midst thereof. Moreover from the possession of the Levites, and from the possession of the city, being in the midst of that which is the princes, between the border of Judah, and the border of Benjamin, shall be for the prince.

79 Hebrews 8:8 *For finding fault with them, he saith, behold the days come, saith the Lord, when I will make a new covenant with the house of Israel, and with the house of Judah.*

80 Jeremiah 31:38-40 is a possibility? *Behold, the days come, saith the Lord, that the city shall be built to the Lord from the tower of Hananeel unto the gate of the corner. And the measuring line shall yet go forth over against it upon the hill Gareb, and shall compass about to Goath. And the whole valley of the dead bodies, and of the ashes, and all the fields unto the brook of Kidron, unto the corner of the horse gate toward the east, shall be holy unto the Lord; it shall not be plucked up, nor thrown down any more for ever.*

81 Jeremiah 30:1-11 *The word that came to Jeremiah from the Lord, saying, Thus speaketh the Lord God of Israel, saying, Write thee all the words that I have spoken unto thee in a book. For, lo, the days come, saith the Lord, that I will bring again the captivity of my people Israel and Judah, saith the Lord: and I will cause them to return to the land that I gave to their fathers, and they shall possess it. And these are the words that the Lord spake concerning Israel and concerning Judah. For thus saith the Lord; We have heard a voice of trembling, of fear, and not of peace. Ask ye now, and see whether a man doth travail with child? wherefore do I see every man with his hands on his loins, as a woman in travail, and all faces are turned into paleness? Alas! for that day is great, so that none is like it: it is even the time of Jacob's trouble; but he shall be saved out of it. For it shall come to pass in that day, saith the Lord of hosts, that I will break his yoke from off thy neck, and will burst thy bonds, and strangers shall no more serve themselves of him: But they shall serve the Lord their God, and David their king, whom I will raise up unto them. Therefore fear thou not, O my servant Jacob, saith the Lord; neither be dismayed, O Israel: for, lo, I will save thee from afar, and thy seed from the land of their captivity; and Jacob shall return, and shall be in rest, and be quiet, and none shall make him afraid. For I am with thee, saith the Lord, to save thee: though I make a full end of all nations whither I have scattered thee, yet will I not make a full end of thee: but I will correct thee in measure, and will not leave thee altogether unpunished.*

ENDNOTES

Also: Jeremiah 33:1-26 *Moreover the word of the Lord came unto Jeremiah the second time, while he was yet shut up in the court of the prison, saying, Thus saith the Lord the maker thereof, the Lord that formed it, to establish it; the Lord is his name; Call unto me, and I will answer thee, and shew thee great and mighty things, which thou knowest not. For thus saith the Lord, the God of Israel, concerning the houses of this city, and concerning the houses of the kings of Judah, which are thrown down by the mounts, and by the sword; They come to fight with the Chaldeans, but it is to fill them with the dead bodies of men, whom I have slain in mine anger and in my fury, and for all whose wickedness I have hid my face from this city. Behold, I will bring it health and cure, and I will cure them, and will reveal unto them the abundance of peace and truth. And I will cause the captivity of Judah and the captivity of Israel to return, and will build them, as at the first. And I will cleanse them from all their iniquity, whereby they have sinned against me; and I will pardon all their iniquities, whereby they have sinned, and whereby they have transgressed against me. And it shall be to me a name of joy, a praise and an honour before all the nations of the earth, which shall hear all the good that I do unto them: and they shall fear and tremble for all the goodness and for all the prosperity that I procure unto it. Thus saith the Lord; Again there shall be heard in this place, which ye say shall be desolate without man and without beast, even in the cities of Judah, and in the streets of Jerusalem, that are desolate, without man, and without inhabitant, and without beast, The voice of joy, and the voice of gladness, the voice of the bridegroom, and the voice of the bride, the voice of them that shall say, Praise the Lord of hosts: for the Lord is good; for his mercy endureth for ever: and of them that shall bring the sacrifice of praise into the house of the Lord. For I will cause to return the captivity of the land, as at the first, saith the Lord. Thus saith the Lord of hosts; Again in this place, which is desolate without man and without beast, and in all the cities thereof, shall be an habitation of shepherds causing their flocks to lie down. In the cities of the mountains, in the cities of the vale, and in the cities of the south, and in the land of Benjamin, and in the places about Jerusalem, and in the cities of Judah, shall the flocks pass again under the hands of him that telleth them, saith the Lord. Behold, the days come, saith the Lord, that I will perform that good thing which I have promised unto the house of Israel and to the house of Judah. In those days, and at that time, will I cause the Branch of righteousness to grow up unto David; and he shall execute judgment and righteousness in the land. In those days shall Judah be saved, and Jerusalem shall dwell safely: and this is the name wherewith she shall be called, The Lord our righteousness. For thus saith the Lord; David shall never want a man to sit upon the throne of the house of Israel; Neither shall the priests the*

Levites want a man before me to offer burnt offerings, and to kindle meat offerings, and to do sacrifice continually. And the word of the Lord came unto Jeremiah, saying, Thus saith the Lord; If ye can break my covenant of the day, and my covenant of the night, and that there should not be day and night in their season; Then may also my covenant be broken with David my servant, that he should not have a son to reign upon his throne; and with the Levites the priests, my ministers. As the host of heaven cannot be numbered, neither the sand of the sea measured: so will I multiply the seed of David my servant, and the Levites that minister unto me. Moreover the word of the Lord came to Jeremiah, saying, Considerest thou not what this people have spoken, saying, The two families which the Lord hath chosen, he hath even cast them off? thus they have despised my people, that they should be no more a nation before them. Thus saith the Lord; If my covenant be not with day and night, and if I have not appointed the ordinances of heaven and earth;Then will I cast away the seed of Jacob, and David my servant, so that I will not take any of his seed to be rulers over the seed of Abraham, Isaac, and Jacob: for I will cause their captivity to return, and have mercy on them.

82   Daniel Chapter 9

83   1 Chronicles 5:4 *The sons of Joel, Shemaih his son, Gog his son, Shimei his son.*

84   Hebrews 8:5 *Who serve unto the example and shadow of heavenly things as Moses was admonished of God when he was about to make the tabernacle: for see, saith He, that thou make all things according to the pattern shewed thee in the mount.*

85   Ezekiel 43:3 *And it was according to the appearance of the vision which I saw, even according to the vision that I saw when I came to destroy the city, and the visions were like the vision that I saw by the river Chebar.*

86   Hebrews 10:14 *For by one offering He hath perfected for ever them that are sanctified, see also: Heb 10:3-4 But in those sacrifices there is a remembrance again made of sins every year. For it is not possible that the blood of bulls and of goats should take away sins.*

87   Daniel 9:25-27 *Know therefore and understand, that from the going forth of the commandment to restore and to build Jerusalem unto the Messiah the Prince shall be seven weeks, and threescore and two weeks: the street shall be built again, and the wall, even in troublous times. And after threescore and two weeks shall*

ENDNOTES

Messiah be cut off, but not for himself: and the people of the prince that shall come shall destroy the city and the sanctuary; and the end thereof shall be with a flood, and unto the end of the war desolations are determined. And he shall confirm the covenant with many for one week: and in the midst of the week he shall cause the sacrifice and the oblation to cease, and for the overspreading of abominations he shall make it desolate, even until the consummation, and that determined shall be poured upon the desolate.

88 John 12:12-16 *On the next day much people that were come to the feast, when they heard that Jesus was coming to Jerusalem, Took branches of palm trees, and went forth to meet him, and cried, Hosanna: Blessed is the King of Israel that cometh in the name of the Lord. And Jesus, when he had found a young ass, sat thereon; as it is written, Fear not, daughter of Sion: behold, thy King cometh, sitting on an ass's colt. These things understood not his disciples at the first: but when Jesus was glorified, then remembered they that these things were written of him, and that they had done these things unto him.*

See also Zechariah 9:9 *Rejoice greatly O daughter of Zion, shout O daughter of Jerusalem, behold, thy king cometh unto thee: He is just, and having salvation; lowly and riding upon an ass, and upon a colt, the foal of an ass.*

89 Mark 4:4 *And it came to pass, as he sowed, some fell by the wayside, and the fowls of the air came and devoured it up* and Mark 4:15 *And these are they by the wayside, where the word is sown, but when they have heard, Satan cometh immediately, and taketh away the word that was sown in their hearts.*

90 Genesis 3:17-19 *And unto Adam he said, Because thou hast hearkened unto the voice of thy wife, and hast eaten of the tree, of which I commanded thee, saying, Thou shalt not eat of it: cursed is the ground for thy sake; in sorrow shalt thou eat of it all the days of thy life; Thorns also and thistles shall it bring forth to thee; and thou shalt eat the herb of the field; In the sweat of thy face shalt thou eat bread, till thou return unto the ground; for out of it wast thou taken: for dust thou art, and unto dust shalt thou return.*

91 Ezekiel 11:23, the third vision. *And the glory of the Lord went up from the midst of the city, and stood upon the mountain which is on the east side of the city.* (Mt of Olives)

92 Exodus 20:25-26 *And if thou wilt make me an altar of stone, thou shalt not build it of hewn stone: for if thou lift up thy tool upon it, thou hast polluted it. 26 Neither shalt thou go up by steps unto mine altar, that thy nakedness be not discovered thereon.*

"BEHOLD, I HAVE FORETOLD YOU ALL THINGS"

93 2 Samuel 7:16 *And thine house and thy kingdom shall be established for ever before thee: thy throne shall be established for ever.*

94 Hebrews 7:14-15 *For it is evident that our Lord sprang out of Juda; of which tribe Moses spake nothing concerning priesthood. And it is yet far more evident: for that after the similitude of Melchisedec there ariseth another priest.*

95 It is by no means certain, but taking the 'reed' to be about 11ft, this would give a total strip about 50 miles long x 20 miles wide (80 x16 km) for this holy oblation. Given that Israel at it narrowest point is about 9 miles, and at its broadest is about 70 miles, this will mean some changes to borders to accommodate these new dimensions.

96 Although it is very probable that this comes from the only natural water source in Jerusalem, called the *Gihon Spring*, currently underground. Originally this was a small 'gusher' pushing water up as a fountain. Where this spring appears may be what the builders eventually use to pinpoint where the holy house is to be located, and the earthquake that will change Jerusalem's topography may also reinvigorate this spring so that it now issues out above ground. In any event we can be sure that the new location for the inner Temple will be on the exact spot of that of Solomon's Temple, which is not necessarily on the present site of the Dome of the Rock. See Psalms 46:4.

97 It is very unlikely that this is the same Zechariah who the Lord mentions in connection with the slaughter before the altar in Matthew 23:35.

98 Ezekiel, and John in Revelation for example.

99 Matthew 11:14 *And if you will receive it, this is Elias which was for to come.*

100 Deuteronomy 27:13-15 *And these shall stand upon mount Ebal to curse; Reuben, Gad, and Asher, and Zebulun, Dan, and Naphtali. And the Levites shall speak, and say unto all the men of Israel with a loud voice, Cursed be the man that maketh any graven or molten image, an abomination unto the Lord, the work of the hands of the craftsman, and putteth it in a secret place. And all the people shall answer and say, Amen.*

101 Revelation Chapters 17 and 18. Babylon seems to be held responsible for the idolatry of the whole world at this time, and perhaps the wickedness of Israel is represented in Zechariah's vision as having been returned to where it belonged. Whilst Israel was cleansed of idolatry in

its exile (which is true, for despite its religious arrogance, it never again returned to the idolatrous worship described in Ezekiel Chapter 8) Babylon has yet to answer for the widespread idolatry that it spawned.

102 As in Nebuchadnezzar's dream, and according to its interpretation by Daniel.

103 Isaiah 11:1 *And there shall come forth a rod out of the stem of Jesse, and a Branch shall grow forth out of his roots.*

104 Paul describes this combined ministry in Hebrews Chapters 5-10 at length, when speaking of the Lord's heavenly intercession for us all. Melchisedec was both King and Priest of Salem (Jerusalem) in the order named after him.

105 On the tenth day of Tevet because on that day, Nebuchadnezzar laid siege to Jerusalem. In Tammuz because in that month, the walls of the city were breached. On the ninth day of Av a fast was instituted because on it the Temple was destroyed. On the third day of Tishrei a fast marked the death of Gedaliah, who remained in Judah after the Destruction of the Temple. These fasts were to be turned into *feasts of celebration to the Lord*, and are still observed by some Jews.

106 Matthew 21:1-14, John 12:14-16.

107 This was Tunguska in Russia, in 1908. Although disputed, the remains of Sodom are thought by some to be located at Tall-al-Hammam in Jordan, on the site of a similar 'natural' disaster, or airburst. Skeletons were excavated there, lying unburied where they died, displaying similar signs of trauma as those described by Zechariah, probably caused by a sudden burst of intense heat, but with no crater found in the area.

108 Revelation 17:16-17, *And the ten horns which thou sawest upon the beast, these shall hate the whore, and shall make her desolate and naked, and shall eat her flesh, and burn her with fire. 17 For God hath put in their hearts to fulfil his will, and to agree, and give their kingdom unto the beast, until the words of God shall be fulfilled.*

see also *Alpha and Omega* for a fuller explanation.

109 Matthew 23:2-7 *Saying, The scribes and the Pharisees sit in Moses' seat: All therefore whatsoever they bid you observe, that observe and do; but do not ye after their works: for they say, and do not. For they bind heavy burdens and grievous to be borne, and lay them on men's shoulders; but they themselves will not move them with one of their fingers. But all their works they do for to be seen of men: they make broad their phylacteries, and enlarge the borders of their garments, And love the uppermost rooms at feasts, and the chief seats in the synagogues, And greetings in the markets, and to be called of men, Rabbi, Rabbi.*

110 Romans 11:25-29 *For I would not, brethren, that ye should be ignorant of this mystery, lest ye should be wise in your own conceits; that blindness in part is happened to Israel, until the fulness of the Gentiles be come in. And so all Israel shall be saved: as it is written, There shall come out of Sion the Deliverer, and shall turn away ungodliness from Jacob: For this is my covenant unto them, when I shall take away their sins. As concerning the gospel, they are enemies for your sakes: but as touching the election, they are beloved for the fathers' sakes. For the gifts and calling of God are without repentance.*

111 Hebrews 8:8 *For finding fault with them, he saith, Behold, the days come, saith the Lord, when I will make a new covenant with the house of Israel and with the house of Judah: Not according to the covenant that I made with their fathers in the day when I took them by the hand to lead them out of the land of Egypt; because they continued not in my covenant, and I regarded them not, saith the Lord. For this is the covenant that I will make with the house of Israel after those days, saith the Lord; I will put my laws into their mind, and write them in their hearts: and I will be to them a God, and they shall be to me a people:*

112 Revelation 20:11 *And I saw a great white throne, and him that sat on it, from whose face the earth and the heaven fled away; and there was found no place for them.*

113 Revelation 21:1-2 *And I saw a new heaven and a new earth: for the first heaven and the first earth were passed away; and there was no more sea. And I John saw the holy city, new Jerusalem, coming down from God out of heaven, prepared as a bride adorned for her husband.*

www.ingramcontent.com/pod-product-compliance
Lightning Source LLC
Chambersburg PA
CBHW051750040426
42446CB00007B/292